O LORD, SUPP... THE ... of this troubleous life, until the shades lengthen, and the evening comes, and the buisy world is hushed, the fever of life is over, and our work is done. Then, Lord, in thy mercy, grant us safe lodgeing, a holy rest, and peace at last. Through Jesus Christ, our Lord. AMEN.

Dances

PROGRAMME

PARHAM HOUSE.
December 30th, 1924.

Cesca's Diaries: A Love Story. Volume I

ISBN: 978-1-9161978-5-5

Copyright © Sarah Courage

The editor Sarah Courage asserts her legal and moral right
to be identified as the originator of this work.

Printed by Gipping Press Ltd, Needham Market.
www.gippingpress.co.uk

These two volumes
are dedicated to
my mother

Acknowledgements

I would like to thank my mother, for entrusting me with the diaries and for answering so many of my queries. And the Tunbridge Wells Family History Society, Air Marshall Sir Ian Macfadyen KCVO CB OBE for showing us round RAF Cranwell, Noel Stephens of Worplesdon Golf Club, who lived at the house by the fifteenth tee, the Lang's home, Mingary. Suzy Powling for her valiant attempts at editing some of the diaries. My cousins for photographs and details for the Family Tree.

Thank you to Danny Cuff of Gipping Press and Matt Pilling of Owl Bookbinding for their huge enthusiasm in this project and their skills.

However, my husband Charlie deserves a medal for supporting this project over the last six years. I cannot thank him enough for his patience assembling the family tree, his computer skills, and the scanning of countless photographs for me.

I would have been lost without his steadfast presence by my side.

The Taylor family at Harmondsworth

Captain Harold Taylor and Violet
Ursula Hunnybun Wedding Day

Unexpected transport for a Married Couple

Captain Rev. Taylor Chaplain in
Royal Field Artillery 1915-1918

The Craven Hunt Meet at Cheam School 1935

Cesca with Pat Ainslie 1911

CESCA

1904-1999
A Love Story
Her edited diaries 1924-1948

This book, divided into two volumes, is the consequence of my mother giving me boxes and boxes full of Grannie's diaries. Also photograph albums, scrap-books and other memorabilia. I was so excited that I slipped down the last few steps of the attic hurting both ankles! These diaries have been my bedtime reading shedding light on large parts of her life of which I knew nothing at all. Deciding to transcribe and edit her twenty diaries was an easy decision but deciding what to edit out of so much material rather a challenge. And has taken me over six years of research and hard work. She was a much loved and wonderful grandmother to me. I have found it fascinating through her own diaries, to have an insight into her life as a young woman in the 1920's, and a wife to her darling Billy and mother of four during World War II. It is obvious that Bill and Cesca's relationship was a passionate one for many years and they both found the inevitable many partings distressing even heart breaking.

The fact that Grannie did not clear out these diaries but kept them, demonstrates to me that she felt they were important to her. Due to living in so many different houses, she was almost obsessive in her desire to clear out, sell or discard possessions all her life!

Unfortunately only one of the thousands of Bill and Cesca's letters written daily to each other survived, found tucked inside her 1935 diary.

Francesca Mary Bisshopp, known as Cesca, (Grannie-Ma or Frankie 1 by her thirteen grandchildren) was born on August 26th 1904 in

Tunbridge Wells. Her father, my great grandfather, Francis Robert Bryant Bisshopp was by then a Senior Consultant Physician. He was born in 1859 at South Lambeth, London. His only sibling was the Rev'd Hammond Butler Bisshopp. His parents were Dr James Bisshopp (1822-1909) and Eliza Anne Bisshopp (1823-1897).

Cesca's mother, my great grandmother, Mary Emily Fanny nee Taylor, was born in 1864 in Kensington. She was the daughter of John C. Taylor, gentleman, and Elizabeth Taylor (Foy). Francis and Fanny were married on September 16th 1891 in Harmondsworth parish church, near Staines. John Taylor, a wealthy man, a publican no less, was the owner of the King's Arms, Knightsbridge and Lord of the Manor of Norwood. The ceremony was conducted by her brother, the Rev J.C. Taylor, Vicar of Harmondsworth [whose son Harold was Jimmy Taylor's father] and the Vicar of Saxmundham, the Rev G.F. Richardson. Fanny suffered many miscarriages before giving birth at the age of forty-one to Cesca, a little red headed daughter. The birth took place at home at Parham House, Mount Pleasant Road, the house built by Dr Bisshopp in 1902, to replace Belvedere House.
The 1901 census, taken at Belvedere records James Bisshopp, aged 78, widow, born in West Burton Sussex, surgeon and living with him was his son Francis, aged 41, a physician surgeon and Francis's wife Mary F. Bisshopp, aged 38, and two servants.

Cesca, five weeks old, was baptised on the 28th September 1904 at Holy Trinity Church, Tunbridge Wells. Cesca would doubtless be startled enough to say 'Mercy!' seeing how Holy Trinity Church has been altered. The exterior remains unchanged. However it is a church no longer within but instead a cinema and theatre complete with a café and bar with gaudy lights!

Her education took place almost entirely at home after a short unhappy time at a local day school where she was physically bullied. She was knocked to the ground and suffered a nose bleed. Her

Cesca fishing 1909

Cesca with peke and hen

Cesca and Pat Ainslie 1910

Cesca 1911

Cesca with bicycle

Cesca with Bogey 1922

mother, horrified and furious removed her and employed a series of French governesses. One of whom, Suzanne Ploquin, became a friend and Cesca remained in close contact with her until her death. Cesca had a pretty voice and took weekly singing lessons in London and was also taught all aspects of needlework. In 1909 when she was five years old, Tunbridge Wells received the "Royal" prefix and James Bisshopp, her grandfather died on March 3rd, the funeral being held at King Charles the Martyr. A Dedication Service was held on November 1st of a new pulpit in memory of Dr James Bisshopp. It is still standing to this day.

The photo album of 1909 find the family staying at Tom-na-bat House, Tomintoul, Scotland from July 30th- September 8th for fishing and shooting. Tomintoul was then reached from London by an overnight sleeper train to Ballindalloch Station, a further sixteen miles by motor or mail coach. Tomintoul being situated at 1,170 feet above sea level, the motor in those days, was liable to frequent breakdowns owing to the steepness of the hills and dangerous bends. In 1910 Edward VII died on the 6th May and George V was crowned. That year the annual holiday was spent in Argyllshire at a hotel in Kilmelfort. Photographs can be seen in 1910-1911 of Cesca with Pat Ainslie playing together as young children. Pat and Hugh Lang were to become ardent suitors in 1925. These annual forays to Scotland staying in different houses or hotels, continued until 1933 according to Francis Bisshopp's Game Book.

The census for Parham House on 2nd April 1911 records Francis Bisshop, aged 51, Physician, Mary Bisshop, aged 47, Francesca Bisshopp aged 6, Charlotte Voulatum, aged 23 governess, born Paris, French.

Also three servants comprising: Annie Funnell, cook, 46yrs, Edith Brett parlourmaid, 29yrs, and Annie Hall, housemaid aged 31yrs all from Sussex. Parham House is noted having 16 rooms excluding scullery, office and bathrooms. The house was named after the family seat of the senior branch of the Bisshopps, Parham House, near Pulborough in West Sussex. After the house was sold in 1933 it was rebuilt brick by brick and can be found in Forest Road, 241, and known as Laurel House. The Ritz cinema was built on the site subsequently demolished over 60 years later.

The Great War, or WWI, started to make an impact in Tunbridge Wells a month after the assassination of Archduke Ferdinand on Thursday 30th July. The band of the Royal Irish Rifles was about to strike up for its usual morning performance in the Pantiles when the bandmaster was handed a telegram from the adjutant, telling them to return to barracks immediately and the band at once packed its instruments and headed for the railway station. The council struggled to fill the gap at such short notice but secured the services of the celebrated orchestra known as Batty and his Band to fill the gap! The congregation of St. Augustine's Catholic Church were invited to sponsor Belgian refugees and were asked "to state the number of rooms available, the class of person desired, whether food, or lodging or both will be given and for how long and whether payment is desired."

And as local men joined up, so the town began to fill up with encampments of troops from other parts of the country, training and preparing for embarkation. The first to arrive was a detachment of 350 territorial Royal Engineers from Birmingham who set up rows of bell tents and a field kitchen on the Common. *The Courier* archly reported in late October; "The military are quite an attraction to the feminine portion of the community and the 'glad eye" is used with great effect when the shades of night are falling fast!" No blackout was considered necessary in the town. As winter arrived, tents were no longer an option and the town's Chief Constable began requisitioning church halls, public rooms, the skating rink and a large number of empty private villas. Rents to private landlords were initially 3s.4d per man per day but subsequently cut to 1s.9d. To feed the new troops, the

Army Service Corps rumbled into action and set up food kitchens and large gas cookers were installed and lorries delivered carcases of meat, sacks of potatoes, vegetables and trays of loaves each day to warehouses in Goods Station Road. Each man was entitled to 1lb meat, 1½ lbs of bread, 2 oz bacon, 2oz sugar, 1oz jam, 1oz cheese, ½ oz of tea and a suitable quantity of salt, pepper and mustard. There were, it was said, very few complaints.

The General Hospital set aside 50 beds for the wounded, this left only 40 for general patients. But these were soon taken up by injured Belgian troops and space for more was found at the Eye and Ear Hospital and the VAD Red Cross Hospital in Chilston Road. There were already shortages of medicines and drugs as many were manufactured by German companies.

Pat Ainslie's elder brother, Lieutenant Denys Alfred Lafone Ainslie, 1st Bn Devonshire Regiment was killed in action aged 20 during the 1st Battle of Ypres 24 October 1914. One of the Drewe's sons was also killed, (the Drewes were a local family, wealthy and hosted wonderful dances at Wadhurst Hall).

In October 1915, there were two events that probably had the most impact on Tunbridge Wells during the Great War. The bombing of the town by a lone Zeppelin, in Calverley Park; and the accidental sinking of HMS Hythe at Cape Helles, Gallipoli, with the loss of 129 local men. At about 8.00 pm 28 October , the former Dover-Calais ferry steamer was about to land the troops it was carrying, when a much larger empty troopship, HMS Sarnia, collided with the Hythe carving it in two. It was very dark, all lights having been dowsed and both had been travelling at about 12 knots. The Hythe sank rapidly in about 10 minutes, taking with it 155 of the 275 men on board. The only officer to die in the disaster was Capt. David Salomons of the philanthropist Salomons family from Broomhill. His father Sir David Salomons arranged and paid for a Memorial to the 129 dead and is now in St Mathew's Church, High Brooms.

Cesca was sent to Paris at the age of seventeen to be "finished" in 1921. She already spoke fluent French and returned many times in the 1920's with her mother for deliciously extravagant shopping trips. Both Cesca's parents were wealthy. Francis Bisshopp was admitted to the Royal College of Surgeons in July 1885. He had a great many rich patients and practised at Guy's Hospital from 1886. And held successively the posts of resident physician, house surgeon and resident obstetric physician. Probate records show that Francis died aged 87 years 26 December1946 at Tunbridge Wells Hospital, Kent. He left an estate valued at about £44,000, (equivalent to around £1.5 million today) and was buried in the Tunbridge Wells Cemetery 31 December 1946. Fanny was rich in her own right, and they both indulged their only child. Near the end of her life in 1946, Fanny had moved from Belstead House near Ipswich to The Chestnuts, Cumberland St. Woodbridge. [The house still stands but is now named Athenrye and is a large old red brick Georgian house divided into flats]. She died there on 4 January 1948. Probate records Fanny leaving an estate valued at about £51,000.

The first surviving diary is 1924, The Sloane Diary purchased from Truslove and Hanson, a thick, green, tooled leather volume with marbled end papers. She writes in black ink, a day to a 5' x 4' page, and there are lists of Dances attended, books read (John Galsworthy and PG Wodehouse amongst them) and Christmas presents given. Cards, book-markers and garters were popular presents for female friends. Cigarettes, stockings and cards were given to men friends. Her father received a collar for Nigger, his black cocker spaniel. She was presented at Court in May.

The first week of January was taken up with parties and dances. The Guthrie's on the 3rd, Mrs Johnston's on the 4th a Fancy Dress Ball on the

5th not in bed before 3.00am most nights. In fact on Sunday 6th, Cesca writes "Felt awfully seedy in the morning and couldn't eat any breakfast. John, Mother and I went off to church but I had to come out before the service started. Couldn't even see Mother or John. Walked slowly home and rested on the sofa…Didn't feel very well."

On Tuesday, she had breakfast in bed as the Drewe's dance was taking place that evening at Wadhurst Hall. This house and estate was bought by Mr Julius Drewe in 1898 for £47,000. The house was demolished in 1948 after being used as a prisoner of war camp. Hans Rausing, the Tetra Pak billionaire has built a very unusual palace there all on one level.

The first surviving photo scrap book of Grannie's is dated March 1922. On 1 October a little black cocker spaniel puppy, Bogey, appears when Cesca was 18 years old. Other photos of the Eridge Races, the Frant Horse Show, trips to Cambridge and Grantchester, Wimbledon, the month of August at Lake Vyrnwy Hotel for shooting. Young men feature, Ronnie, Mac, Rex, John, Guy and Geoff Walford and girls too, Betty Walford and Barbara, Vi and Mary, Peg and Joannie.

Then during August and September, Northumberland, with her parents, the dogs, Bogey and Bruce, visiting Otterburn, Hexham, Corbridge and Jedburgh. Dr Guthrie, John and Jack were amongst the shooting party. Ferreting was another occupation!

The scrap books for 1923, 1924, 1925 and 1926 are also full of photos of race meetings, the meet after the Eridge Hunt Ball, Brussels, Eights Week Oxford, tennis parties, Muntham Court, Cambridge May Week and Henley featuring both Pat Ainslie and Hugh Lang and of course the annual six weeks grouse shooting in Scotland. Hugh and his Bentley, Edmund and his Amilcar, Pat and his Talbot, Henley and

Cranwell and the first photos of Bill dated July 1925. There is no doubt that Cesca was not just an attractive young woman with the most unusual titian hair but very slim, beautifully dressed and with an irresistible effervescent personality.

But enough background from me. Read for yourself in her own words and I hope you all find it as interesting and illuminating as I have.

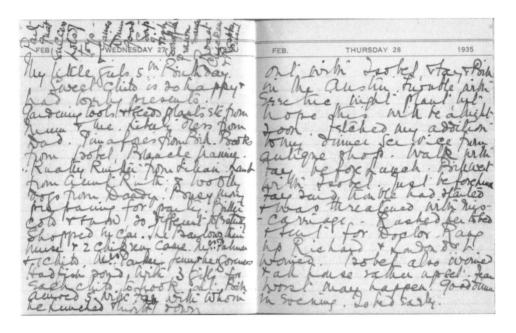

A sample of one of Cesca's diaries

1924 Parham House, Tunbridge Wells.

This is the earliest surviving diary and is crammed with details of dozens of dances, dinner parties, hunt balls, point-to-points, England v Scotland rugger at Twickenham, Oxford and Cambridge cricket, Opera, theatres, tennis tournaments, shooting parties and frequent visits to London for fittings and shopping in Bond Street and Fortnum & Masons. Poker patience, bridge and mah-jong are played in the evenings. Cesca sews, has singing and piano lessons and illuminates texts. She adores her black cocker spaniel, Bogey [given to her in October 1922] who is left with the keeper, Harrison, pitiful howls, when Cesca and her Mother leave for Paris and Brussels in February.

Cesca has a wide circle of friends and at least a dozen men friends to dance with and to accompany her to the above engagements and sporting events. Guy, Rex, Gerald, John, Jack, Peter Knox, Mac, Dick, Martin, Jim, Lamont, Bickerton and Noel Halsey. Cesca's Mother at 61 years old had the exhausting task of chaperoning Cesca often not home until 4.00 or 5.00 in the morning, sometimes three dances a week!

Cesca and her Mother left for Paris by the boat train on Friday 15 February and had the best crossing having feared it would be rough. Got through the Douane without any trunks being opened and had very comfy First Class seats to Paris and reached the Bedford Hotel, 17 Rue de l'Arcade that evening.

They went to the English Church on Sunday and Cesca noted that 'the same foul young curate still there and oh so admired by all the rows of wretched English girls.'

Lots of delightful shopping in Blvd des Italiens, Rue Royale, Rue de Rivoli, Rue de Saint Honore for hand painted long necklaces, bags, brooches, scent, talc, a hat for 225frs, a pair of grey silk stockings at 21frs and seven pairs of gloves. They went to Madam Chevrier where they ordered dresses, one in blue velvet for her 'robe d'interieur' as Madam called it! A sweet pair of mules, white and gold trimmed with turquoise blue feathers, two pairs of lovely garters at 15frs a pair and Mum bought her another hat as she liked it awfully, brown straw with sweet brown and green leaves and ribbons. They had wonderful seats at the Opera, the best in the house for only 40frs each.

At the end of the week Cesca was sad to leave Paris and take the train to Brussels from the Gare du Nord. A foul journey as 'the most repulsive Flemish brutes in the carriage' refused to let them have the window open even an inch, even though they had the window seats. They stayed at the Brittany next to the King's Palace and it snowed. They saw thousands of paintings in the Palais des Beaux Arts, mostly of the 'vulgar Dutch and Flemish school', were impressed by the beautiful buildings and the cathedral but not the people, awful. And the country is very depressing after the war. They both bought lace and Cesca is pleased to leave for home via Ostend though she has enjoyed her fortnight away. The sea this time was terribly rough and they were both awfully sick, 'fed the fishes till we got to Dover. The stewardess did nothing but eat chutney and curried rice and beer. An unhappy four hours.'

Bogey nearly went mad with delight to see Cesca again and Cesca too!

Jack invites Cesca to the Royal Artillery Dance, Shoebury on Thursday 20 March so after buying a new tennis racquet and a Mahjong set from Lillywhites, she and her Mother travel down to Southend by train and stay at the Palace Hotel, huge and quite comfortable.

'It was fun, wore my blue velvet, and I felt like being thoroughly bad. And when I got there I was going to make things hum and I did'.

At the end of March the search is on for a flat in Mayfair and they look at several at eight guineas a week for when she is presented at Court. Her Mother settles on 23 Hertford Street from 14 May. Cesca thinks it is divine. Writing paper is ordered from Smythsons. Court gowns are chosen in Sloane Street at the end of April, Mother's black and diamante and Cesca's a dress of flesh pink with a silver lace train over pink chiffon and a flounce of ostrich feathers. A shock to hear that Court Presentation is brought forward from 26 June to 21 May with only a week's notice. A lot of scuttling around to get everything done. Long white kid gloves, plumes and veils bought and curtsies practised with the Dancing Mistress, Adele in Bond Street. Photographers booked and a present from Mum of a lovely pink, mauve and blue feather fan.

Wednesday 21 May The Court

Up at 11.30. Went up Regent Street to get some flesh net for shoulder straps. Had a quiet lunch with Mum and Dorothy and then rested till 3.00 when Dad arrived and woke me up by falling down the steps. Had a bath and changed as far as I could, as the dresses didn't come until 4.30. At 4.30 Mr Gerard the coiffeur from Smiles arrived and did Mum's hair first and then mine. Did it frightfully tight and then attached the plumes. Had tea altogether at 5.15. Hogben arrived to see me in my dress and thought me "Really beautiful Miss Cesca!" We went off in the car to Bassano's in Davis Street, then Mansell and Fox in Piccadilly and then Hay Wrightson in Bond Street. I like the way the latter photographed us better than the others. The people in the crowds were awful, all thronged up to see us and made remarks! Home at 7.30 and after dinner at 8.30 Auntie Fan called for us in the car and took us along. The queue was prodigious, all the way down the Mall nearly as far as the Cenotaph. Everyone staring in at us! Arrived at the Palace at 9.30 and then we had to wait till about 11.00 before it came to our turn to make one curtsy. The whole Palace is marvellous, too wonderful for words. I enjoyed myself most frightfully. We came fairly near the end, I wasn't a bit frightened and made my curtsy awfully well! The King looked awfully tired and the Queen lovely. She is has perfect skin and the sweetest smile. Then we had a wait and finally we had to process down the corridors, with the King and Queen first then Prince Henry and the Duke of Connaught and all the Royal Party. It was an awful job after supper getting away from the Palace and all very tired.

Thursday 22 May
Didn't get up till noon. Went out and had a light lunch at Fullers. Returned some fans to Duvelleroy that were sent on approval, and then went to the Goldsmiths Company and took Mum's diamonds to be repaired. Came in and had two letters, one from Martin asking me to the theatre on Saturday and a dance and also to the Sandhurst Dance on June 9. Also had a letter from Mac.

Saturday 24 May
A wet morning, I went off to Bakers and bought a lovely new pair of shoes. Mum went off home by 10.40. I came home and changed. At 1.45 Martin arrived and took me off to "Toni" at the Shaftesbury. A wonderful show, I simply loved it. Martin most awfully nice too, I do like him so. Wanted me to dance and dine with him somewhere but had to get home by 5.40. Anyhow I am going to the Sandhurst dance on the 9th and the Gymkhana show when the King is coming down, it will be fun.

Monday 26 May
Went to Oxford by the 3.05 had to change at Bletchley and got to Oxford at five. No Peter to meet us alas! Got to the hotel about 5.15, The Oxford. Quite nice, near the Randolph, but very small.

Got a nice comfy room though, we had scarcely arrived when Peter turned up and dragged me off to the " Eights" at once. We motored down there in the GU and then crossed the river in the ferry and went on to the Green's barge. Enjoyed it frightfully was introduced to the rest of the party Mrs Martin, Rupert and Beatrice Martin.

Wednesday 27 May

Peter came round at 10.30 and took Mum and me off in the car to Queens. Showed us all over Queens. Peter then took us to have coffee at The Oxford, the place for such things. He then motored us to Woolvercote to the Trout Inn, the sweetest spot I've ever been to I think. Got back at 12.30 changed. Then Peter took us to Christchurch where we went to Gerald's rooms and had lunch there. Gerald was frightfully nice, Nora was there and two girlfriends of hers. Changed and got down to the Queen's barge for the races. After the races went to home in the car, changed into thick things and Peter fetched us again and we went off to Magdalen bridge. Then we had a picnic up the river in two punts. Peter and Rupert, Barbie, Mrs Martin, Mrs Sawyer, John Coldham, George Cookson, Mum and me. It was wonderful.

Wednesday 28 May

Peter came for us again at 10.30. He and I wandered round Oxford then had some coffee at 11 at The Oxford with the Martins, then he took me in the GU to Iffley. Lovely drive, then I dashed home, changed and we went off to lunch with him in his rooms at Queens. Another boy was there called Edward Cary Coker who rows in the Queens boat. Very nice looking. Then we motored down to the Queen's Barge, had tea after at the Queen's Pavilion and watched the cricket. Changed and Peter came for us, then went off out to dinner with the Martins at the Eastgate Hotel at 7.00. Went off to the theatre and saw "The Bad Man". Very good indeed, home at 10.15.

Thursday 29 May

Peter came round as usual at 10.30. Peter and I went shopping in the car and got together a whole lot of things for our picnic. We packed them all up and at 12.00 started off. Mum, Mrs Martin, Rupert, Barbie and the chauffeur in Mrs Sawyer's car, and Peter and Henry Ellishaw and me in the GU. We went to Burford, a sweet village about 17 miles from Oxford and visited the charming old church. Had a priceless picnic lunch and then motored home again. Had tea, rested and changed. We went off in a raging thunderstorm to Queens and dined there. The party was Mrs Martin, Rupert, Barbie, Mum, Mrs Hugh, Christopher Lee, Mrs Bennett, Jock Goldie and Peter and me. Then came the dance at Queens. Clifford Essex Band and awful fun. Kept up till 1.30. Peter is too sweet for words. I'm a bit in love I think with him.

Friday 30 May

Felt rather tired. Got up at 9.00 after breakfast and started packing. Peter came at 10.30. I forgot to say yesterday that my photo was in the *Queen*. Terrific. I went off with Mum and took some photos, two of Queens and one of Mum. Then we packed and had lunch and just had time to go to Christchurch and see the cathedral there. Peter came round to say goodbye. I've never felt more like crying in my life and of course I couldn't! But I think I showed it a bit. Got to the flat teatime. Felt flat too.

Tuesday 3 June

Got up about 8.30 and had four letters one from darling old Mac. Very nice one too. Kennion is to take me to a show tomorrow night. Then changed and wore my presentation dress which really looked lovely. Jim Reed came to dinner at 7.30. I do like him so. So does Mum. Very nice dinner and left here in the car at 8:45 and got the Skinners Hall at nine. And it was the most wonderful dance. Great fun and danced until 3.30, home at 4.00 Wonderful!

Wednesday 4 June

Only had about three hours sleep and got up and was dressed by 12.30. Peter arrived to lunch soon after and was awfully nice and cheerful but I think he was a bit tired. Rested after he left. Had a quiet tea with Mum. Wore my blue velvet again. It looks quite nice still. Dick Kennion arrived to dinner at seven. Gosh he is tall. Mum likes him awfully. Had quite a good dinner and then we went off to 'Tonight's the Night' at the Winter Garden Theatre. It was great fun I loved it and he was so awfully nice. He brought me back here, then dashed off for his train.

Thursday 5 June

In morning Mum went to Hamptons and I called on the Hartnell's at 10, Bruton Street. Miss H very nice indeed. Showed me her flat and met him, he showed me some of his manikin's and dresses.

Saturday 7 June

Got up early and packed. Left here and went to Charing Cross and caught a train at 10.30 down to Tunbridge Wells. Frightful crowd owing to Whitsun.

Monday 9 June

Had to rise with the lark. Got up at 7.00 and Dorothy finished my packing. I had breakfast and motored over to Tonbridge with Dad catching the 8.43. Had letter from Mac, hadn't time to read it till I got on the train. Awfully thrilling. Got a taxi to London Bridge and went to Waterloo. Caught the 10.30 down to Camberley. Frightful crowds but as I went 1st.Class wasn't troubled much. Met Joanie Horden at the station and she motored me over to Frimley. Quite a decent little pub but pretty dirty! Had a nice room though, she's awfully nice. Had a scrap lunch together and then went off to RMC, met Martin and his friend Disney Barlow. And then met Mr and Mrs Hicks very nice. The show was wonderful and after tea went to Martin's rooms, then saw the chapel and the stables. Dashed back with Joanie, changed, had supper and dashed back to RMC for the dance. They had over 900 people there and very good floor and lovely room and sitting out places. Clifford Essex band, danced nearly all the time with Martin, three with Disney and two with Pat. Met Lamont there, he swears he wrote, still very struck! I loved all of it. Home at 4.00.

Tuesday 10 June

Joannie and I were both woken by tanks going to Aldershot. Made the deuce of a row Got up at 8.30 had a bath, breakfast and packed. She drove me to the station at Camberley. Caught the 10.44 up to Waterloo. Couldn't get a porter for love or money so had to carry everything. Awful sweat! Got home in time for lunch. Mum turned up a bit later. Jim came round later. Has asked me to "Diplomacy" tomorrow night. Wish it were last night again.

Wednesday 11 June

Feeling quite fit and went to Madame Racon for a fitting. After lunch at Harrods took a taxi home. It simply poured. Rested all afternoon then changed and at 4.30 Aunt Edie had tea here. Showed her over the flat. At 6.00 changed into my blue velvet and at 7.00 Jim came to dinner here. Frightfully smart all 'in tails'! We left at about 8.00 with Mum who went on to 'London Life' at Drury Lane while we went to 'Diplomacy' at the Adelphi. Splendid show loved it.

Thursday 12 June

Pouring wet morning again. It is the limit this weather. Wore my brown dress and hat and thick winter coat and went to Cannon Street. Had lunch there, the best lunch I've had for a long time. Then caught the 1.44 down to Woolwich. Mac met us at the station and took us up to the 'shop' deposited us in Mansell's hands and then he changed and blacked his face! We watched their Wild West show in which Mac, Mansell and Riddle were performing. Lots of sideshows too but the The` Dansant show was really awful fun. Danced with Mac and Kennion who was very nice, lost my temper completely with Mac.

Saturday 14 June

Packed up. Mum left and caught the 10.41. I went to Mme Racon's and tried on the dress. Then went to Thierry's in Regent Street, saw some shoes that I rather liked, black satin ones and very cheap too so bought them. I took a bus to Cannon Street and caught the 12.44 down to Tunbridge Wells. Had lunch, saw Dad and my little black dog! Rested after tea and then changed into my green dress and my white shawl. Drove over to the Podmore's at Moatlands at 7.30. Had dinner, then played games and had the gramophone. Dick and I danced. Got home at about 11.00.

Monday 16 June

After breakfast packed and Mum and I came up by the 11.56. Train packed but we went Ist class so all was well. Heard from Peter about next Monday. We all are dining at the Piccadilly first, then going to 'Tonight's the Night'. After tea went to Racon's. Had letter from Dick Kennion and one from Mac. Rather upset poor darling.

Tuesday 17 June

Got up after breakfast in my new dark green dress and went off to Hay Wrightson's for a complimentary sitting for the papers. Great fun. Mrs Wrightson is so nice too. Then went to Truefitts in Bond Street and had my hair cut. Had 3 inches taken off and the girl did it up a new way for me. Dad came to lunch and spent part of the afternoon with us. Mum and I went out in the park after tea.

Wednesday 18 June

Lovely hot day. Went to Swan and Edgar to have my petticoat pleated. Came home along Piccadilly and then changed, wore my green dress again. Mum and I went off out to lunch at the Albemarle Club in Davis St.

Thursday 19 June

Got up at 9.00 after breakfast. We went off to Wembley for the day. Loathed the approach by tube and all the awful people but thought the exhibition itself marvellous though places such as Canada, India and Australia didn't interest me much. I don't think they would unless one's been there. But the Rodeo at the Stadium was too wonderful for words. I was terribly thrilled. Mum was a bit nervous. The bands too were excellent and what interested me very much was the old English house by Maples & Co. Charming. Didn't care for the Queen's dolls house.

Friday 20 June

Another nice hot day, still rather tired after Wembley! Mum and I went out shopping and got photos at Hay Wrightson's. Took some lovely lilies and carnations to Auntie Fan and booked a table at the Piccadilly for Monday night. Had a rest and then went to Queen's Club for the Tennis Tournament. Great fun.

Saturday 21 June

Mum wouldn't let me stay up to see Mac, so went down to Tunbridge Wells and got here at 11.30. Dad terribly grumpy and cross, simply don't know what's wrong with him. It's awful.

Monday 23 June

Had a busy morning getting things ready for London. Went up by 11.56. Found lots of letters, unpacked. Terribly hot. Went off to Mme Racon's at 3.00, Mum's dress very nice. Changed and got to the Piccadilly to find Mrs Martin, Rupert, Barbie and Peter there . Had a good dinner and then all went on in two taxis to the Winter Gardens. 'Tonight's the Night' was wonderful. I loved it and cried with laughter. Distinctly heard Martin's voice in the stalls. Looked for him but couldn't see him. Peter insisted on our going on to the cabaret show and dance. Met Martin and enjoyed it frightfully, Martin wanted me to go on to a nightclub with him but Peter took me home!

Tuesday 24 June

Terribly hot day. Mum went off to the Horse Show at Olympia with Aunt Edie. Dad and I came back to the flat. Find Mac waiting, he said he had got seats for the 'Whirl of the World,' a most excellent show. Enjoyed it awfully but left before the end and went on to the cricket match at Lord's, but found it all over alas, so came back to the flat. Went and sat in the Park and talked a lot. Mac left at 7.00 and then I had a quick change. Wore my new black dress with the flowers at the hem and dined with the Pontifex at 20 Roland Gardens. Rather dull except Gerald who was there, they were all going on to the Asquith's dance.

Friday 27 June

Feel much better and got up early. Packed and left the flat at 10 and caught the 10.40 home. After lunch Dad went off up to Cambridge for a dinner at Trinity. After tea Hogben and I marked out the court. It was lovely being in the garden with Bogey.

Saturday 28 June

Had a busy morning getting ready for the tennis party. Helped Hogben put up the net. Picked the strawberries. Brushed Bogey and went out shopping. Peg came to lunch, looked very nice in white. I changed and then she and I had a singles set. Peter, Gerry and Mrs Kenyon came. At 4.15 Mrs Podmore, Dick, Mrs Brooks, Col and Mrs Mitchell and Mr and Mrs Palmer came. Played v Peter and Peg. Beat them 6-1.

Sunday 29 June

Nice day again. After lunch Dick came and fetched Mum and me and took us over in the 'Standard' to Moatlands. Played tennis quite a bit, had tea there and saw Dick's pigs and horses. Dick motored us home again and is coming to lunch Wednesday.

Monday 30 June

In morning practised and wrote to Mac, a very long letter as had a thrilling one from him this morning. Bought a book on dog training for Dad's Birthday. After lunch, changed and wore the green dress. We motored over to the Hon. Mrs Fields at Ballard's for her garden and tennis party.

Tuesday 1 July

Came up to town with Mum and Dad. Said goodbye to my little Bogey again who was so sad. To the shoe shop and chose a pair of spats, white ones, very smart. Then went to Burlington Arcade and got a pale grey and blue waistcoat and a grey tie for the Garden Party. Dad had lunch with us. I'm so glad he's coming with us on Saturday. Mum and I went out to Racon's and I settled on a long green organdie dress to be made. Then went and got a divine green hat in Sloane Street.

Wednesday 2 July

Went to Bond Street where at last I got my green shoes at Randles. Lovely ones! Dick motored up from home to lunch and got here late. After he took me in the car to Hay Wrightsons then to Dorothy Stewarts in Davis Street where I had my hair shampooed with pine and water waved. She did it beautifully, home at 4.15. Dick took us out with car in the Park and then went off home.

Thursday 3 July

Went out to lunch with Auntie Fay. Got home at 3.00 and rested. Wore my pink presentation dress and Gerald came and we went off to dinner with Mrs Levy who had 24 to dine. A Mr Pacey took me in and on my right sat the Hon Bobbie Harris. Very nice. Lord Cottenham and Miss Low were there etc. wonderful dinner. Left at 9.45 and walked to Hyde Park Hotel wonderful dance, enjoyed it frightfully danced with Gen Gillespie, Gerald, Major Foster, the Hon Bobbie Harris and Mr Dorian Williams etc. Left at 3.00. Gerald brought me home then he motored all the way back home.

Friday 4 July

Woke up at 8.30 but did not get up until 11.00. Then I tried on my new dress for the garden party at the Palace tomorrow. It's pale almond green organdie embroidered in white. I'm wearing green shoes and a green hat with gardenias and tulle and flesh stockings. Dick Kennion came and we had a sandwich lunch, then went off down to Wimbledon. Couldn't get seats alas, so stood for over three hours. I was nearly dead! Got home at 7.15 and then went out to dinner at the Piccadilly with Dick and Mum.

Saturday 5 July

Spent morning in bed. Dad came to lunch at 1.00 very smart in top hat, frockcoat and white spats. Changed into my new green organdie dress and new green hat and shoes. Left here at 3.00 and got to the Palace 3.15 for the Garden Party. Quite a nice day but rather cold. I enjoyed it awfully as did Mum and Dad. Met Mrs Levy and Mary and Winnie and also saw the Drewe's. Left at 6.00 changed and went home by 7.30 train.

Monday 7 July

A letter from Gerry still as mad on me as ever! Went up to town by 11.50, had nice invite from Mrs Lyall asking me to the Eton v Harrow with her but I am already going. Eve and Lily came to dinner and stayed till 11.00. Dad came up and joined us for dinner with Hugo and brought me a letter from Mr Bickerton, the man I danced with at the Dubuisson dance. Awfully thrilled!

Tuesday 8 July

Lovely hot today, went off to Lords at 11.30 with Mum. Enjoyed it awfully, had lunch there.

Wednesday 9 July

Had a letter from Mac at breakfast, and was going to Lords with Mum when Peter came and suggested to go to Wembley instead. At 1.45 Peter came and marched me off to Wembley. I have never been so frightened in my life of those terrible switchbacks! I was too frightened to scream. We only went on the racer and Jack and Jill. The latter I loved so we did it twice. Then we came home, and Peter changed here then we went and dined at the Piccadilly and then to the opera at Les Maestro and heard the Magic Flute by Mozart. Lovely music and enjoyed it frightfully. Peter went down to T.W. by 12.30 train.

Friday 11 July Eton v Harrow

Got up at 9.00 and my pale green organdie dress with green hat and green shoes and went off to Lords at 11.00. At 11:30 met Jim under the clock and left Mum who went and sat with Harold and Ursula who gave her lunch. Jim and I went on the Mound. Then as lunch looked horrid at Jim's club we went to the Piccadilly Grill Room and lunched there. Then returned to the match then Mary and Mrs Levy, Jim and I had tea at his club and then home at 7.00.

The hectic social whirl continues, weddings, tennis tournaments and dances. The flat in Hertford Street is given up on 23 July. Cesca buys a darling mascot, a solid silver owl for Peter Knox's 21st on 5 August. She enjoys the evening awfully sitting next to Peter at dinner and at cards. The Wellington Williams dance at Shenfold was wonderful. Cesca wore her pale pink presentation dress, white stockings and silver shoes, her fan and a lovely pale pink rose on her shoulder. Everyone there and the place looked too lovely for words. The Clifford Essex Band played and Searcys did the supper and breakfast. She danced with Jim the most 'who got awfully struck' and tried to kiss her once. Danced five times with Dick, and four times with Peter etc. Lost my reputation completely with Gerald by going into his room while he changed his socks. She simply loved it and stayed till 5.00.

Cesca's Mother has given her a baby gramophone, a beauty. For Goodwood Cup day she wears the pale green organdie dress, matching shoes and hat but for the drive in the Citroen a long coat and felt hat. They nearly have a crash at a turning near Colmans Corner but arrive safely after a drive of seventy miles. Tickets for the Paddock and Grandstand, awfully dear at two guineas. She won 21/9 and due to the crowds did not get home until 10.00.

A few days later she writes, 'oh how damn dull it is after London!'

Another garden party at Mrs Barrows with a string band, clock golf, croquet and tennis followed by Lewes Races in the Citroen where they had to eat their sardine sandwiches and bath buns. The parents seem to be trying to sell Parham House and Cesca and her mother look at Cowden House and Holmsly several times but are advised by Hamptons that Parham is unlikely to sell before the spring. Tennis Tournaments are played and Cesca and Noel Halsey, rather nice, 'play jolly well getting into the semi finals'. He promptly invites her to his tournament in four days time. Heavy rain in between find Cesca and her Mother feeling so bored they go up to London for the day. Cesca has her hair washed at Vasco's and a water wave set for 8/6. Ruinous! Met Mother for lunch at Stewarts and then bought the prizes for her Birthday Tennis Tournament. Three pairs of stockings purchased for 17/6. Then for her birthday, Mother bought from Plucknets the most lovely solid silver gilt engine turned toilet table set. Simply lovely. £13.00. Home about 6.30 [having had a thoroughly diverting day!]

Thursday 21 August

In the morning Mum and I had the surprise of our lives. Dad mysteriously said he had something to show us and took us into the drive and there was a lovely brand new car for us! An Austin five seater 12.16hp. Dark blue with lovely fittings and all simply beautiful. It's only done 250 miles so we have to go very slowly as yet but it's divine. After lunch it took me over to Lamberhurst to Noel Halsey's Tennis Tournament. He is such a dear and I like his mother and grannie awfully. Played badly. Everyone kept their own score and it was rather complicated. I met Mr Fane again, he is awfully nice and just a bit struck on me I think. He wanted to bring me home on the back of his bike as the car did not turn up till 7.15.

Friday 22 August

A busy morning with Mum. Rested all afternoon then Dick arrived to stay for the League of Mercy Ball at Wadhurst Castle. Changed into my sparky dress and wore a lovely rose on my shoulder. Dance very well done at the castle. Danced ten times with Dick, three with Mr Fane who I rather got off with. He is just the type I get thrilled by. Rather fell in love with him. I did not want to a bit but couldn't help it.

Saturday 23 August

I was up at 10.00. Dick not until 11.15! Went down the town and met lots of people. Everyone turns and stares at Dick and last night everyone was asking who he was. Wore my new blue dress and left in the Austin arriving at the Castle at 1.45 for Capt and Mrs Watson Smyths American Tennis Tournament. The ground was impossible! Absolutely thick mud. Played very well at first but got so tired. A terrible thunderstorm stopped everything. I talked a lot to Mr Fane. Have got it worse than ever. Dick held my hand in an absurd way coming home in the car, last night too. He is a dear thing.

Monday 25 August

The new maid Marjorie is here and is such a nice girl. She is awfully good at sewing and cutting out and was with the Countess of Antrim for sixteen months. Had such a nice letter from John. How I wish he was here. My last day of being nineteen. I am getting old!

Tuesday 26 August

Today I am twenty! Woke up and found heaps of letters. Dad gave me £10 and Mum the gramophone and the silver gilt toilet set. Spent a very busy morning preparing for our Tennis Tournament. Turned out a lovely warm day. Peg came to lunch and then everyone else, eight couples. I played with Gerald who really plays well and we got fourth place. Finished about 8.15 and enjoyed my day very much.

Mary invites Cesca to stay at Muntham Court for a week. [This was a colossal mansion belonging to the Thynne family surrounded by beautiful grounds but sadly demolished in 1961 to make way for a crematorium]. She is met at Worthing station by Lady Bearsted in their car, a Napier. They all play tennis, some play squash and ride, play pool and dance to the gramophone and are taken to Lewes Races by Mrs Levy where Cesca is given a ladies pass and won 12/-. Home by train on Thursday 4 September. So dull at home!

More tennis with both Dick, 'felt rather fond of my great big Dick today' and Noel Halsey, 'I like awfully'. Cesca with her Mother stay with the Stanley-Clarkes at their charming old manor house in Bulford and are collected from the station by Auntie Baba in the Standard. They go to a Gymkana, visit Stonehenge and play tennis on the Garrison hard courts. Dinner parties and the brigade sports followed by church at the Garrison. This Cesca enjoys as they sit in the front pew and process out first down the aisle in front of everyone! She walks up Beacon Hill, a good six and a half miles. They return home on the 15 September via Golanski where she chooses some furs to be sent down. Dad goes off to Yorkshire for a holiday 19 September for 10 days. Cesca makes new curtains for her bedroom in a deep shade of rose and bought a lovely bit of brocade gold and old rose and made a lovely cushion and altered all the pictures in her room too.

The clocks go back one hour 21 September and Mac leaves for India 23 September whereupon Cesca burns all his old letters with her old curtains. Cesca and her Mother settle to go to Italy for sixteen days leaving on 6 October and in preparation Cesca goes to Randalls and buys a pair of shoes, lovely crocodile and antelope, flat heeled for 55/- and a book, *Things seen on the Italian Lakes*. Dad returns on 1 September 'looking ever so fit and brown as a berry'. A new fur smart choker is ordered from the fur shop on the Pantiles for eight guineas. Both Dick Kennion and Tony Richards come down to see her before she leaves on Monday 6 October for Paris with her Mother. She arranges to leave Bogey with Harrison.

Monday 6 October

Up early, finished packing and left home in the car with Mum and Hogben at 9.45. We had to wait a good time before we could embark on the boat. Very rough sea, have never seen it so rough, so went and lay down at once and fortunately were both all right. Had nice First Class carriage to Paris and no difficulty with the douane. Arrived at Hotel Bedford at 6.45.

Tuesday 7 October

Had breakfast in bed. Mum went off to the Bank and I went straight to Madame Chevriers and ordered a dress and coat and will return with Mum later to choose material. Then Mum and I went out and saw darling Paris. I changed £1 for 84 francs then went to Lyse Berchous where I found such lovely evening dresses. Couldn't make up my mind but finally settled on a deep beige one heavily embroidered in silver. A beauty and suits me. 1,300 francs, very dear but lovely and so original. Chose material and left Paris for Gare de l'Est at 8.30.

Wednesday 8 October

When we arrived last night at Gare de l'Est found we had to share our couchettes with two deadly German men. I felt I'd sooner walk than be bottled up all night with those two brutes so I seized hold of a man and he like an angel gave me two couchettes held for two people who never turned up so Mum and I were installed with a Swiss man and his wife. However I did not sleep at all as they all snored so. Arrived at Basle 6.15 then lovely Lucerne. A good breakfast and hot bath at the Schweizerhof and I felt fine again. Poor Mum not too grand however.

Thursday 9 October

Woke up early, had breakfast and left Lucerne and got lovely First Class seats all to ourselves to Lugano. Passed through the most delightful countryside and then through the St Gothard tunnel, nine and a half miles long. Directly we arrived the other side it was hot. Extraordinary! Had a two hour wait for the steamer and I got a bit of a shock as Mother went for a walk and fell down, while I looked after the luggage. She is so stiff in the knees, poor dear. We enjoyed the steamer trip very much. Then took a priceless little railway to Menaggio which is the sweetest spot surrounded by very high mountains and a deep blue lake. All up the side of the mountains are terraces where vines and brilliant yellow pumpkins grow and tall green cypress trees and little pink and yellow villas peep out.

Friday 10 October

Mum and I had a quiet morning then went for a walk behind the hotel in the afternoon. The hotel is fairly full of old fossils and honeymooners. We were spoken to by some priceless old souls staying in the hotel.

They spend a delightful ten days in Menaggio taking the steamer across to Varenna and Belaggio in wonderful hot weather. Belaggio is full of Huns and good shops selling tortoiseshell. Mother buys a pair of combs for 50 lira and a cigarette case for Auntie Fan. Cesca buys a choker necklace of round blond tortoishell beads for 105 lira. Cesca goes to the bank and gets 102 lira for £1 and then shops for Christmas presents in the Sicilian shop. On their return to the hotel the old padre there tells Cesca that to obtain the best tortoisehell one has to skin the poor animal alive at Naples where it is done. She now regrets buying the necklace. On 17 October, their last day, Cesca hates the thought of going but is comforted by the thought the supper dance is only a week away. She and her Mother have been very close this trip and has confided in her things Cesca had not known before. They set off by steamer and train, first class carriage all to them selves, through the customs and passport controls to Basle and stay at the Three Kings. Quite a nice hotel but very German. The next morning after breakfast in a very pretty dining room overlooking the Rhine, they travelled to Paris in a crowded first class carriage full of French who refuse to open the windows. Sickening as it was so hot. She was pleased to leave Switzerland, so expensive, pro German and all hemmed in too. Arrived at the Continental.

Cesca felt the' hotel was ruinous as they charged 15fr for breakfast, awful and is full of Americans who throw their blessed dollar about and in consequence everything has gone up'. They return to Madame Chevriers and Mother has a coat fitted to match her dress. Her blond dress is lovely with a pleated side and a long coat to match. A charming hat is purchased in Hubert's in brown with feathers. They enjoy a musical comedy in a tiny theatre and find all their new clothes looking very nice at their last visit to Madame Chevriers. On 22 October they leave the Continental and have a carriage to themselves all the way from the Gare du Nord to Calais. 'The sea was mountains high and I have never known such a frightful crossing. I never thought we would get into Dover harbour it was so bad. Everyone was sick and a poor old American lady was flung right off her berth to the other side of the ship. It was awful. Had tea at Dover and were met at Tonbridge by Dad and Hogben with the car so all was well'. A General Election was called on 19 October, Mother voted before they left for London. [Cesca at 20, could not vote as women over the age of 21 were not given the right to vote until 1928]. A wonderful result, 408 Conservatives, 150 Labour and 37 Liberals. Bogey is collected from Harrison after his bill is paid of £1.10.0 for looking after him. Cesca has a singing lesson in London and is frightened as the room is full of people listening and her teacher ties her up with a belt so she cannot breathe. Cesca is now having weekly singing lessons in London and is practicing daily. Garceau is pleased with her. She has lunch with Aunt Edie and is encouraged to tell her all about 'her boys' as Aunt Edie calls them. The Spa Dance and the Bartleys Dance both take place in November and Noel Halsey and Dick Kennion are in attendance. Noel invited her to dine before the Bartley Dance, her Mother rang to say no but he 'wangled her so all was well'. The Halseys lay on a prodigious dinner of eight courses. Letters from Jack from India and from John and Martin inviting her to the Sandhurst Dance. Cesca is very busy sending out invitations, about 100, to her dance at home on 30 December.

Noel comes to supper 30 November and they played foolish games. She does like him frightfully. Answers are pouring in for the dance. Great excitement! Mary Levy is engaged to Stuart Montagu, Lord Swaythling's son. Too thrilling for words! Cesca goes up to London with Mother and goes first to get a collar for Nigger from Burlington Arcade. Then to Mary's and found them all terribly excited. Mrs Levy delighted too. Lunch with Mother at Searcy's but the concert is cancelled as Garceau has such a bad cold.

Wednesday 3 December

Spent busy morning with Kathleen packing all my things together for the RE Ball at Chatham. Left after lunch in the car for Chatham, Dick did not arrive until after we us at the hotel. He and I went for a walk up to the Barracks. Changed into my new beaded brown dress which looked really lovely. We were twelve for dinner. I sat next to Dick and Morris. All great fun but I didn't dance enough with Dick. I got on rather well with Morris, almost too well as he is a bit of a lad. I liked Foster very much too and have invited him to our dance.

Mother's birthday on 8 December and has quite a lot of presents, mainly books. Kathleen starts to make Cesca's fancy dress costume, My Columbine! On 10

December, terrible fog but Mum and Cesca go up to London and the 10.8 train is very crowded and does not arrive until 1.00. They go to Gamba to buy Cesca's evening Columbine slippers, pale pink ones. Then to Smythson's where they ordered writing paper and looked at programmes [dance ones]. Very late home due to the fog. The following day, joy of joys! A letter from her Martin saying he has tickets after all for the dance at Sandhurst. She goes to look at programmes locally for the dance and bought a Christmas present for Mother, a book on Italy and the Lakes. On Tuesday 8 December, Kathleen packs up Cesca's things and she leaves in the car to have lunch with Joannie and then they leave together in Joannie's car, 'Little Nell' for the Sandhurst Dance. Martin and Mr and Mrs Hicks come down to tea at the Duke of York where they are staying. 'Wore my new beige and silver dress and danced with Martin nearly all the time. Martin was such a dear'. They leave at 12.30 the next day and have lunch at Guildford, foggy and dark and home at 4.00. Then Dick Kennion turned up on his way back from Chatham. 'I loved last night. It was fun and Martin does dance divinely and seems quite fond of me. But Dick is nice!' Cesca stayed the night in London for Lady Ferguson's dance returning the next day for the Wadhurst Hockey Club dance where she danced with Dick most! On the 23 December another dance at the Pump Rooms where she dances mostly with Edmund Horden, seven times! 'I like him frightfully and he dances simply wonderfully. He is really a dear'.

Christmas Day, a very windy morning and a sore throat prevents Cesca from attending early service. Suzanne, her French governess, is staying for Christmas. Mum gave her a lovely case to hold her gramophone records and also gave her records, 'It had to be you' and 'Oh Eva' and a book on illuminating. £5 from Dad. Then she went with Mum and Dad in the afternoon to visit the Hospital and go round all the wards. On Boxing Day Cesca is taken to a fancy dress dance at the Spa with Edmund Horden and they dance together a good deal. She found the dance really thrilling but there were some awful people there and a good few quite drunk.

Tuesday 30 December

Woke up very early with excitement and could not sleep again. Busy doing final arrangements for the dance, caterers and moving furniture. Terrible night with pouring rain and gales. Met Tony and he and Hogben moved the furniture and Dick arrived in time for lunch. Lunch went off rather badly as Dick and Tony did not hit it off. I went for a rest and Dick and Tony both went fast asleep in the library. After tea I changed and wore the Columbine dress that Kathleen had made me, pale pink and it looked very nice. Dad wore his MA robes, Dick was splendid in Pickwickian brown velvet and a colossal black hat. Made him look eight foot! Tony was very good as a Persian prince and Averil a pretty disgusting sight in Empire period with very low neck, her hair looked lovely but I wished she had worn more clothes. The dinner party was great fun. Then afterwards to my astonishment I saw Hogben dressed up in a clown's outfit that he had kept secret from me! He took us in two car loads to Calverly and brought us back. The band arrived about nine and everyone arrived and I danced five with Tony, four with Dick, four with Edmund etc. The band was splendid and so was supper. We kept dancing until 2.45 and then went home and danced to the gramophone and talked. Averil was the only failure. She flirted and behaved vilely with everyone she could lay her hands on.

After lunch the next day, Averil having left in a taxi and the furniture having been moved back by Hogben and Tony, Cesca and Tony go for a walk before she sees him off on the 4.48.
'How I loved it all last night. It's been such a very happy year for me. Wonderful! Goodbye 1924'.

1925 Parham House

Wild, wet and windy weather ushers the new year in and Cesca continues to attend dozens of dances throughout the first six moths of the year interspersed with singing lessons in London at Garceau's. The Stanley-Clarkes come to stay for a few days in February. Mahjong is played most evenings. Then Cesca and her Mother take the train up to Cambridge on Friday 13 February at the invitation of Tony for several days.

The next day whom should they meet but Mr and Mrs Ainslie and Pat who Cesca has not seen since she was six. 'He is a dear and very good looking'. They go down to the river and watch the bump races.

Sunday 15 February

Another lovely morning. At Magdalene to see Geoff Pontifex's rooms. Saw all over the College which is lovely and quite one of the nicest. Pat Ainslie came to lunch. Have lost my heart to him. He's a perfect sort of person. Loves to be alive like me. Has got the most ripping car too, an Eric Campbell. It's wonderful. He took me in it and it went like the wind.

Monday 16 February

Had letter from Dad enclosing one from Jack. (Got it badly, poor Jack!)

Cesca is still having weekly singing lessons in London. Besides Jack there are amongst her boyfriends, Dick, Noel, Jim, Guy and Edmund. On 24 February she receives a letter from Pat A. 'Too thrilling for words! Asking me up to May Week. Isn't it just too wonderful! So excited about Pat. Went for a long walk with the dogs and wrote to Pat accepting'.

Wednesday 25 February Cesca goes up to town and then meets Edmund and Joannie and another RAF lad called Knox for the Rugger at Twickenham RAF v RM won by the RAF, a very thrilling match. They then take a taxi to Piccadilly 'where we danced and had tea. There met another RAF lad called Alec Ryde. Awful bounder but a nice bounder. Such fun dancing with Edmund again'.

Saturday 7 March

Dick and I changed and went off to the Spa dance with Joannie and Edmund. Had great fun. Tore along the passages upstairs and knocked on people's doors. Nearly got turned out. Such fun.

Monday 16 March

Dick's 21st party at the Savoy Hotel. Wore brown evening dress and sat on Dick's right. Danced downstairs. All men danced frightfully well. I loved it all and Dick was such a perfect host. Feel a deeper heart beat than ever.

Friday 20 March

Shock! Misery! Guy returns from Australia to announce he is engaged to an Australian girl. Felt awfully upset and could not sleep.

Monday 23 March

Hectic rush packing, Florence helping me. Three letters from Mac, Jack and Rex. No time to read them. Off to Tonbridge and Dover. Dad was beastly when we said goodbye. Peeved at our going I suppose. Splendid journey and wonderfully smooth crossing, arriving very fresh and fit at Calais.

Bedford Hotel at 6.45. Such fun being in Paris again.

A happy week in Paris ordering dresses and coats for Mother and Cesca from Chevriers and also from Dellas which was very thrilling with lovely things. Fittings follow and a very good lunch at Pruniers recommended by Peter. Awfully good cooking, Cesca chose 'Sole Prunier'. They also lunch at Lucca, very good but dear. On Saturday they enjoyed lunch at Samaritaine which was very good indeed and not dear. The Opera for Samson and Delilah and a visit to the Louvre and shopping for gloves and scent. The Hordens and the Timberlakes join them for tea and dinner at the Hotel Bedford. Home on Monday 30 March having packed one dress from Dellas. A good journey home, train empty and another smooth crossing, no trouble with the Customs. Dad met them at Tonbridge and Dick rang inviting her to the Gunner's Point to Point which she had to refuse as she was going up to town!

On Sunday 12 April Monkey and Peg fetch Cesca in his new Darracq, sports model, and they motor down to Eastbourne in just over the hour. 'Wonderful time considering the crowded state of the road! Such fun. It goes like the wind. Touched 70mph several times. Monkey CAN drive. Had tea at the Grand and raced a car all the way home, finally passed it'. On 29 April Cesca develops shingles on her face, neck and back. Her face in an awful state and Dad orders her special lotion for it. She refuses to see anyone for a week.

By the 21 May the painters have finally finished painting the greater part of the ground floor and it looks charming. Friday 22 May The Skinners Ball. Cesca stays at Hans Crescent and wore her brown beaded dress. Jim dines with her and 'was awfully smart and very nice. I loved the dance. Great fun and danced mostly with Jim who was sweet and asked me to stay. Bed at 4.30'.

Saturday 23 May London Oxford.

Woke and had breakfast in bed. Then Peter rang to say he would call for me and Mother at 3.00. Mum decided to go down by train to Oxford, left at 2.30. I went to lunch at the Levy's. Returned to hotel and was sitting waiting for Peter but the idiots in the hotel had told him I had gone with Mother. Did not know what to do, felt awfully lost. However took next train down to Oxford arrived at 6.00. Peter turned up at 7.00 having had an awful adventure. Lady Diana Cooper ran into him at Maidenhead and completely smashed up his car and hers. Poor Peter awfully upset. Went after dinner to the Trout and danced. Next day went down to Queens, met a Mr Jock O' Gilvie, an American very amusing and he punted Marjorie and me down to the races to the strains of a gramophone.

Tuesday 26 May

Lovely morning all seven of us to breakfast at the Trout. Great fun. Perfect morning. I like Edward Carey Coaker awfully. He has a sweet Alsatian. After lunch at the George we all went down to the races. I wore my new muslin. Queens did very well got bumps everyday. Had dinner at Queens in College. A Mr Beresford, the chaplin, very good looking but did not like him. He ran down the Bullingdon Club and made me very angry.

Thursday 28 May

Queens Ball. The previous evening all the men had got very drunk at a bump supper next door and John came in drunk. I was furious. The most happy day I've had for ages. Down to breakfast Peter first to turn up looking very bright but with a gash across his cheek. Then John to whom I did not address a word! John very ashamed of himself. Then Chris and Edward. Peter bought us lovely flowers and cherries. We went down to the river, Peter and Marjorie in one canoe. John, Chris and I in another. I hated it and insisted on getting out and led Chris a wild chase round an island. On getting off the island and crossing some punts, I caught my heel and did splits and fell in the river. Chris saved me however and I was taken back to the Clarendon (*Cesca never learned to swim*). Had some coffee and made it up. Rested in afternoon, changed into blue bridesmaid frock and went with Mum and Marjorie to Queens for dinner with Peter. Oh the dance was fun! Danced with John most, he dances too wonderfully and is so nice. I like him desperately. Then a good bit with Peter who was perfect dear and is v. fond of me. Three with Chris. He is very struck on me. Home at 2am.

Friday 29 May

Alas all over! Wonderful, wonderful Eights week. Peter has asked Mum and me for next year however. Cheers! Home at 4.00, sad saying goodbye to Peter. Dick turned up for tea, dear old Dick!

Thursday 4 June The 4ᵀᴴ June

Stay Levy's at Lowndes Square. Mrs Levy, Betty Style and Winnie and me all motored down with Bud in the Daimler. Arrived at Eton at 12.15 and met Jack very smart all dressed up. Lunched with housemaster Mr Young, very terrifying. Watched the cricket then tea in Jack's room. Lovely tea lobster and asparagus, banana mess cake, iced coffee and I don't know what. Dinner at the Etonian Country Club, lovely place by the river. Saw procession of boats from the lawns. After dinner saw the fireworks, too wonderful for words. Betty Styles, such a nice girl, has asked me to her coming out dance 22 July Maidstone. Went home to TW by 4.30.

Saturday 6 June

Dance Metropole Brighton. Had my things packed and went off in car with Mum and Dad, dropped off at the Rectory and played tennis. After lunch Edmund took me out in his new car, an Amil car, very fast and nice. More tennis then changed into pink for dinner. After dinner set out in the cars Freddie Settrington and me the dilapidated Bentley, Edward and Marjorie in Amil car. Home at 4.30am after a paper chase.

Friday 12 June

Went up to London and met Mum and Douglas Bisshopp, cousin from Tanganyika. Quite nice tall and good looking but rather old. Had lunch at Piccadilly grill. Then we all three went to Liverpool St. and I caught my train, Mr Ainslie wasn't there, I had expected him to meet me. The car met me at Harlow. Both Mr and Mrs Ainslie awfully nice and lovely house and garden.

Saturday 13 June [Pat Ainslie became the Watson's family solicitor]

Perfect day and had everything packed up after breakfast. At 11.00 Pat in Hugh Lang's Bentley and Cynthia Watson [Cynthia Watson and her brother Michael were in fact Rupert and Virginia Watson's father and aunt] the other girl in the party arrived. I like her frightfully also like Hugh Lang though he is very different to what I expected him to be. Six foot four, fairish and lovely figure. We motored over to Cambridge, Cynthia, Hugh and me in the Bentley, the Ainslies in the other car. Our three rooms are very nice with a sitting room. Lunch at Varsity Arms then off to watch the polo in the Bentley, the four of us. Great fun. Then to Pitt club lawns for the races Oh such fun. Then they had a bump supper and we dined at Varsity Arms. Then to the theatre.

Sunday 14 June

All motored back to Harlow in the Bentley for lunch and friends came over and we played tennis. All played pretty well. I played very well on the whole. During dinner awful tragedy, some of Mrs Ainslie's chickens were killed by a fox, she was awfully upset and no wonder. Back to Cambridge at 11.00 in the Bentley and sat next to Hugh. Like him most awfully.

Monday 15 June

We went round to Pat's rooms first thing then went round the College. Collected our lunch and got a punt and Pat punted up the river and we tied up on the bank. Then Pat and Hugh bathed and sunk the punt amongst other excitements. We then went onto Grantchester and had tea there. We dined at the Varsity Arms then Mrs A went home and we got to the ball at 10.00, wonderfully well done and perfect floor. Pat is not a good dancer and nor is Hugh but they are both such perfect dears. Cynthia and I got to bed at 7am.

Tuesday 16 June Christ's and John's College Balls
Slept till 11.00 then Pat and Hugh took us to lunch at the Varsity Arms. Watched tennis Cambridge v All England great fun. Wore my pink dress for dinner at Hugh's rooms in the Silver St. Very nice rooms and good taste. He is so nice, so is Pat. Then went off to Christ's Ball, lovely floor and better than last night. Danced only with Pat and Hugh. Pat got rather struck. Went on after supper couldn't get in so had to get over 8ft wall. But Hugh caught me and Pat pushed. It was a lovely ball. I loved it all.

Wednesday 17 June
After the dance we went in Pat's car to breakfast in the Bellvue Hotel. So funny having breakfast in evening dress but great fun. Hugh v tired and Pat rather cross. I never went to bed at all. Packed and Pat came round and we went to say goodbye to Hugh. I hated it. He is one of the nicest people I've ever met. Pat and I fitted ourselves into the Americ Campbell with all our luggage and a bicycle strapped on. Mrs A, Cynthia and the chauffeur in the Swift. Lunched at Rowney Bury. Cynthia left and Pat and I went out and shot three rabbits. Then caught the train to London, rather wonderful journey with Pat. Home by 6.16 and met by Mum and Dad.

Cesca receives a letter from Pat asking her to Henley 'so sweet of him'.

Wednesday 1 July
In London shopping after Lady Court Hope's dance. Went with Mother and bought a long thick winter tweed coat in blue for

36

Cesca and Belinda the Bentley 1927

Joannie, Pat & Cesca on Hugh's Bentley

Edmund's Amilcar 1925

Edmund, Cesca, Joannie & Pat 26.8.1925   Pat & Cesca 1925 Parham

Bill, Cesca, Brian Knox Cranwell 1925   Cesca's Mother Fanny Oxford
1925

Cynthia Watson, Hugh, Cesca,   Cesca, Henry & Alice Stanley-Clarke 1925
Mrs Ainslie 1925

Scotland for £3.10s very nice. Then ordered from Gerrards a coat and skirt in same blue tweed. Back to Hans Crescent to dine alone with Mother.

Thursday 2 July Henley

The most lovely day I have spent for a very long time. Left the hotel 9.30 for Paddington and caught 10.10 to Henley. Met at the station by Pat in his car, very smart. Motored us to Phylliss Court club where we sat on the lawns and watched the racing from the banks. Had lunch with Pat, and then of course saw Hugh. I went on the Umpires launch, marvellous fun. Saw a lot of Hugh and of course Pat. They are darlings both of them and Pat is too good to me for words. They are both coming to Scotland. Just missed the 8.00 home so had dinner at Charing Cross. Home very tired but very happy.

The following day Dick collects her and they motor over to a dance at Groombridge Place. A marvellous dance all done by the MayFair Co. 'Oh it was such fun. Only thing was we had a thunderstorm and it came through the Marquee. Home at 4.30'.
The next day cricket Kent v Warwick with Dick. Cesca is very, very tired.

Friday 10 July

Off to Eton v Harrow at Lords with Jim. Wore my pink dress and brown hat with roses. Had lunch at Jim's club and wandered around, saw loads of friends. Had tea at old Etonian's tent with Jim and Cynthia. Then met Hugh terribly pleased to see him and he came and sat with us. Back to Hans Crescent and wore my blue. Dined at West Halkin St, Joanie, Edmund and Brian Knox. Motored down to Hurlingham and J's and E's cars. Lovely dance but, too crowded to dance. Edmund and I danced together so happy, bed 4.30.

Saturday 11 July

Eton v Harrow with Monkey. A draw at lunchtime. Had lunch in old Harrovian Tent. Met up with Hugh, he was late and I upset. Watched cricket from free seats and he gave me lovely tea at Carlton club. Then Mum and me came home. Dad v. cross. And next day had terrible row with Dad after lunch.

Then more tennis parties, county cricket matches, dances, fittings and shopping in London with Mother. On Wednesday 22 July Cesca stays with Lord and Lady Bearsted for the Styles dance. Betty looked charming and Cesca dances mostly with Dick.

Tuesday 28 July London Cranwell

Cesca's first encounter with Bill. Note the misspelling 'Pierson' instead of Pearson. There does not seem to be any mutual attraction.

After two fittings rushed to join Joannie for lunch then she motored us up to Cranwell met Edmund on way in Grantham. Bill Pierson-Rogers and Brian Knox met us at the Mess. Then onto to Sleaford to change. Sent wire to Mother. Dined at 7.15, Edmund, Brian and Bill and his sister Pat dined with us. Quite nice little hotel. Then to Cranwell for concert which was awfully good.

Wednesday 29 July Flying Display and Dance RAF Cranwell

A lovely day had breakfast with Joannie then motored over to Cranwell in our best bib and tucker for the display. Edmund looked wonderful. Sir Philip Sassoon inspected them all and the band played. Oh it was wonderful. Then watched the flying. Edmund and Brian both flew. Helped Edmund pack and had lunch in Mess. Then changed later and wore my new green dress, suits me so I'm told. Motored to Cranwell through an awful thunderstorm. All boys waiting and looking very smart. Danced with the General and various officers, five with Bill, five with Brian who is a dear, and about eight with Edmund. Sat out with Edmund who is so wonderful. I do love him so and he loves me. To bed at 5.00 Oh! such fun.

Thursday 30 July

Everyone rather cross and tired. Joanie and I motored down together to Eaton Socon, Bill escorting us on his motorbike then Edmund and Brian arrived. I went with Edmund. Brian with Joannie. Got back to London and rang up Mum, found she had fallen downstairs and hurt herself. Felt worried. Had dinner then motored home. Poor little Bill went home, he is so in love with Joannie.

Saturday 1 August

Lovely day. Joannie asked me to join her and Edmund for the Light Aeroplane flying tests at Lympne. Mum said I could so Edmund fetched me in the Amilcar. Such fun. Saw Sir John Salmond and Sir Philip Sassoon there. The flying was marvellous and all the machines terribly interesting, especially so as E. explained everything so marvellously. He is so wonderful. So happy, a wonderful day!

Cesca leaves for Muntham Court to stay for a week on Wednesday 5 August. Lots of tennis with Winnie, Margery and Vi and Bobbie, Jane and Jack and dancing in the evening to the gramophone, singing old songs and playing priceless games! She returns by train on Wednesday 12 August and immediately starts to get her things ready for Scotland leaving on Friday 14 August. However there is time for Edmund and Joannie and the Andersons to dine and all go to Cabaret Girl at the Opera House in Tunbridge Wells.

Friday 14 August Leave for Edzell, Scotland

Up frightfully early, had breakfast and finished off all our packing by 6.30. Left home by 7.15 with three trunks, two suitcases, hat box, fishing rods, gramophone, mah-jong set and Bogey. Reached London 9.00 and Euston 9.15, where we met Uncle Henry (Stanley-Clarke) very fit and cheerful. Comfortable carriage all to ourselves, all the way up thanks to Bogey who did not allow anyone else in the carriage. Had lunch and dinner on the train. Arrived Bridge of Dun about 10.00. Then 10 miles drive, Dad met us with

car. Very tired and felt miserable as have to share a room with
Mum. Got to bed however and slept solidly.

Saturday 15 August [A devastating fire in 1952 destroyed a large part
of this substantial hotel].

Woke up at 8.00. Most heavenly spot this is. The Panmure hotel too
is most comfortable and food excellent. Have interviewed the
manager and he can give up rooms for all our guests. Wire from
Jim delighted and surprised accepting my invitation up here.
Spent morning with Mum quietly unpacking and out for short
walk. Then after lunch a long walk along Esk river. Mum in car to
fetch Dad and Uncle Henry who shot four brace grouse and a hare.
[Fordoun Hill Moor, 2,000 acres]. Met nice couple staying Col and
Mrs le Rossingnol.

On Sunday they all go to church opposite the hotel. 'An amazing service'. After
tea a visit to Edzell Castle ruins and Bogey and Dad's spaniel Nigger meet and
the result was quite satisfactory though Bogey does not love Nig much. On
Monday 17 Cesca walks all day with the guns, roughly 12 miles. Hot but lovely
and the sea is visible from the moor. Eight brace and two hares. Cesca was not
a bit tired. The next day Cesca helps Dad pack up seven brace to Mrs Levy, Lady
Amhurst, Dr Chisholm etc. On Wednesday 19 August Pat arrives before
breakfast by the 7.05 train, and is looking very fit. He went out with the guns
and they all return soaked to the skin with only two and a half brace. After
dinner Cesca and Pat go out for a walk down the river. 'He is a perfect dear, so
young and fresh. Wonderful'. The next two days fishing and walking and Dad
beats Uncle Henry at golf both days. On Friday evening the Rossignols have
invited them all to a dance they are giving at the Memorial Hall. They motor
over in the Rossignols' Lanchester. The dance is amusing, good floor and band.
Danced all the time with Pat.
Another day on the moor on Saturday, six brace and two hares. 'Perfect day
and not tired at all. I do love the moor, the heather, everything. It's near to
heaven'.

Monday 24 August

Perfect day. Went off up the moor with lunch, Henry, Pat, Dad and
Smith the keeper. Four brace and a hare shot. Rained in morning,
enjoyed the day but felt very tired owing to wet feet. Pat shot very

well. On our way home we met Edmund and Joannie who had arrived from Stirling looking very fit and happy. In evening danced with E and Pat. Oh I do love this place and feel so well and strong and happy.

Tuesday 25 August

Went to Montrose in the Amilcar with Edmund, Joannie and Pat. Frisked about on the sands, built sand castles. Home to lunch. Went out later and unfortunately Edmund sprained his ankle which is sickening as he will not be able to shoot tomorrow if it is not better.

Wednesday 16 August My Birthday

I am 21. Seems so funny. Had lovely presents. Cheque £100 from Dad and an awfully nice seed pearl necklace. From Mum a lovely pair of field glasses from Dollonds, and a fur coat to come! A wristwatch from Uncle A., a camera from Barbara and a lapis lazulite necklace from Pat, sweet of him. After breakfast Dad and Pat went off to the moor and we all went off at 11.30 in Edmund's car with the lunch. I ricked my ankle after lunch and fainted which was trying. Walked all afternoon and Pat shot three grouse with two shots. After dinner we all danced in the ballroom. Pat seems rather fond of me, also E.

Thursday 27 August

We all fished on the West Water in the morning and came back on back of a wagon. Helped Edmund clean his car and tighten up bolts and screws. Edmund left after lunch for Kent. After tea Pat and I went out with Bogey by the river. Had lovely walk and long talk. Returned about 6.30 and found Hugh had arrived looking very fit and nice. After dinner we danced later.

They all go out on the moor including Joannie who walks very well. Hugh shot well and Dad very badly and Pat did not have much. Cesca's heels hurt and her ankle still. 'Hugh is so nice and Mum and Dad have lost their hearts to him. Pat of course too can do nothing wrong'.

Saturday 29 August

Decided to go out for the day and left in Hugh's car at 10.30. Went to Aberdeen where Pat and Hugh went to see some friends. Joannie and I bought some lunch for a picnic. Motored to Banchory, Ballater, Balmoral, where we had lunch and saw the Queeen. Braemar and home via Glenshee and Brechin. Over 170 miles and was fun. Mum very peeved with us because we were late home. Danced in the evening.

Sunday evening they played consequences 'and laughed and laughed and made a frightful noise. Hugh is a perfect dear and Mum and Dad like him most frightfully and Pat too, who can do nothing wrong. I quite agree'. Cesca helps Joannie pack on Monday and sees her off at the station and Hugh, Pat and Dad go off shooting and have a good day. After tea she helped Hugh pack, had dinner then he left at 9.00. 'Pat and I both miss him frightfully'. The next day, more birds are packed up and sent to Aunt Edie etc. 'Jim arrived at lunchtime very well and fit. Went for long walk along the Esk with Mum and Dad to the Pools of Solitude. About six miles. I miss Hugh awfully'. On Wednesday Pat, Jim and Dad with Cesca have a good day, seven and a half brace. Jim and Pat both shot well. The next day, after lunch Pat and Cesca went for a long walk 'and had a long talk about things in general and us in particular'. The following day, Friday, They all went for a long walk to Mooran Bridge about five miles away. 'I had a row with the family and walked off alone. But was caught up by Pat so walked back with him'. They had another walk together after lunch and 'talked all by ourselves'. After tea, Jim and Cesca went out alone. 'It's so funny. They both are jealous of one another and like to be with me. Jim is nice but gets on my nerves a bit. Pat is wonderful' Cesca on Saturday a very windy day for their big day of driven grouse divides herself between Jim and Pat all day. A Mr Garvie never touched a feather all day and was thought very dangerous indeed. Six brace are shot and no one shooting well.

Sunday 6 September

Pat's last day. What misery. Ah! Pat packed and then after lunch we went out for a long walk as it's the last one. He is the most wonderful man I have ever met. Don't know what I shall do when he's gone. After tea, Jim and I went out. Like him too very much but it would be nicer if he was not here just now.

Monday 7 September

Oh what misery. Simply could not stop crying. Thank heavens I have got bites all round my eyes which helped matters and the family didn't guess at least, I hope not. Pat left by 9.45 train. What shall I do now? Jim and I went for long walk. He was so nice and kind to me too. I'm sure he guesses about Pat. There was a very good entertainer in the evening, most amusing. It helped to cheer me up.

Shooting again on Tuesday and the birds terribly wild. Only shot two brace. Jim very nice, much nicer without Pat. Jim had early dinner then left by the 8.05 for Euston. Cesca finds it awful now everyone has gone and misses Pat so.
A letter from Pat is a comfort and she starts to pack. She takes Bogey for a walk along the river, 'all full of memories. Oh! Wonderful Edzell'.

Thursday 10 September

Our last day at Edzell. Finished packing. In afternoon Dad, Mum and I went for our last walk. Coming home along the Brechin Road saw an old man on a seat looking terribly ill. Dad turned back and he died immediately. It was awful. Mum went to the Doctors and I stopped a car and sent man in it to the police and then ran and got help. I have never seen anyone dead before. It was awful. He was a Mr Sharp of Dundee.

Friday 11 September Leave Edzell

I slept nearly all the way home. We changed at Bridge of Dun and there picked up a colossal salmon sent on by Pat and weighing over 19 lbs. The dogs were very good and we had a carriage to ourselves all the way to Euston. Had breakfast there, bought papers and then by taxi to Charing Cross arriving home by about 12.00. Spent the rest of the day getting straight and turning out drawers etc. It is hateful being down south again, after wonderful Scotland, feel flat now.

Letters from her beloved Pat arrive frequently and Cesca thinks he is wonderful writing so often. He invites her to stay at Rowney Bury on 30 September. Mum and Cesca travel up to London to Golanski's in Liverpool Street to choose a fur coat for her birthday. 'Wonderful of Mum, Marmot full length done in lines, with Russian collar and crepe de chine lining. Too lovely'. On 18 September Mother opens a bank account for Cesca, £100 to start it and with her Father's £100 has £200! 'Uncle Hammond arrives to stay, looks well weighing 12 stone but is madder than ever we all think'. Cesca is given the most beautiful RAF badge brooch by Edmund. 'Lovely one, so good of him'. A card from Hugh sent from Pisa. He has driven over 1000 miles and is on his way home.

Wednesday 30 September Harlow.

Finish my packing and said goodbye to Mum and Dad and went to London. First booked in my luggage at Charing Cross. Then to Goldsmiths left Mum's diamonds and fetched my pearls. Then to Liberty, Fortnum & Mason. Then had my hair cut, singed and brushed and bought a brush for £2.3.0. Lunched with Mary at 8 Grosvenor Crescent, then bought some gloves and picked up my hat and ordered woollen combies. Then picked up my luggage and met Pat at Liverpool Street and travelled down to Harlow together. After dinner danced till 10.00.

Cesca finds Mr and Mrs Ainslie charming and so nice to her. Loves the place and the weather is perfect too! They visit Cynthia Watson at the Chantry. In the afternoon they go to Wembley in the car for the Torchlight Tattoo, dinner at the Stadium Restaurant. Cesca finds it all simply wonderful, heavenly evening and confesses to be so in love with Pat. The next day they lunch with Pat's cousins at Knebworth Manor House, have tea with Cynthia and then change to go out after dinner to a dance at Hatfield Broad Oak given by the AASCRETA. Pat very smart in Mess kit. Heaven. On Saturday Pat and Cesca went out beagling at the Swire's place where they saw lots of hares and enjoyed the run enormously. A dinner party is held that evening and they dance afterwards. On Sunday they drive up with Mr and Mrs Bernie Ainslie to Cambridge and have lunch in Pat's rooms at Pembroke. Home in the evening for a walk and more long talks together which Cesca loves. The days go by in a golden October haze, driving with Pat, his fox terrier Sam on her knee and the car doing 40-50 mph, Oh!! Heaven! Had a picnic lunch near Manuden. Perfectly wonderful. Picking walnuts and spend lots of time alone together. They leave Harlow on Wednesday evening for the Savoy, meeting Mr and Mrs Bernard Ainslie there and have a wonderful dinner. 'Danced in the ballroom, such fun and most amusing people there and lovely dresses'. The wonderful week comes to an end and after a sleepless night, her packing finished by the maid, and long farewells to Mr and Mrs A. who both have been so kind, she leaves for the station with Pat. 'Have never felt more miserable leaving Pat standing on the platform looking miserable too' The next day Cesca is reluctantly having her things packed to stay at Rogate with Dick Kennion who fetches her at 9.40 in the car. Cesca observes the Kennions live very simply and she feels the house is very cold.

The next day she receives a letter from Pat and wishes she was with him. In the evening they proceed slowly in several cars to the dance at Shalford Park as there was frightful fog. 'I was frozen even though I had on my new fur coat. Danced all the time with Dick who got v. foolish and in love'. The following morning Cesca admits she did not enjoy last night as Dick was so tiresome and she missed Pat and felt so cold she could not sleep. Dick drives her home and then stays the night leaving early the next morning for Chatham. Another letter from Pat, who is back at Cambridge.

On Thursday 15 October Cesca went down to the fur shop on the Pantiles about a fur for herself. 'Rather lucky as a lady is trying to sell a Canadian sable stole. I may buy it, remodelled and cleaned for £20'. This she duly decided to do for £19 and feels much cheered. Up in London on 20 and 21 October staying with Aunt Edie for Rose Marie at Drury Lane. 'A wonderful show. It was pouring when we came out and finally got back to A. Edie's by 6.30. To my surprise saw a Bentley outside, gave me an awful shock and thought of Hugh. When we got upstairs there were both Hugh and Pat waiting to see me'! This development gives Cesca a lot to think about. However she and her Mother spend the next day shopping in Bond Street and Harvey Nicholls before returning home.

On Saturday 24 October Cesca writes 'this day 11 years ago Pat's brother Denys was killed in action and felt awfully sorry for the Ainslies'. The letters from Pat arrive regularly all through November, but Dick continues to annoy her even in a letter 'filled with amazing cheek'.

Saturday 14 November Pat to stay

Spent busy morning with Mum discussing the plans for the weekend. At 11.15 Pat arrived in the Eric Campbell having left at 7.00 to motor down. How wonderful. Went out for a walk with him and had lunch early. Then went off beagling in the car but could not find them. Back to tea at 4.30. In evening after dinner Pat and I went to the Bartley's dance which was rather a poor show.

Sunday 15 November

Lovely morning. After breakfast Pat, Mum and I went to King Charles where we had the most shockingly poor sermon I have ever heard. Pat and I hated it. After lunch, Pat and I went off in the car to Withyham, Hartfield and the forest. Had a wonderful time and home to tea at 5.00. In evening Pat and I went to the Sunday evening concert at Opera House. Very good.

On Monday more motoring together. After lunch another long walk and then after tea Pat had to leave. 'Hated his going'.

Tuesday 17 November The Peach Ball, Claridges

Lovely day and feel so happy. Off to town by the 9.50. Tried on my dress at Margaret Marks. Then to Garceau and had nice singing lesson. Then to Hans Crescent where I found Mother unpacking, and we went together to lunch with the le Rossignols at 17 Chapel Street where they have a charming house. Retuned to Hans Crescent after another fitting and found Pat had arrived. My Pat and I went out to tea. It is fun being in town together. Back at 6.30 and changed into my new peach dress. Sweet it is and we went out to dine with the Fergusons. Enjoyed the Peach Ball very much and made £6 selling peaches.

Wednesday 18 November

Pat was wonderful to me last night. Had breakfast together then Mum came down. Went shopping together and then lunch together, such fun. Then watched the rugger match with Dick who was so unkind and drove abominably. I was so frightened. Took taxi back to Hans Crescent and found Pat alone. Then Hugh arrived and I spent nearly an hour in Belinda with him looking for an all night garage. He is so nice, old Hugh. Came back to find Mum and Pat anxiously waiting for us. We all changed and went off after dinner to a very good revue 'By the Way' and then on to the Café de Paris which was wonderful fun. Just Hugh, Pat and me.

Cesca feels very flat now Hugh and Pat have gone and hopes they returned safely to Cambridge in Belinda. She buys a new hat, lovely and very expensive at three guineas. Cesca enjoys a day's shooting at Burwash with Dad but wishes Pat had been there too. His letters continue to arrive every few days. Cesca whilst taking Bogey out for a walk on Sunday 22, saw Edmund who cut her dead and did not stop. 'That settled me with him forever. The rude man'. She has not heard from Hugh and can't make it out. Two days later, a frightful blow. A letter from John saying he is engaged to a girl called Joyce Flanagan and not coming home. Even shopping in London cannot cheer her up but her Mother on Cesca's return is very understanding and terribly kind. She cries herself to sleep. Snowing and bitterly cold for Queen Alexandra's Funeral on Friday 27 November. Just before dinner that day, an express letter from Pat came. 'Darling Pat is an angel to write at once and cheer me up'.

Wednesday 2 December

Very cold day, wore fur coat and brown dress. Went up to town First class from Tonbridge. Went to Debenhams to look at dressing jackets and chose three on approval. Then to Garceau for my singing lesson. He says I must sing at the concert. Oh misery! Then to Les Lauriers in Jermyn Street and found Pat, my Pat waiting for me. Love him so. Had lovely lunch then to Charlot's Revue at Prince of Wales. Enjoyed it awfully. Very well staged and acted. Pat so nice to me. To tea at Ridgeways then taxi (heaven) to Charing Cross and Pat saw me off.

Cesca receives three letters from Pat over the following week and also one letter from Hugh. On Saturday 12 December Cesca goes up to town again for Winnie Levy's dinner party for 18 followed by dancing. Cesca wore her peach dress and enjoyed it all very much. The next day she and Winnie went to a marvellous concert at the Albert Hall. Then they went out to dinner with Lord Bearsted at Hamilton Place. On Monday 14 December Pat fetches Cesca from the Levy's and after parking the car in a garage in Shaftsbury Avenue they go shopping at the Army and Navy Stores for Mrs Ainslie. They lunch at Les Lauriers and then to a show at the Coliseum. Pat sees her off on the train at Charing Cross. On Thursday 17 December, Cesca so frightened she can hardly breathe, at the thought of singing in front of 57 of her Mother's friends that afternoon. Tony arrived the previous evening and will sing too and has a divine voice. Cesca wears her black frock, Tony very smart in dark blue. However it all goes off very well and everyone says they have enjoyed themselves.

Friday 18 December

I am so looking forward to Hugh coming to stay tonight. Did some shopping with Mother and ordered some biscuits for Mrs Levy and Mrs Ainslie. At 5.30 Hugh arrived but not in Belinda but in Morris Cowley, as Belinda is being painted. Hugh is so frightfully nice. Changed into blue dress and Hugh very smart in tails and very smart waistcoat. After dinner left for the Wadhurst Hockey Club Dance. Very good band. Home at 2.00.

Cesca and Hugh go to the Opera house after a walk on the common, and see a very poor Revue. Such a poor show it was really very funny. Home to tea and Dad home from a good day's shooting at the Drewes, 96 pheasants. Hugh changed into a dinner jacket, Cesca her black and Gerald and Muriel join them for dinner. After dinner they go to the Spa dance which was great fun. Snowing. The next day, very wet followed by thick fog, a miserable afternoon and Hugh left at 3.30. Cesca hates to see him go, he is so awfully nice and the family like him too.

Monday 21 December

Letter from Pat and by parcel post a lovely present from him. A pair of sweet Copenhagen china owls and two KG Almanacks. How he does spoil me and I don't deserve it. A letter from Jack sending me a huge box of chocs from Fortnum & Mason unfortunately liqueur again so shall change them. Busy morning packing up parcels.

Presents and cards from Cesca's girlfriends pour in and a huge box of chocolates from Hugh weighing seven pounds! Cesca has changed the liqueur chocolates for a lovely pair of check stockings 14/- and some Dubbin 1/6 for a pair of shooting boots Dad is giving her for Christmas. Mrs Ainslie sends Mother a huge turkey for Christmas and a hat pin for Cesca. Suzanne arrives at 7.15 Christmas Eve, tired out after a frightful crossing and goes straight to bed. Christmas Day dawns with an old fashioned white Christmas. Snow thick on ground and all over roofs and trees. Looked lovely but so cold. She did not go to church till 11.00. Suzanne remains in bed until lunch. Monkey comes down bringing Cesca a present of some mother of pearl opera glasses. Pat is off to Switzerland for ten days.

Cesca dines at Somerville on Boxing Day and enjoys it awfully and comes home by taxi at 10.00. On Sunday afternoon, Brian Knox collects her for tea at Withyham with Joannie, Edmund and lots of others and they play mad games. Their differences forgotten, Edmund takes her home in the Amilcar.

Monday 28 December Rowney Bury

After lunch just caught the train, frightfully crowded platform and was late at London Bridge so had to fairly fly for my train. Did it quarter of an hour! Pat met me at Harlow in the new 20hp Austin. Mr Ainslie came up by the same train and gave me a lovely bottle of Rimmels Lavender Water. Danced to the wireless in the evening.

Tuesday 29 December

Spent the most wonderful hour of my life in Union Wood with Pat. I have never met anyone so determined so had to give way much against my will outwardly. I wonder though if I do mind so very much? In afternoon went out shooting again but seemed to spend most of the time enjoying each other's company. After dinner we went to the Territorial Dance at Hatfield Broad Oak. I enjoyed it awfully.

Wednesday 30 December

Mrs Ainslie, Pat and I went up to town in the car and after lunch in Grosvenor Square, Pat and I went off to Olympia for the Circus. I had never been to a circus before so enjoyed it awfully. The lions were wonderful, about 65 of them and some very good clowns. Left London about 6.00 and back at Rowney Bury at 7.00.

Thursday 31 December

Pat's cocker puppy arrived at 10.00. He is to be called Bogey II, too sweet but very nervous and shy. He has a lovely coat and head but seemed rather seedy so we took him to the vet after lunch. He said it was only the journey and he needed rest. In evening after dinner we went off to the Albert Hall for the Happy New Year Ball. I thought it a wonderful show, spectacular lights and wonderful dresses. But rather dud people and a girl there called Veronica Biggin who smelt of coal tar soap. Spent an hour of heaven with Pat before going to bed at 4.30.

1926 Parham, Venice and Scotland and an Engagement.

Cesca seems much in love with Pat but almost as fond of Hugh and is so far successfully juggling her two suitors. Her social whirl continues much the same as last year, her Mother valiantly in tow as chaperone. The New Year begins with Pat staying for the West Kent Hunt Ball at Somerhill, '300/400 there and great fun'. Cesca wears her new green dress with green satin shoes, rather becoming! And dances mostly with Pat and enjoys it all awfully. She admits to loving Pat more and more each day and finds him so good looking. They take the opportunity in Pat's car to have half an hour of bliss. Cesca loves being in town with Pat and going for long walks with him. In fact lovely to be with Pat anywhere. Pat stays over a week at Parham, shooting with Cesca's Father at Burwash where they shoot seven pheasants, three rabbits and a woodcock in wet conditions. They see a pantomime, Alice in Wonderland and Peter Pan at the cinema. They drive out to Ashdown Forest where they spent an hour alone. 'Absolute heaven'. Pat leaves on 9 January. Misery! However three days later 12 January the Eridge Hunt Ball and Hugh, Betty and Blanche come to stay! 'Felt the same old thrill coming back, that divine going to a dance tonight feeling'.

Tuesday 12 January
Betty Styles arrived at 3.30 having motored over from Maidstone. Blanche was met at the station at 4.00. Hugh arrived in Belinda at teatime and had to go round to Blundells garage because of Belinda being too big to fit into our garage. Wore my black, Mother said I looked awfully nice. After dinner went in two carloads, the Chrysler and our car. Danced with Hugh ten times, seven with Peter, four with Geoffrey and one with Captain Gosling. I did love it and enjoyed it more than any other Eridge Hunt Ball. Missed Pat of course, but I have Hugh and like him terribly.

Wednesday 13 January
Hugh and I to the meet at Eridge Green. Finally hounds moved off and we followed in Belinda but lost them. Hugh left at 5.30. Do miss him so.

A dance on Thursday 14 January at Cowfold, but after a heavy fall of snow
Cesca wonders how she will ever stay with Jim Reed at the Warren, Handcross.
However she travels by train to Three Bridges and is met by Jim in a lovely
Sunbeam car. A lovely big house and she has a lovely room, all pink with a big
fire. Mrs Reed very nice to her. 'I enjoyed the dance awfully, danced mostly
with Jim and drove home alone with Jim, about six miles, snowing hard. Jim
seems very fond of me and I like him too'.
The next day, after breakfast, Jim sees Cesca off at the station. 'He was very
sweet to me. He is a good sort and can't help loving me'.

Wednesday 20 January

A letter from Pat rather upset me and all my calculations for he has
told old Hugh everything. Felt exceedingly cross about it.
However on thinking it all over realize it's not so bad as I thought
it might be. At least I hope for the best. Wrote to Pat and told him
how peeved I was about his telling Hugh.

Tuesday 26 January

Left home by the 2.52 and caught the 4.15 down to Harlow with
Mrs Ainslie and Pat met us. Changed and wore my green and after
dinner we went to the Essex Hunt Ball at Down Hall. Danced most
with Pat and sat out a lot. I love him more and more. We arrived
back at 5.15 all pretty weary. It was a wonderful dance.

Cesca arrives home the next day at lunchtime, feeling more dead than alive and
goes straight to bed. Mrs Ainslie comes to call Thursday afternoon. 'Mum
awfully pleased'. Letters from Pat arrive at least weekly and also one letter
from Hugh who has been ill with jaundice on top of 'flu. Visits to London with
weekly singing lessons and much shopping, especially for shoes, (six pairs) from
Fortnum & Mason and Fauchon.
'Dad in a fiendish temper. Don't know why'.

Thursday 18 February Cambridge Lent Races

What heaven! Cambridge again, and Pat! Mum refused to go up
early and I was rather pleased. So got to London Bridge at 1.30,
then to Liverpool Street and arrived at Cambridge at 3.58. Pat
fetched me and we went to see the last division to return. Picked
up Mum and then went to tea with Pat at Pembroke. Such fun.

Tore back to the Varsity Arms at 7.00 and Tony came to dine. Pat came in after dinner. He looks very tired from the rowing, poor dear.

The next day Cesca and her Mother have lunch in Pat's rooms and watch the races after picking up Cesca's camera from the Varsity Arms. Pat 'rowed over' and rowed jolly well too. After dinner Hugh and Pat came in Hugh having just returned from Worplesden. 'How I love it all'. On Saturday another day of watching Pat row, visiting Hugh's rooms, rather dark and gloomy. Then spent a wonderful hour together in Pat's rooms. Hugh and Pat both lunch with Cesca and her Mother at Varsity Arms followed by more races where Pat rows in great style. Pat joins Mother and Cesca for dinner.

Sunday 21 February
Our last day at Cambridge. Seems dreadful it has gone so fast. Now all training is over, Pat came to breakfast then we all went to Kings for Chapel. Lovely service. Hugh and Pat both came to lunch again. Hugh took me out in his new Bentley. He has only got a chassis so far. No body to it. It was rather unsafe but such fun doing 50mph with nothing to hold on to! Met Pat further on and he took me over to Harlow for tea. Mr and Mrs Ainslie away so were all alone. Great fun. Returned to Cambridge and Pat dined with us.

On Monday, a perfect warm spring day but are leaving Pat and Cambridge. Miserable day! Cesca goes to his rooms to say goodbye. Misery, misery! Hell! However she admits it has been wonderful and they are home by 3.15 being met by Hogben. 'Mrs White [cook] came in drunk and Mum gave her notice'. Consequently their planned trip to Italy is postponed as a new cook will have to be found. Dad has been a terrible temper for three days and won't speak to Cesca or her Mother. They assume it is gout. They have lovely long talks about the past and the future. 'How I love my Mummy'. Wednesday 3 March Cesca dashes to London and after some shopping and her singing lesson at noon with Garceau, she posts her music back to herself and runs like a hare to Harvey Nicholls where she tidies herself to meet her Pat, a little late for lunch, at Les Lauriers. He takes her to Red Boots at the Winter Garden, front row seats and she loves it all. During the next ten days Cesca receives no less than seven letters from Pat and feels she is the happiest girl in the whole world. A day trip to Bexhill by train with Mother, to escape the workmen and smell of paint, cheers them both as they lunch at the Sackville and walk in the sun. 'Felt blissfully happy, everything bathed in light and warmth'.

A three night stay at Bulford with the Stanley Clarkes is rather fun and includes an RA concert in the Mess, RA Harriers Point to Point and the RA Hunt Ball where she wears her peach dress. Furious to have to leave early as there is an excellent floor and the Clifford Essex Band. Then off by train 19 March with Uncle Henry to Sandown for the Grand Military where she meets lots of people including Hugh and Dick and returns home with Peg and Monkey having loved the day. Her bedroom is looking very smart with the new carpet.

On Saturday Cesca leaves for London and is met by Pat who after lunch, go to Waterloo together in a frightfully crowded train to Twickenham for England v Scotland Rugger match. They meet Hugh and after a thrilling match, England was beaten, Hugh motors them back to Dover Street. After collecting Pat's car, Cesca and Pat motor down to Harlow where Cesca stays for a week. Pat gives her several fishing lessons on the lawn and she is also given bridge lessons by Mr and Mrs Ainslie in the evenings when they are not dancing or dining in London.

Thursday 25 March

Pat and I wandered out into the wood. He loves me so and I love him and everything seemed very near. In fact I said yes, but don't know if I really meant it forever and ever and ever. It's too big to think about and my heart is overflowing with happiness, love and gratitude to him for making me so happy.

They return to Parham together by train on Saturday after watching the Boat Race, thrilling as Cambridge won by six lengths.

Monday 29 March

Lovely day and I feel so happy. Went up to town with the luggage First Class with Pat. Had carriage to ourselves and heaven! Left our luggage at the Langham Hotel and then Mum met us for lunch at the Piccadilly Grill. Had lovely lunch and felt frightfully well and happy. Pat and I went to the cinema then returned to the Langham and changed for dinner, then Mum, Pat and I went to *Hayfever*. Had very good seats in first row of stalls. We all loved it and afterwards we saw Mum into a taxi and went off to the Café de Paris and loved it.

Tuesday 30 March

And today it is all over. I have left and said goodbye to Pat for six weeks as when he returns from Devon on the 15 April I don't think I can face the misery of parting all over again.

However all is not lost as Hugh comes to stay on Sunday 4 April leaving the following Tuesday after the Eridge Races and enjoying a wonderful dance at Shenfold! Belinda has still not got her body yet. Cesca is down 5/- and Hugh 15/- at the end of the days racing. Captain and Mrs Gosling dined at Parham before leaving for the dance. 'It was a heavenly dance. My card was full at once and I danced ten with Hugh and one each with Capt. Gosling, Gerald, Maurice, Dick etc. Had supper with Hugh and breakfast with Gerald. I do like Hugh awfully. We got home at 5.00 when it was quite light'.
Hugh leaves after lunch in Belinda. 'Like him most awfully'. On Friday 9 April, Tony comes for the day and tells Cesca all his news, the most exciting being his engagement and that he is blissfully happy. Monday 12 April, a sad day leaving Bogey with the keeper, Harrison, as Cesca and her mother leave for Paris and Venice on Friday 16 April. A change of heart finds Cesca meeting Pat in London on Thursday for a show *'Is Zat So'* at the Apollo. She packs a lot of shopping in at Randalls, Fortnum & Mason, Fauchon, Gerrards, and Truslove and Hanson. Pat had poor fishing in Devon as there was no water. They enjoy the show and Pat sees Cesca on to her train home. 'He was so sweet'.

Friday 16 April

Left home after final packing at 9.30 in the car for Tonbridge arriving at Dover at 11.30. Went for a short walk, then boarded the boat at 12.00, then as it looked very rough Mum and I went downstairs and prepared for the worst. But all was well and we had an uneventful journey. We arrived at the Bedford and had a lovely room on the first floor. Changed and dined at 7.30.

Saturday 17 April

Paris again! A lovely morning. What fun! Went to Chevriers and found it has been taken on by her old tailor who was very pleasant and anxious to please so we gave him an order for one dress each. Then to Dellas and saw lots of lovely dresses and I ordered one lovely evening dress. Then we wandered and wandered and loved it all. I bought some stockings for 29frs and changed £2.10 at the bank for 144frs for each £1. Lunched at the Grand Vatel which I loved, then back to the Bedford.

Sunday 18 April

We left the Bedford and went to the Gare de Lyons and found our wagon lit all to ourselves, very comfy, clean and nice. We left at 11.15 and began our long journey to Venice having both lunch and dinner on the train. Fell asleep in our wagon lit soon after the Swiss border and slept well.

Monday 19 April

Woke up with the train still jolting along, dressed and washed (more or less!) Through Verona and Padua and finally about 11.00 arrived in Venice and took a gondola to the Grand Hotel. My first impressions of Venice were very poor. I suppose because I was tired. It was rather cold, very smelly and to me seemed full of decay, disease and dirt. All the houses too seem to be falling down though the hotel is very nice. We unpacked, had lunch and rested till dinnertime. All Americans and English in the hotel. Heard mosquitos all night.

The next morning after a good rest, Cesca's impressions of Venice have improved, 'a wonderful city'! But she thinks St Marks is need of a clean up and smells tremendously of incense. They have tea at Florians, poor and very expensive. [Nothing changes}. Their visit coincides with the Natal Day of Rome. Bands and excitements in the Piazza and the Fascists holding a demonstration and all was confusion. They watched it all from the top of St Marks. The noisy demonstration went on all day so they retreated to the hotel where Cesca found a letter from Pat. In hot sunshine they take a steamer up the Gran Canal to see all the palaces and then over to the Lido. On Friday pouring with rain, and everything sopping they visit the Ducal Palace full of wonderful treasures. On returning to their hotel they found a grand luncheon in honour of some ambassador, taking place and had fun watching all the people. They take in the Accademia, the English Ideal tea Rooms, S. Georgio Maggiore, saw the King leaving his palace and into his motor boat for Mestre. On Wednesday they take the steamer over to Murano to see the glass but were not allowed into the factories and Cesca found the 'island dull, hot, filthy dirty and smelly. Lots of beggars were sitting in the streets showing their diseases and filth'. They took the next steamer back!

On their last day Cesca is sorry to be leaving as Venice is beginning to grow on her. They buy some interesting Venetian glass and then pack. The train left on Friday at 7.30 and was very full, hot and stuffy. They arrive in Milan at 2.30 and stay at the Hotel Europa, very comfy, unpack and set off to visit the Cathedral. It is the third largest in Europe and Cesca and her Mother climb the 500 steps to the top but felt so sick and giddy they came down again. On Saturday 1 May they leave the hotel at 3.30 after visiting an old monastery seeing Leonardo da Vinci's famous fresco The Last Supper.

Their wagon lit is comfortable and the train passes through lovely scenery. Sunday 2 May Cesca and her Mother arrive in Paris and go straight to the Bedford for two nights and are alarmed to hear there will be a General Strike in England. [This lasts for nine days 3-12 May badly affecting all forms of transport]. Predictably they spend all Monday shopping, trying their dresses, some already finished ready to be sent round to the hotel. Cesca buys a mac as it is raining and dashes out to buy nine pairs of gloves, stockings, and a pretty pair of pink slippers, scent, cigarettes and sweets for Pat.

Tuesday 4 May

Heaven knows if we shall ever get home again due to the Strike. We caught the only steamer of the day, a bad crossing and I was sick! Then we sat in the train for Victoria for two hours hoping it might leave. Suddenly we saw Hogben who had motored down with Dad to fetch us so were home by 8.30. So glad to be back.

[No newspapers or letters or transport and the government enlisted middle class volunteers to maintain essential services]. Pat rings Cesca to say he and Herron, a friend, are in town working the underground. The following day he rings again to tell Cesca he is now a special constable. This she thinks is very foolish. On Sunday 9 May Cesca suddenly hears Pat's horn and nearly jumps out of her chair! He was discharged as special constable and had motored down to stay the night before returning home to join his territorials. 'It is too wonderful to see him again. Pat had to leave at 11.00 but we had some wonderful time together before he left and I felt quite limp'.

Tuesday 1 June and Pat's 21st Birthday. Cesca has sent him a photo of herself and a book, Memories. Cesca's new hat came. 'It's such fun and makes me look quite beautiful. I shan't recognise myself. It is well worth three guineas'. [A pretty feather in different shades of green and pink was found tucked inside this diary?]. She spends the day at Withyham for Edmund Horden's birthday playing tennis but found she was bored and 'wanted only Pat or Hugh or even

Jim, sensible men'! The Skinners Ball in London with Jim on Tuesday 8 June is great fun. Bed at Hans Crescent 3.30.

Friday 18 June MAY WEEK CAMBRIDGE!

Day dawned with pouring rain. However it cleared later. A rush to get everything packed ready to leave with Mum by 9.53 to town. Then from King's Cross to Cambridge. Mum saw me off. Pat met me looking terribly nice, frightfully good looking and so smart in new grey check flannel suit. How I love him. We went straight to Pembroke and had lunch there. Wonderful lunch a deux. Of course I succumbed again as usual and love him more than ever. Then went to 3 Paunton Street and was welcomed by Mrs Stockbridge. Eustace and Audrey there and both awfully nice, though not well dressed. Dined at Varsity Arms.

Saturday 19 June

There is not a moment for anything. Out shopping with Pat, Eustace and Audrey in morning and met Sam, Herron and Jock. Then back to change into my pink dress and panama hat as it is hot. Then we lunched at the Varsity Arms and met the family in force. Mrs A. so sweet to me. Then watched the tennis at Fenners, wonderfully good. Then went down to the Pitt Lawns and watched the races. I let off my *pistoletto inoffensevo*, bought in Venice, with great success!

Cesca and Pat went down to Harlow on Sunday for lunch with the Ainslies followed by a large party of twenty-six for tennis in the afternoon. It was very hot and she played badly. On Monday they go to a Gymkana and Pat and Eustace volunteer to lie in a manure heap and be jumped over. 'I did laugh'. They go up river to Grantchester by punt and took supper with them. Great fun. On Tuesday 22 June they set off after breakfast for a picnic to Icklingham in Eustace's car.' Saw Hugh in evening dress at 11.00 just going off to Henley. We then returned and changed. I wore my pink and we dined with Pat. Oh how I have loved it all. The Pembroke Ball was wonderful, I only danced with Eustace and Pat and Pat nearly all the time. I got so, so happy that I went and did it, got engaged definitely! How awful! We told Eustace and Audrey and drank no end of toasts to celebrate'.

Wednesday 23 June

Woke up at 11.00 after two hours sleep. Far, far too happy to sleep at first. Just think, engaged to Pat! Eustace and Audrey have been so sweet to me. Had a motor picnic at Quy but it was rained off so we went to a flick, then played poker till it was time to change. Wore my pink and mauve and dined for the last time in Pat's rooms. Then went to King's Ball. Such a lovely dance in such a lovely hall too. I loved it and danced nearly all the time with Pat. Had time together under big trees in grounds. Oh what heaven! Home 6.30.

Thursday 24 June

Rested for short time, then dressed and packed. How awful it is to leave Cambridge. I suppose I shall never come up again. Certainly not with Pat and now we are engaged not with anyone else. How I love him and how I have loved May week and how quickly it has all gone. Pat and I had lunch together and spent a most wonderful half hour alone together. I love him more and more. We all set off for Harlow in two cars and then an awful thing happened. Pat and I were alone together with Mrs A. and Pat made signs to me he was going to tell her of our engagement and did. Oh it was so awful. She said we were much to young and didn't know what Mr A. would say. I was so tired and upset I burst into tears and couldn't stop. I cried all the way home on the train and then I told Mum who was sweet.

Every thing seems to be much calmer after a good night's sleep. Cesca spends the morning in bed writing a very difficult letter to Mrs Ainslie and to Audrey and a long one to Pat. Then off to London in the afternoon to stay with Winnie Levy for Lady Ferguson's dance in Hans Place. Cesca wears her new pink dress and enjoys the dance most awfully dancing mostly with Edmund who Charlestons wonderfully! The next morning to distract herself further she buys a pair of satin shoes from Fauchon and returns home on a very crowded train. The following Tuesday 29 June, a letter arrives from Pat and she writes to him, then has her things packed to leave after lunch by train to Woking via Waterloo. She was met by Mrs Lang's chauffeur, Harvey, in the Delage, [a luxury French motor car]. Then to meet Mrs Lang in Woking and on to Mingary.

[Mingary is a large mansion beside the fifteenth tee, now divided into flats. Hugh's father also called Hugh, was captain of Worplesdon Golf Club 1915-1916 and was instrumental in holding a meeting at Mingary to establish a special fund to meet the expenses of the Club. He contributed £50 in 1918 and again in 1919]. She took Cesca all round her lovely garden and house, most attractive with a view of the golf links in the distance.

They leave Mingary for Henley the next day in the Delage with Jessie Hudson, Mrs Lang's stepdaughter. Arrived at Henley and were met at the Armistice Hotel by Hugh and the Richards. Then they went to Phyllis Court and had a lovely picnic lunch in the car, then did not see Hugh again until after the race at 5.50. Hughie was so nice and after the last race we motored back and they were a merry party after dinner. They return to Henley again the next day. It was very hot and Cesca wore her black and Hughie met them both as usual and they went to the Stewards Enclosure. Cesca leaves the next day for London staying at Hans Crescent for dinner for twelve with Pat and the Ainslies at the Carlton Club and *Lady Be Good* at the Metropole.

Cesca returns to Henley with Pat on Saturday and they join Hugh in the Stewards Enclosure for prize giving. Pembroke was beaten by Jesus by just three feet. Pat and Cesca motor back to Mingary and then the next day to Henley again Hugh having arrived in time for breakfast. They decide to motor over to Henley all together in Belinda. 'Lovely drive. The car is divine and goes so beautifully'. They return for lunch and play tennis and in the evening mad games.

Cesca's social calendar seems to be fuller than ever! Theatre, dinner parties in London, a wedding, Eton v Harrow with Hugh and the next day with Pat who has bought a blue two seater Talbot for £125 and more theatres and dinners. Sunday 11 July, Cesca admits she is glad to be home after having been on the go ever since June 16. There is plenty of County Cricket to watch with Dad, tennis and tea parties not to mention the Sussex Yeomanry Ball. Cesca is filled with longing to return to stay with the Ainslies for the dance at Hyde Hall. 'It was absolutely wonderful seeing him again. The dance was wonderful, to bed at 5.00'. Cesca shoots her first bunny and feels most awfully pleased about it! Pat returns to Parham with Cesca and spends five days with her playing in tennis tournaments most days. Pat leaves and Cesca miserable to see him go, but packs up to go by train to stay at Townhill, Southampton with Lord and Lady Swaythling [their son Stuart Montagu is married to Mary Levy] for tennis and dancing for the weekend.

Sadness for Cesca as her friend Mary Montagu gave birth to a stillborn boy on Saturday 14 and is terribly ill and a marvel they saved her. Then more sadness as Bogey goes to kennels with Harrison. [Bogey and Dad's dog Nigger do not like each other]. Dad has now left for Scotland.

Wednesday 18 August
This time tomorrow I shall be in Scotland. How divine and how I'm longing to be there. Mother and I left home by 8.00 pm and had dinner at Euston. Most awfully comfortable sleepers and I slept very well.

Thursday 19 August
At 8.50 we reached Perth where we left our sleepers and boarded another train to Coupar Angus. Then changed arriving at Blairgowrie at 10.00. Dad fetched us at 10.30 in the hotel car and we motored 13 miles to Kirkmichael to the Aldchlappie, a small inn. Quite nice, clean and comfortable and we have a good sitting room in the front.

Friday 20 August
Too wet to shoot this afternoon as planned. Sickening.

Saturday 21 August
Pat arrived before I was down. He had motored the 28 miles from Perth and looked tired. After breakfast we set off for the moor at 9.45. It was very windy but fine. Great fun and we got eleven grouse, two black game, three hares and a rabbit. Pat shot a stoat and shot very well indeed. Felt tired at the end of the day but after a bath quite fit.

The next few days are uneventful, shooting and fishing, bridge in the evenings.

Thursday 26 August
My birthday. I don't feel 22 somehow. I had £10 from Dad, £5 and a silver comb from Mum, pink enamelled powder box, initialled with a C from Pat. We went shooting and shot eight grouse, two black game and one snipe.

Friday 27 August
Went to Ashintully in the Talbot with Pat and had an enjoyable morning's ferreting getting 23 rabbits. Went out again after lunch

in the car with Pat and had a lovely time together. How I love my
Pat.

Sunday 29 August

A perfectly glorious day, hot and misty. After Mum and I had
darned Pat's socks and stockings, went off with Pat on the
Pitlochry road for about six miles. It is a ghastly road, nothing but
potholes and loose stones so we turned back. We took Mum over
to tea at the Spittal of Glenshee. A ripping drive as the road is
good.

Tuesday 31 August

This afternoon we went into Blairgowrie to meet Hugh who
arrived in Belinda. We shopped for films and razors and back in
time for tea. Fished again in the evening.

Thursday 2 September

An awfully hot day for the Drive. Wore brown coat and skirt and
had breakfast at 8.15. Set off at 8.45, Mum, Dad and Hughie in the
hotel car and Pat and I in the Talbot. There were 15 Beaters, a horse
and man. Such fun and I loved it all. Total bag 45 grouse, four
black game, one snipe, thirteen hares and four rabbits. Mrs
Griffiths collapsed due to the heat.

Friday 3 September

Pat and I set off with Hugh in Belinda to Gleneagles for lunch. We
arrived rather late as we had to stop for petrol at Perth and send
off some grouse. I was quite pleasantly surprised at Gleneagles. I
expected it would be vulgar and awful people about but there
were none. Attractively decorated and a good luncheon. The boys
swam in the pool there. Had tea then motored back.

Tuesday 7 September

Decided to go for a drive all day in Hugh's Bentley. We went first
to Pitlochry where we looked at tweed but did not like any of it.
We then went along the Upper Tummel through the Pass of Killie
Crankie, then on to Aberfeldy then all along Glen Lyon. Over the
mountains to Loch Tay to Castle Hotel where we had tea and
home via Aberfeldy, 125 miles.

Thursday 9 September

Pat and Hugh went off to shoot with the Ivory's at Glenisla. Mum, Dad and I went off in an Austin 20 to the Braemar Games 28 miles away. Awfully heavy traffic, thousands of cars around the Devils Elbow. Had a picnic lunch in the car. The games great fun but very hot. Saw the King and Queen there in state, a la Ascot. I loved it all.

Friday 10 September

Very sad as Hugh leaves this morning. Pat and I helped him pack and saw him off to Mull in the Bentley.

Thursday 16 September

Set out to shoot low ground. Dr and Mrs Griffith brought out that beastly dog Bob who spoilt the whole morning's shooting by tearing about disturbing all the birds for miles around. Finally Dad insisted on his being sent back to the kennels. A miserable morning for us all. In afternoon Pat got most of the shooting and shot very well.

Friday 17 September

Went fishing with Pat in the Ardle and caught one trout of fair size. After lunch went into Blairgowrie with Pat and Mother to have the car seen to and buy cartridges and films. Then back to find Hugh here. He is at the Spittal of Glenshee for the night as he is shooting with us tomorrow.

Saturday 18 September

A damp morning but turned out a lovely hot day. We were seven guns including Hugh and Pat and had a very jolly day getting 13 brace grouse etc. Hugh stayed to dinner and then set off in the car to Perth.

Monday 20 September

Mum's last day. How I hate her going. Felt so miserable that I cried my eyes out and Pat had to try and comfort me. He is a darling, he and I went out together after Mummy had gone.

Tuesday 21 September

A most perfect Autumn morning, lovely sun and light on the hills but very cold and frosty. Poor bag up to lunch but in afternoon shot three partridge, 11 rabbits, one pigeon and one snipe.

Thursday 23 September

How sad, our last drive. Set off at 9.00 in Pat's car. The Ramsays in theirs, bringing a beater. Have had a job to get enough beaters so I had to flank which meant a lot of walking and I felt dead tired at the end of the day. Total bag eight brace grouse, one greyhen, one hare, 12 rabbits. A very jolly day for four guns but I was tired.

Friday 24 September

The most miserable day! Woke up feeling wretched and tried hard to control myself but in vain. Could not stop crying and presented a miserable face at breakfast. Both Dad and Pat tried to console me but it was no use. When I said goodbye to Pat it was more than I could bear. He was a darling and did try to comfort me. Dad was very tactful and was very sweet to me too. Pat left at 5.30. Feel the most wretched of girls.

Saturday 25 September

Dad and I dined at Perth at the Station Hotel on fried sole then got into my sleeper and Dad had a first class reserved for himself. Had comfortable journey to Euston, slept splendidly and felt better in the morning. Very comfy sleeper with boiling water. We travelled across London and breakfasted at Charing Cross, fried sole again. Then caught 9.15 home. Hogben and Bogey met us at the station. Mum very fit and everything very comfortable at home.

Tuesday 28 September

A nice but very cold day. Had two letters from Pat that cheered me up enormously, one from Aberdeen and one from Carlisle. He is sending Mum a salmon, it arrived tonight, a beauty.

Saturday 2 October

Mother and I went up to town by the 10.07 to Charing Cross. Booked luggage there and went to Golanski's where in a few moments I decided on a magnificent black seal musquash coat. Most attractive one and not nearly so expensive as other places. I longed for a grey squirrel one but can't afford it. Met Mum for lunch at Mazarin's café then went to Hans Crescent and had a rest. I waited and waited for Pat and finally he arrived at 7.15 looking very tired. Took taxi to the Savoy and dined with the Ainslies.

Wednesday 6 October

Mother and I went up to Mrs Walters with a huge parcel of things for a bazaar. Then we left the car and took Bogey and walked right through Eridge Park then caught the bus home to tea. To my utter surprise found Pat waiting in the library. It was such a lovely day that he decided to come over in the car, such a darling. Pat stayed to dinner.

Sunday 10 October

I dragged Pat off to church at King Charles this morning as it was Harvest Festival and I thought he should go. Poor Pat it was a dreadful long service. Mum felt ill and he and I come out before the sermon. After lunch Pat and I went out in the car and spent the afternoon together. Then home to tea. Pat had to leave after supper.

Monday 18 October

I caught the 10.46 up to town, took my luggage over to Charing Cross and then to Adele Colliers where I had my first Charleston lesson. It is absurdly difficult though it looks so easy. Then over to lunch with the Levy's. Then home by the 4.25.

Thursday 21 October

Letter from Pat. Went off to town by the 9.53. Very cold. Mum and I were both so cold we had to have some Bovril. Went to Debenhams where I bought a new nightie then to Marshalls where I bought some angora knickers. Then to Adele Colliers for my Charleston lesson.

Friday 22 October

Busy morning packing for Harlow. Dad and I caught the 2.58 for London Bridge and only just caught the 4.18 for Harlow from

Liverpool Street. Clements, chauffeur, met us and in fact we were too early as Mrs Ainslie out at a Bridge Tournament and Mr Ainslie and Pat still in town. Dad and I had tea together and Mrs Ainslie arrived at 5.30 and Pat at 6.00. Had a great fun dinner party of eight including a Miss Carmen Gilbey who I liked. [She was born 2 June 1894 and died at the age of 87 and was Tom Gilbey's great aunt]. Sat next to Pat and Mr Ainslie. Dad seemed to enjoy it all.

Saturday 23 October
Breakfast at 8.30 and we left at 9.00 in the Austin for the shoot about nine miles away at Lamberts Farm. Six guns including Mr Hoare and John Buxton there. Dad left after lunch in the Talbot for home. I stood with John Buxton twice who seemed rather struck and the rest with Pat. Bridge after dinner.

Sunday 24 October
After breakfast Pat and I took Mr Ainslie to golf and Mrs Ainslie to church. We then had the morning to ourselves and made use of it as had not been alone once this weekend. I do love him so. After lunch Pat and I went over to tea with Mrs Lafone at Knebworth, a big party there. It was great fun.

Monday 25 October
Left Rowney Bury with Pat at 9.30 and as train was late, took Pat to Law Courts then booked my luggage at Charing Cross. Then lunched with Pat at Marchesis. Felt positively miserable and cried like a child of three. Left Pat, both feeling miserable, and went to Golanski where I settled on some grey squirrel fur for my new coat. Then home at 6.30.

Tuesday 26 October
My darling sent me the sweetest letter to cheer me up but it made me cry all the more.

Wednesday 27 October
Mum asked me to come up to London with her. We went to see about Mum's investments first. Then to Hamptons about the house. Then to Gerrard's where I have at last settled on a coat to be

dark blue edged with grey squirrel and lined with crepe de chine in the same colour. I really enjoyed my day's shopping.

Wednesday 3 November

Have seen Pat again today wonderful. Went up to town, rushed about shopping till 12.00 when I had my lesson with Adele Collier's assistant. Got on very much better today so will not have any more lessons. Found Pat waiting at Marchesi and it was lovely seeing him again even though it was for such a short time. I left him at Chancery Lane and then to Bond Street in search of a hat. I went to Mary Richardson's where I ordered a very smart blue felt and velvet hat, very dear four guineas. Then I went to Roskys and got a green one for Win's wedding for £2.12.6. Tea with Mrs Levy and home at 7.00.

Saturday 6 November

Last night and this morning had dreadful rows with Mum and Dad. I said I would leave the house and get a job. Oh it was misery and all my fault but I was feeling so seedy, did not know what I was doing or saying. Anyhow made it up in the evening and all was well.

Tuesday 9 November

Had rather awful row to make Mum to come up to town and felt quite worn out afterwards. However packed up and went up to town with Mother by the 11.00 train. Went to Rubens Hotel and left my suitcase then Mum and I went to Hans Crescent and booked rooms. Then to Bayswater Synagogue for Winnie's wedding. Winnie looked awfully nice and her bridegroom looked a cheery sort. Mary and Stuart Montagu and all their friends there. The bridesmaids looked pretty in blue chiffon and yellow roses. The reception was fun. I knew lots of people there. Winnie left looking sweet in green velvet. I arrived at Rubens, Mrs Ainslie and her brother Admiral Lafone there. He is rather a dear. After dinner Pat and I went to the theatre to see *'And so to Bed'*.

Wednesday 10 November

Woke up feeling seedy with sore throat. Pat and I had breakfast together then he left. Admiral Lafone and I went out to do his Christmas shopping, I rather enjoyed it. We went to Aspreys and then Hamleys for toys then to Gorings for Crepe de Chine. Then lunch with Mrs Ainslie at Rubens, home afterwards feeling so tired and rotten.

Thursday 18 November

Packed up and went out shopping at Harrods then went to Gerrards for fittings. Left shoes at Randall's and Fortnum & Mason. Found my Pat waiting for me at Marchesis. Had the most excellent lunch there and I do so love being with him. He is giving me such a lovely oval gilt mirror for a Christmas present. I saw and chose it at Harrods. Mum and I went to The National Gallery then home.

Thursday 25 November

I went up to London in a dense fog by the 11.04 train not arriving at Charing Cross until 12.40. So rang up Pat and suggested lunch. We had it at the same place and had a long talk. Went to tea with Mary and Stuart came in and we chatted together. Then went round to Lowndes Square, awful fog and very nearly got lost. Changed, wore pink dress. Jock Backhouse came to dine. I did enjoy the dance so. Tom Barlow, or course, was there and he stuck close as usual. He does bore me. I loved the dance.

Tuesday 30 November

Awful dark day. I illuminated in the morning. Lady Swaythling has invited me down to Townhill on December 31st for the New Year.

Friday 3 December

Jessie packed Mum's things and mine and we went up to town by the 10.08. Went to Hans Crescent and unpacked. Then to Gerrards and Katinkas and had to take both my new coat and dress back as they were all wrong. Then lunched with Pat, such fun. Then I shopped until I met Mum at Gunters for tea. And afterwards she gave me the sweetest bird in Copenhagen china just to cheer me up as I am dreading tonight. Rested and changed and at 8.00 went off to dine with the Skipwiths. Deadly, loathed it and them. Dance at Chesnil Galleries rather awful too. Fortunately knew a few people there. Awful, awful pictures on walls, made me blush.

Wednesday 8 December

Mum's birthday. Mum had some quite nice presents. 15lbs. walnuts from Pat. I gave her a book Night of London by H V Morton and a waste paper basket. Dad gave her lovely books.

Thursday 9 December

Spent a lovely day today. We all went up to town by the 9.58. I went to Burlington Arcade to change hankies for socks for Pat. Went and met Dick Kennion who is as asinine as ever. Then met Mum and Dad at the Piccadilly and had excellent lunch there. We then went to the Duke of York's and saw 'The Queen is in the Parlour' by Noel Coward, I loved it.

Thursday 11 December

Woke up with a horrid head that continued for the rest of the day. Spent morning busily shopping for Mum but by afternoon it was so bad I had to go and lie down. Rested till 4.15 when I heard the Bentley, so dressed and came down to find Hugh had arrived. He was looking tired too and had a head as he had been to the Black Prince Ball last night at the Ritz. General and Mrs Knox came to dine and were rather boring. I am afraid Hugh did not get on with them very well.

Sunday 12 December

My headache gone thank goodness. Hugh and I went out for a walk. Then I gave him a lesson in the Charleston. Mr and Mrs Harold Taylor came to lunch from Sevenoaks. Like him immensely, he is a solicitor too. Then Hugh and I went over in Belinda to call on the Williams in very thick fog. Hugh and I played bridge in the evening v Mum and Dad.

Monday 13 December

Hugh and I went out for a walk. He has asked me to go to Mingary for the night on Thursday. I have accepted as Mum says I may. I expect Pat will be cross however. Hugh had another Charleston lesson and left after lunch. Spent the rest of day packing up Christmas presents and writing letters and cards.

Thursday 16 December

I went up to town by 10.08. Had fitting at Gerrards and lunch with Hugh at Piccadilly at 1.00. We then set out on our shopping expeditions. We went first to get opera hat, then notecase for Win. Then Harrods for boots for Mrs Lang. By that time it was five so went to Poland Street Garage where we fetched Hugh's suitcase and then to change at 39 Cleveland Square. Hughie and I went to dine at the New Princes then went to the '*First Year*' at the Apollo which was a very good show. I laughed and laughed. Then H. and I went on to the Cafe de Paris. Saw Lord and Lady Brecknock there and the Prince of Wales and Prince George. Rather fun. Then motored home in the Lanchester at 4.00 in the morning.

Friday 17 December

I couldn't wake up this morning, in fact didn't until 10 and then found a letter by my side from Pat. Felt so cross with him. Hugh and Mrs Lang both down before me, Mrs Lang is such a dear and motherly to me. She had the sweetest peke puppy. Hugh and I went out for a long walk all over the golf links and Brookwood Cemetery and home for lunch. [Brookwood Cemetery, also known as the London Necropolis, is the largest cemetery in the UK covering 500 acres]. In afternoon he took me to Brookwood Station and there we said goodbye. Hated it and feeling as if I didn't want to go and stay with Pat. Wanted to go on staying at Mingary. First class carriage to myself. Then taxi to Liverpool Street and there met Pat who I was furious with. Arrived at Harlow at 7.00 and bathed and changed. Danced after dinner.

Saturday 18 December

Woke up feeling awfully miserable with such a lot of worry on my mind. Don't know what I ought to do. However went out shooting with Pat to their shoot. Party of five guns. A lovely fine day but very cold. Four brace of pheasants, a few partridges, hares and rabbits. Enjoyed it very much. Had a hot bath and felt sleepy. Dined and played bridge. Feeling a bit more settled now.

Sunday 19 December

I think there is something between Pat and me. I know what it is but I won't admit it. No. Pat and I took Mrs A to church and then were alone together. I do love him again now but not as much as I should. In afternoon went out for a walk with Pat. He is a darling.

Monday 20 December

Woke feeling less muddled and more certain of myself. Pat and I left Harlow together, and travelled up in an empty carriage. I love him again as much if not more than ever. However I wish I were not so changeable. Did some shopping in Bond Street and the Copenhagen shop. Home by 5.00.

Tuesday 21 December

Had such a lot of presents from Auntie Cassie, from Winnie, Peg, Mary, Blanche, all very nice things. I took more illuminated book markers to Saltmarsh and found a few had sold. I changed after tea and went to meet Pat's train at 6.55 and we walked home together. Changed my dress and dined at 7.45 then went over to Burwash in the car with Hogben driving – misery! Got there dreadfully late. About 70 people there I should think. Danced nearly all the time with Pat. Had long talk to Pat, love him so and then to bed at 2.45.

Wednesday 22 December

I felt so miserable and had such a bad night that I simply couldn't get up to see Pat off. More letters and cards arrived and also in the evening I had a most lovely red and gold travelling clock in a crocodile case from Hugh. He does send lovely presents. Went to bed early.

Thursday 23 December

Frightfully cold with snow on the ground. Had charming French novel beautifully bound from Suzanne Gallois. Letter from my darling

Friday 24 December

Christmas Eve! Felt rather miserable which I shouldn't, I know. But then a letter came from Pat – the most divine letter and I now feel completely happy.

Saturday 25 December Christmas Day

Mum and I went down to early service at King Charles, quite a few people there. Dad has given me £5. Read Copenhagen China and wrote to Pat. Rather dull. I wish I were young again then I would enjoy Christmas like I used to.

Friday 31 December

Had my things packed up and went up to town by 10.07. Was met at Waterloo by Pat. Took my luggage across to Waterloo then went to Fenwicks in car. Spent short time in the Park together. Then lunched at Café Mazarin. Pat saw me off from Waterloo to Southampton. Arrived there 5.30 met by Father William in the Morris. Quite a nice cheery crowd there. Lord Shaw, Lord and Lady Swaythling, Vi and Jack, Mary and Stuart, Harvey Adams the singer, rather nice and a wonderful dancer. Great fun and loved it all. Saw New Year in singing Auld Lang Syne. I was between Lord Shaw who kissed me and Father William. Wished Pat had been with me, he is my all now and so to bed.

1927
Parham, Cannes, Scotland

Saturday 1 January Townhill

Vi and I went to talk to Mary. She was in bed and is expecting a baby in August. I wondered how Uncle Hammond was, looked in the Times. To my horror, see he is dead. Shall have to go home which is sickening. Danced after dinner, mostly with Hervey Adams who Charlestons divinely.

Tuesday 4 January

Everything is terribly depressing. Dad is depressed and gloomy and Mum and I too. Also I don't love Pat as I should and feel discontented with my engagement. Mum and I went out in the afternoon, both draped in black.

Wednesday 5 January

Mum and Dad have gone to Uncle Hammond's funeral via London and Henley to Nuffield. Snowing hard and me all alone. Mum and Dad home about 7.00, both worn out after their long day. Only five at the funeral. They are glad to be home.

Cesca is very depressed all that week and receives a cross letter from Pat which does not help. Pat stays at Parham for shooting, then the next day up to town to see 'The Constant Nymph', a wonderful play. Several days are spent with her parents in St Albans going through Uncle Hammonds effects and Cesca learns she has inherited a lot of his silver. Most of his things are ghastly however. Cesca stays with Pat at Harlow for five days for shooting, freezing cold in six inches of snow, lunching with the Gilbeys, Lady Goschen's dance and then the following night the Essex Hunt Ball at Down Hall. On Wednesday 26 January she stays with Aunt Edie for two nights. Cesca loves staying there, so comfy with breakfast in bed. She returns from collecting her umbrella from lost property in Lambeth to find Hugh had been waiting for some time, the Bentley outside and Hugh chatting to Aunt Edie. They have a delicious lunch at the Piccadilly and then see 'The Ghost Train', very thrilling and terrifying! They dine together with Aunt Edie. On Friday 28 January after viewing the Flemish and Belgian Exhibition, Cesca meets Pat for lunch and told him all about yesterday. He was very angry and said goodbye very upset. Letters from both Pat and Hugh arrive at Parham House regularly.

Wednesday 9 February, another delicious lunch with Hugh followed by 'The Gold Digger' at the Lyric. They motor down to stay with Hugh's Mother who is so sweet to Cesca and after lunch see a film about India. Home in Belinda, in time to change for dinner. Do love being here so with Hugh. On Friday 11 February they motor to Parham for the West Kent Hunt Ball. She loved the dance and danced mostly with Hugh. On Sunday 13 Cesca admits to feeling divinely happy yet worried to death and miserable. Hugh departs, and writes Cesca a sweet letter arriving on Wednesday 16 February before she goes up to town to lunch with Pat. 'Not very happy somehow'.

Monday 21 February

Quite the most miserable morning. Pat left and I felt wretched again. Not so much at his leaving but at the hopeless prospect of a three years wait and no friends to help as he is so jealous. Told Mum all about it and she was sweet to me. My trouble is that I don't know my own mind at all. It is all so very difficult.

Wednesday 23 February

This afternoon quite the most miserable. I went up to London with Mum not knowing what to do about Hugh. Went to meet Hugh at Hyde Park Hotel. Waited ages not knowing what had happened to him. Finally had the wits to look for him in the Lounge Grill and found him. We then walked in the Park for two hours and tried to thrash things out. Have decided not to see him for two months. He took me to Charing Cross and left him, miserable.

Thursday 24 February

Had frightful bad night and could not sleep. Told Mum all about it and we thrashed it out together but like me she is very worried. She saw Hugh last night, standing still looking dazed, at Charing Cross after I'd left him and spoke to him. If my mind were more decided I'd know what to do at once. As it is, Hugh is terribly unhappy and Mrs Lang too and I am all to blame, but nothing can be done as I am engaged to Pat.

After Cesca and her Mother talk things over it is decided finally that Mother will write to Mrs Lang and see her about it all one day next week. On Sunday 27 February after another bad night, feeling sick all morning, Cesca goes to church and prays for help in this awful muddle and mix up and indecision. She feels worse after lunch and is sick with worry and misery. But by the end of the day, Cesca has come to the hard decision that to end her engagement to Pat is the only thing to do. Mum thoroughly approves of her plan and has given her excellent advice and help.

[Pat Ainslie and his wife Ursula, and second wife Doreen are found in the visitor's book for Belstead, Tostock and the Lodge. He lived in Surrey until his death in 1999.]

Thursday 3 March

This has been a ghastly day. Up to town with Mum. Mum went to see Mrs Lang and I to lunch with Pat which I simply dreaded. Ghastly. Can't write it down at all. Bumped into Father William who I had to tell the whole story to. I could not help it and he was so very kind. We went to Christies and looked at the pictures together. Went to the 'Beaux Stratagem' that was quite wonderful if I could love anything again.

The next day her Mother goes to see Mrs Lang again. She and Hugh are staying at the Park lane Hotel and later I saw them from the window at Stewarts. Poor Hugh looking like nothing on earth. Cesca and her Mother have booked seats for Cannes leaving on 17 March and will be thankful to be out of England.

Thursday 17 March

Left home at 9.45 after having said goodbye to the servants, Bogey and Dad. Arrived in Dover at 11.30 and bought some dry biscuits as the sea looked rough. However our fears proved groundless and we had a perfect crossing in an hour. Easy journey to Paris arriving at 6.30 and settled ourselves at the Bedford.

Cesca changes £1 for FF123.50 and after wandering about they leave for Cannes at 7.30. A most comfy journey but in spite of the comfort, Cesca is unable to sleep 'for thinking and thinking out her future which seems ever to be one vast tight knot which will not be untied'. Perfect Riviera scenery and brilliant sunshine, blue skies and blue sea and the Hotel Bellevue most attractive and comfortable. They have a lovely room on the first floor with cabinet de toilette complete. Nearly three weeks are spent enjoying being entertained by various friends also staying in Cannes. Opera, the Russian Ballet, tea parties and enough dancing to necessitate a shopping expedition for new frocks. 'An afternoon dress for Mum, royal blue, white and black printed chiffon with a white georgette vest and I got a green georgette evening frock embroidered with pearls and sequins in mother of pearl colours. Also ordered a printed silk frock for me on beige ground. Very nice at FF850 which is cheap'. Cesca hears that Hugh had sailed for America for two months on 27 March and Pat writes a rather miserable letter to her Mother. They discover that Mr Lang is buried in the cemetery in Cannes. They catch the afternoon train to Paris leaving Cannes on Sunday 3 April. After a good night they take a taxi to the Bedford and have breakfast and a good wash then walk and walk but find Paris so very dull after Cannes. Cesca buys some washing suede gloves and some crystal buttons.

Tuesday 5 April

The end of our holiday. I feel sad it is all over. Had breakfast in bed, packed and taxi to Gare du Nord leaving Paris at 10.00. A crowded train and they say sea will be rough. It was awfully rough, so I read the paper hard all the time. Everyone was sick. At Dover had awful time at Customs, perfectly horrid and our fault for not declaring. Arrived home late, rather tired.

Cesca and her Mother are occupied cleaning all Uncle Hammonds furniture, silver and his dinner service, over 100 pieces which has arrived in a filthy state. Cesca hears that Hugh has returned to England 6 May. Cesca writes to Pat suggesting a meeting in London Wednesday 4 May. Mrs Lang invites Cesca's Mother to lunch at the Park Lane Hotel Thursday 5 May.

Wednesday 4 May

I have so dreaded today. It is been pretty awful too. Went up by 10.00 train with Mum and had an argument which did not help matters at all and spent the morning by myself. Felt too upset to eat lunch. Then went to Green Park wondering whether Pat would turn up or not. He did and I spent over half an hour trying to make him realize the position and how he had behaved. It was heart rending and difficult. He does not seem to understand in the least. Felt miserable, then met Mum and talked it all over with her.

The next day Mrs Lang and Mother have a satisfactory lunch together. Cesca is very glad to get yesterday over with and her Mother has written to Pat. A few days later Mother receives a letter from Mr Ainslie which clearly shows he would never have consented to their marriage.

Monday 9 May

It is most extraordinary to wake up feeling all thrilled and that something was going to happen and I should hear from Hugh. Then when Rose brought in my tea there was a letter from Hugh asking to see me in town on Friday 13. I felt so happy until at 10.00 received a registered parcel of all my letters to Pat returned to me with a most pathetic letter from him that made my heart bleed. I wrote to Pat and Hugh and then burnt all the letters.

Cesca is longing to see Hugh but also dreading it because anything may have happened during these last two months.

Friday 13 May Stay Aunt Edie

Today has been so wonderful. I am nearly off my head with happiness. Came up to town with Mother leaving her in Bond Street. Then went to Aunt Edie's where I changed, wore printed dress and fur coat then had hours to kill before meeting Hugh at 1.15 in Piccadilly. Felt terribly shy and embarrassed when we met and he did too. He was looking so nice. We were both so nervous and even though H. had ordered such a nice lunch, we did not know what we were eating. Talked and talked. He still loves me. Then we collected the car and drove about. Then walked around Mayfair and sat in Green Park talking for half an hour, before having tea in the Ritz. It has been so wonderful and I do love him so and it's so hard not to show it yet.

Cesca stays the weekend with Aunt Edie where she is always happy. She receives a letter from her Mother who wishes her to be careful! 'How can I be when I love Hughie so.' On Monday Hugh collects Cesca from Aunt Edie's in Belinda, looking so nice again. They lunch together at Mayfair, then to the cinema and afterwards to tea and dance at the Savoy. 'So lovely to dance with Hugh again'. On Tuesday

Cesca has alterations made to her new tennis dress and in Raynes 'buys the most delicious pair of gunmetal kid shoes. Lovely but expensive £2.10.0 and a lovely pair of stockings to match 12/6'. After having tea with Aunt Edie, Cesca leaves for home. For Hugh's birthday Tuesday 31 May Cesca buys him a rather attractive platinum and gold pin from Goldsmiths Co. During the summer months Cesca and Hugh meet in the West End for delicious lunches or dinners usually followed by a play. They both stay in each other's houses for tennis parties, Wimbledon, Henley and the Derby. By the beginning of July Cesca is desperately happy sitting in the Billiard room at Mingary alone together Hugh tells her he loves her. 'It seems like a dream and too good to be true. It is bliss. Nothing can come between us now'.

Monday 11 July

Mr and Mrs Jewell came in to dinner to discuss Scotland. Dad and Mr Jewell have taken a moor together near Carrbridge for £200. Sounds very good though small and we are to put up at the Carrbridge Hotel. Like Mrs Jewell very much.

Dad has made Cesca very happy by inviting Hugh up to Scotland, because of this she is now looking forward to it enormously. On Tuesday 2 August Cesca goes up to town for fittings for a coat and dress and then to Golanski's for alterations to her fur coat. Then she meets Hugh for lunch at the Berkeley, a most excellent lunch and loved seeing Hugh again. Afterwards they go shopping together at Fortnum & Masons where they buy a leather coat for Hugh.

Monday 8 August

Took poor little Bogey over to Harrison's this morning. He was miserable and so was I. So too were Mum and Hogben. Left at 4.30 and then to Euston on the 7.20 train. Our train very full and Mum and I had sleepers and Dad a 1st to himself. Had good dinner on train.

Tuesday 9 August

Did not sleep much. Arrived at Carrbridge at 7.50 ahead of time. Mr Jewell's dog very good indeed in van all night and Nig with Dad. Hotel about size of Panmure. Had breakfast and unpacked. Had extra chest of drawers put in my room and then had plenty of room for all my things. Out for a turn with Mum after tea. Feel depressed, more or less unaccountably, but because things can never be the same as last year and at Edzell. But I would not have it otherwise.

Shooting, fishing and walking and drives to Inverness fill the days until Hugh arrives on Thursday 25 August. Great excitement just before he arrives, a lorry had fallen over the bridge, took about an hour to get it out. Cesca meets Hugh on the road as she returns from a walk. 'So happy'. The next day is Cesca's 23rd birthday and Dad gives her £10, Mum the fur coat and investments, Aunt Edie three hankies. They all go the Kingussie Sheep Trials, Cesca travelling with Hugh in Belinda. Hugh gives Cesca a large box of chocolates for her birthday. Hugh is not shooting at all well so he and Cesca went to Inverness to shooting school where Hugh lets off 100 cartridges at clay pigeons. One morning they drive to Glenmore and climb Cairngorm starting at 12.45 and did not reach the summit till 4.15. 'Wonderful views and saw ptarmigan and deer. Took one and a half hours to come down. Had awful blisters and nearly ran out of petrol on way home'. Cesca's mother is not pleased with Hugh as he loses the watch Cesca has given him. 'Awful tragedy Hugh having lost his watch on the moor, so after lunch he and I set out to hunt for it. Did it thoroughly and must have walked miles. Then just about to give up when found a match and then the watch where Hugh had sat and lit his pipe. Mum very angry with Hugh'. Cesca's Mother is still angry the following day. Cesca is afraid she does not like Hugh and wishes she did.

Thursday 8 September

Hugh has been able to stay one more night. Mr and Mrs Jewell went over to Braemar and we left about 10.45 stopping for petrol. Caught up with the Jewells and lunch altogether at the roadside. Got to Braemar about 2.00 and left the car in a good place. Saw the King and Queen arrive looking very nice with the Duke and Duchess of York. They stayed some time and we saw very well and took some photos.

Friday 9 September

Dreadfully sad day as Hugh left this morning. Have so loved having him. Was especially depressed by what Mum said about Dad and cried when Hugh left. Felt so angry and ashamed of myself too. Hugh is going to Carbeth. Mum so depressing. Felt so unhappy.

Cesca hears from Hugh a few days later that he has lost her watch somewhere on the road between Kingussie and Pitlochry. She was not surprised as she thought he would lose it. The last part of their stay is spoilt by continual rain, non-stop for 60 hours. Cesca is glad to go home. They leave on Tuesday 27 September, Cesca and her Mother in very comfy sleepers and Dad as usual a 1st to himself. The train arrived at Euston at 8.30 and after a good breakfast she sees off her parents and shopped for the rest of the day in town. She went to Gerrards and Golanski and bought new combinair and new shoes at Fortnum and Mason. Home in time for tea. The new maid Blanche seemed nice. Cesca receives a letter from Hugh enclosing all snaps from Carrbridge. Another two weeks goes by until she hears from Hugh. Mum has given Cesca another £100 for investment in Union of South Africa 5% Insurance stock.

Wednesday 19 October
Spent the day thinking about tomorrow as I had letter from Hugh suggesting meeting at Park Lane – terrified.

Thursday 20 October
I felt so frightened this morning. Longed so for today to be over. But things went off better than I had expected really. Went up by 10 o'clock with Mum, then she took me Barbellian when she fortified me and herself with chocolate. Drifted about in Bond Street to kill time until 1.00 and met Hugh or rather he passed me and I said his name. [?]

Wednesday 26 October
Went up to town with Mum and I tried to make Mum give me pale pink tulle frock but she said 16 guineas was too expensive. Felt very angry and went and met Hugh at 12.45 at The Mayfair. Poor lunch. Think the place has gone down horribly. We then took taxi to a show which I enjoyed awfully. Today has gone off so well.

Tuesday 8 November
Lovely cold morning but foggy. Went to Art School of Needlework about bedspread but very expensive. Then back to Aunt Edie to await Hugh who did not arrive until past 1.00. Went to Hatchets for quick lunch, and there Hughie told me the splendid news that he starts working on Monday next at a shipbroker's office. Most cheerful about it all. Am so pleased he at last has got something.

Thursday 10 November

Lovely morning. Went to Times Book Club and walked down Bond Street. At Gray's I ordered divine new pink evening dress in satin and tulle – too lovely. Felt very happy.

Saturday 19 November

Hugh arrived for weekend in time for lunch having motored over from Mingary. Went and saw Battles of Coronel and Falkland Isles which was very fine. Changed, wore black and went up to dine at Shernfold at 8.15. After a dinner for 14 we danced and played hide and seek and played mad games.

Sunday 20 November

Hugh and I both enjoyed last evening. Hugh and I went up to Shernfold to fetch Hugh's cigarette case he had left there last night and then he had to leave after tea to get back to town.

Wednesday 30 November

I go to stay Frogmore Park for Staff College Ball. Went up to town and took my suitcase to The Cavalry Club. Had lunch at Stewarts and met Peter. Went to Cecil Beaton's exhibition at Cooling's Gallery before having my hair set at Millie's. Went back to Cavalry Club to wait for Wyn and Margaret. Motored down after tea with Wyn and Margaret who were very nice to me. Rather depressing cold house. Changed and looked very nice in my new pink dress. Hugh arrived first. Really rather disliked the others in the party. Dance quite fun but rather sedate.

Cesca stays with Hugh at Mingary having been collected by Mrs Lang. Hugh is working in London, she and Mrs Lang go to the cinema. The next day Hugh and Cesca set off in very cold weather to Parham. Took two and a half hours and find her mother rather cross. They spend the next morning together alone and he left at 5.00 after tea. The following weekend Cesca is very disappointed as she wrote to Hugh yesterday to say she would come up to lunch today to meet him but as she did not hear so concluded he was at home.

Tuesday 20 December

Went up to town by 11.04 which was appallingly late. Took taxi to Lowndes Square and left suitcase and then went and had lunch at

Aunt Edie's. After lunch went to Millie's to make appointment. Met Dorothy for tea and had long talk, or rather she did and I said very little! Then had my hair done and went to see Hugh to make arrangements for tomorrow night. Back to Lowndes Square at 7.00. Changed and dined. Enjoyed Mary's dance. Such a lot of people I knew, Ned, John and Claud etc. Bed at 1.30.

Wednesday 21 December

Had breakfast in bed and spent morning talking to Vi and Mary. After lunch went to Asprey's and bought notecase for Hugh. Came back to Lowndes Square where I had a bath and went to sleep. Hugh came and fetched me and we dined a deux at The Berkeley and saw lots of people we knew.

Cesca busy packing up all her things for Townhill as she is spending Christmas there. Left for Southampton. Met Vi and Jack on the platform. Quite a cheerful party. Danced in the evening and played bridge. Vi and I are sharing a room which is great fun. She enjoys playing tennis on the hard court. They tell ghost stories on Christmas Eve over a huge log fire however Christmas Day does not feel like Christmas. She wishes she was with Mum and Dad and sent them a wire and wrote to them again on Christmas Day. Hugh rings to say he can't come over as too much snow. Thick snow falls again the next day. Cesca goes out for a walk with Ned, Charles and Trevor but get lost and are snowballed by a crowd of urchins and were very late for lunch.

Cesca returns home on Wednesday 28 December.

Cesca spends the last night of 1927 at a dance at Ditton Place – a most amusing small private dance. They see the New Year in with hot rum punch and Auld Lang Syne and danced with the lights out.

1928
Egypt and an Engagement

Cesca returns from staying for the New Year at Handcross and finds her parents both rather cross and cold. A terribly cold thaw and she settles down to letter writing interrupted by Hugh ringing up about plans for the next day in London.

Tuesday 3 January

Went up to town by 10.08, train very late. Shopped at Fortnum & Masons and Bond Street. Aunt Edie's held her New Year's lunch party. This went off better than I expected although Aunt Edie was very flustered. Had my hair set at Millie's and bought this diary and an engagement calendar for Mother and paid Miss Gray's bill. Met Hugh and came home by 7.30. Terrible row on getting home.

Saturday 7 January

Dad went up to match at Twickenham. Mum went to Ben Hur in afternoon and I sat and read and waited for Hugh. He did not arrive till 4.15 having had trouble with the car. Took Belinda to garage. Dad home at 6.30. Played bridge after dinner.

Sunday 8 January

Lovely warm day. Hughie and I took car up to the forest and went for a good walk there. Home to lunch. Afterwards went to Canterbury to have tea with Canon and Mrs Spring, Hughie's aunt and uncle by marriage. Then came home and everything seemed to go wrong with the car. Finally at Pembury all lights went out so had to crawl behind a bus for the last two miles home.

Tuesday 10 January Eridge Hunt Ball

Had hectic morning. Then to add to the difficulties of new servants and putting up five guests, the parlour maid left and made Mum nearly distracted. However all went smoothly. Dollie and Vi arrived at 6.00 in Di's baby Austin. Hugh came by 6.00 train and Jim arrived in his new car at 6.30 and I met Bobbie in the car at 7.00. It was all rather a rush. However I enjoyed the end of the dance very much. Not so much before. Poor Jim sprained his ankle and was in great pain. To bed at 5.30.

Wednesday 11 January

Did not get any sleep as felt so cold. Up at 7.45. Bobbie and Hugh left by 9.00 train. Jim's ankle very swollen so he went home, instead of going to town. Dollie and Vi left about 12.00 after having breakfast in bed. Mother and I dead tired, so tired by the evening that I could not stop crying and had to be put to bed.

Hugh returned the following evening to collect the car. On Friday Cesca went up to London, shopped and then met Col and Mrs Ian Smith at the Naval and Military Club. His regiment is in Cairo and he is writing to the Colonel to tell him Cesca and her Mother are coming out there. She meets Hugh at 6.00 and dines at 'Good Housekeeping' and then motors to Mingary in the new Morris Cowley. Hughie shooting so she returns to town with Mrs Lang in the Lanchester. They lunch at the Criterion and then to the theatre returning to Mingary at 6.30. On Sunday Hugh shows Cesca over the house which is much bigger than she thought. On Monday they both leave for London, Cesca meeting her Mother and lunching at the Criterion. On Wednesday 1 February Cesca is up in London and staying at the Levy's house in Lowndes Square. She has her hair set at Millie's, lunches with Barbara and sees a most thrilling show, The Wreckers. She dines with Mrs Levy, Mrs Vaughan and Vi. The next day is filled with fittings and odd jobs to do for Mother. She changes and dines with Hugh at Mayfair, an excellent dinner and then went to 'Hit the Deck' at the Hippodrome. She hated saying goodbye to Hugh for eight weeks. Before leaving for home the next day, Cesca watches Lord Haig's funeral procession from Mary's balcony. Most impressive. After lunching with Aunt Edie who gave her a sermon about Dad, she has tea with Mrs Levy and is home by 7.00. Two letters arrive from Hugh in quick succession before the great departure for Egypt.

Thursday 9 February

Hogben terribly upset when we left. He and Blanche both quite miserable. Left home by 11.04. Took our luggage to Victoria and met Dad there at 12.30. Had lunch with Dad and then found our seats on the Pulman at Victoria. Dad rather worried about the crossing and about us generally. Arrived Folkestone 3.30. Boat left at 4.00. Arrived Boulogne 5.30 after rather a rough crossing but we were alright.

Friday 10 February

Had dreadful time last night. About an hour from Paris there was a terrible crash and the train stopped but went on again very slowly to Paris. We were told the buffers at the end of our coach had smashed and we were to turn out and get into other sleeper. So by 12.30 we got into fresh wagon lits and were off again. Did not sleep at all. Arrived Marseilles 12.00 and went straight on board. The *Kaisar i Hind* is rather a lovely big boat and very comfy. [This P&O ship was remarkably fast and carried 548 passengers in great comfort having fans positioned all over the ship. The Prince of Wales sailed in her September 1928 for his tour to East Africa]. Mother and I have small cabin with two beds. We went ashore in afternoon and posted our letters home. I loathe Marseilles. I think it is an awful place. Hugh sent me a wire wishing me luck that arrived just before dinner.

Saturday 11 February

The boat did not leave till 5.00 this morning. When Mum and I woke up, it was distinctly rough and we both felt rather seedy. I soon recovered though Mum felt seedy until the evening. Have met Edith Ashfield, now Mrs Erskine and her husband Major Erskine who are off to India. She is much nicer than she used to be. A lot of passengers are still ill as it is rather 'rocky' as the stewardess says. A dance in evening. Most of the men are awful bounders.

The conditions remain rough, cold and windy for the next three days at sea. Deck quoits and bridge are played and Cesca and her Mother are amused that such a lot of passengers are still ill whilst they feel fine. The porthole window keeps banging keeping them awake at night and Cesca finds dancing on deck after dinner a challenge as the ship rolls so. A Mrs Lumb, very well dressed elderly lady is also going to Mena House.

Wednesday 15 February

Was woken many times during the night with porthole window banging. Finally had to shut it. Woke at 5.30 on arrival at Port Said.

Amazing seeing all coal barges coming alongside with yelling screaming Arabs who bring it on board. Breakfast then tipping. Disembarked at 9.30 and went by motor boat to Customs and had to pay 6/6 quarantine tax. Customs a filthy place, then wandered about Port Said, but it is a deadly hole and nothing to see so we took a carriage and got our seats on the train. Had good lunch then a most interesting journey. Passed through fascinating country and stretches of desert with few palms here and there, then cultivated land and flocks of goats and sheep, oxen ploughing and men riding camels and donkeys. Arrived punctually at Cairo at 4.30 and were met by Colonel Mayfield and out to Mena House at the foot of the Pyramids.

Their first day in Egypt is blighted by a fearful sandstorm blotting out everything. Colonel Mayfield takes them in his car, a nice closed Austin into Cairo. Not pleasant owing to the gale and rain. He brought them back to tea and later they walked up to the Pyramids which they thought marvellous. The following day was lovely and sunny. They visit Cairo again and have lunch at the Continental meeting several friends of Mother's. Colonel Mayfield then drove Cesca and her Mother to the Nile Delta Barrier fifteen miles north of Cairo where they have tea and admire the sand dunes.

Saturday 18 February
Perfect day and very hot. Mum and I went into Cairo by 10.00 bus and went to Cooks and then to the Museum for an hour. Saw Tutankhamen's artefacts which were beautifully arranged and very interesting. We lunched at the Kasr-el-Nil Barracks then went to the Sports Club at Gezira and enjoyed the races very much there. Came back at 6.00 and found Bill Pearson-Rogers waiting there. He had sent three wires on getting my letter this morning which we had not received as we had been out. So he chanced it and turned up. Such fun to see him. Dined here and then we went out to Shepheard's where Bill had booked a table and danced there! Then onto Groppi's, most amusing. Loved my evening.

As Bill had spent the night at Mena, he stayed the next day there with Cesca and her Mother. They walked to the Pyramids where photos were taken by Mum and after lunch Cesca went to the Zoo with Bill. He had to leave after tea to get back to Abu Sweir, about 90 miles from Cairo. Cesca so enjoys Bill's company. 'He is such fun'. Cesca and her Mother have a days sightseeing on Monday in Cairo including the Citadel, the mosques and the bazaars. Colonel Mayfield drives them to Heliopolis for tea and back to Mena where they find a wire from Bill saying he will come over the next day for both the afternoon and that night. They meet him at Shepheard's and have lunch together at the Continental returning afterwards to Mena where they spend the afternoon in the gardens. Bill and Cesca return to the Continental for the Shrove Ball. However very crowded so they go on to Groppi's and dance there till 2.00. Back to Mena by car. Wednesday is another day spent enjoying Bill's company until she has to see him off at the station at 6.00. Cesca feels miserable. Cesca and her Mother visit Cooks rearranging their trip to Luxor to go by train instead of by boat on Sunday 26 February as Mother is afraid of the boat getting stuck again. They also book rooms at the Winter Palace there.

Sunday 26 February
Bill rode early before breakfast so all had breakfast at 9.30. Mum went to church and left Bill and I alone so spent morning together at Mena. In afternoon Mum took snaps of us and the hotel and then we had to pack. We then left at 6.30 by sleeper for Luxor, very comfy and I slept at once.

Monday 27 February
Arrived Luxor 7.30 and took carriage to the Winter Palace Hotel. Lovely big hotel on the edge of the Nile overlooking the Valley of the Tombs. Mr Amburg, the manager greeted us (thanks to Bill) and gave us a nice room overlooking the Nile. We unpacked, bathed and I slept till lunchtime. In the afternoon an awful sandstorm blowing. This hotel is crammed with Americans who I think are foul and loathsome. Mr and Mrs Lumb are here however and are so nice. Wrote to Bill.

On Tuesday they engage a dragoman and visit Karnak and the Temple of Luxor by carriage. Cesca does not think they will stay beyond Saturday as the hotel is so full of awful Americans. She receives a letter from Bill enclosing some snaps. 'Letter too thrilling. Don't know what I ought to do'.

The next two days Cesca and her Mother explore the Tombs of the Kings and the Tombs of the Queens reaching the West Bank by sailing boat and riding on donkeys. Cesca admits to feeling very bow legged at the end both days and tired as it was very hot. The scenery is wonderful and Tombs most impressive but the Americans continue to swarm about everywhere. Lots of letters arrive for Cesca, two for her from Bill and one for her Mother. Also one from Hugh, rather depressed, one from her Father and from Peg and Blanche. The Arabia, the boat they were to travel in has arrived in Luxor. They go to have a look at her and were glad they had changed their plans. They spent their last day at Luxor quietly writing letters and playing bridge with the Lumbs. Mother is nervous because she believes the man in the next bedroom is dead as policemen are outside whispering! On Saturday they leave Luxor and have an easy journey by train to Assouan where they are staying at a large hotel the Cataract with 300 rooms. Colonel Mayfield has booked them a lovely room with a balcony. They have tea with the Mayfields who leave for Palestine on Monday. Cesca and her Mother cross the Assouan Dam by trolley, and were also rowed to the half submerged temple of Philae and were impressed by the fineness of both. They returned to the hotel by sailing boat which took about two hours. Cesca thoroughly enjoyed the trip but was afraid that Mother was very frightened. Letters are arriving regularly from Bill. Cesca writes to him and Hugh.

Friday 9 March
Left Assouan after lunch by train. It was terribly hot, over 100 in the shade. The carriage filled with dust and was unbearably hot. A most awful journey though it cooled down as we approached Cairo.

Saturday 10 March
Arrived Cairo at 7.30. Wonderful to see Pyramids again, all the way in the train and felt so happy to be back at Mena again. Before lunch, a letter from Bill who said he was arriving today. Felt so happy when he turned up at lunchtime and we spent the afternoon together. Mother went into Cairo and brought me back three letters, one from Hugh, one from Aunt Edie and Dad.

Sunday 11 March
Bill rode early then we all had breakfast together in our dressing gowns. How I love it all, it's such fun and marvellous sun and blue skies and makes everything so terribly happy. We had tea in our

room as there was such an awful crowd of people everywhere. Played bridge after dinner.

Monday 12 March

We had arranged to go to Sakkara today but due to the roads being closed as all the troops were on manoeuvres so Bill and I went to Gezira to watch the Polo. A lovely lazy way to spend a perfect afternoon. Danced in the evening at Mena.

Tuesday 13 March

It is such fun having breakfast all together in bed every morning and I am as happy as the day is long. Bill and I went to the Museum in the morning, full of Americans again. Then lunch at Shepheard's and then returned for tea with Mother. In the evening went to Groppi's after dinner and danced there till 1.00. The band and floor are perfect, so is Bill so what more can one want.

Wednesday and Thursday Bill and Cesca spend most of their time left together, in Cairo, or watching Polo at Gezira and dancing together in the evenings.

Friday 16 March

Felt tired and miserable when I woke up and later so worried about Bill and leaving him and telling Hugh that I started to cry and could not stop. Bill succeeded in cheering me up but felt so unhappy and tired that he took me to watch the Polo at Gezira. It was lovely but we both felt sad it was our last afternoon together and could not forget the thought of parting tomorrow. Bill had long talk to Mum while I rested. I wrote him a line so he will get it on his birthday this Sunday 18 March. We dance together at Mena till about 12.00. Too sad to sleep.

Saturday 17 March

The most awful day I can remember. Leaving Mena House. Up at 5.45. After packing we had breakfast. Felt so sad. Bill absolutely wonderful trying to cheer me up. We said goodbye and Mother and I left at 7.00 both feeling terrible unhappy. Watched Bill for as long as I could. We arrived at the station, train very full, hot and dusty and took our seats. Arrived in Alex late and had fearful scramble to catch our boat after going through Customs, Quarantine and Passport Offices before boarding *The Vienna*. Found a wire from Bill then dined and went to bed.

Sunday 18 March

Sent Bill a wire for his birthday. Can't bear this boat, it's small, dirty and smells. Just after lunch boat started to roll most alarmingly. Mum and I were both terribly ill until dinner time. The stewards most negligent too. Felt so unhappy.

Monday 19 March

The time on this boat seems interminable but not so rough again. Arrived Brindisi at 12.00 and posted letters there. It has turned much colder.

Tuesday 20 March

We arrived in Venice about 12.00 and disembarked. Then had a difficult time retrieving our luggage before we could reach the Grand Hotel. It is terribly cold here but anything is better than that boat with its disgusting smells and filthy food.

Unpacked and found a letter from Hugh from Cannes which gave me a shock. He has been ill with flu and ear infection and been ordered to rest so will not meet us now in Paris.

The next morning they wake to heavy snow. Cesca writes to Bill and tells him all the news. Also writes to Hugh and tells him on no account to attempt to come to Paris. They leave Venice on Thursday morning by gondola and are terrified all the way to the station as their gondola, shipping water, nearly sank in pouring rain. Cesca and her Mother arrive at the Gare de Lyon in bright sunshine and have lovely big adjoining bedroooms at Hotel Lotti overlooking the courtyard. A letter arrives from Bill from Cairo, followed by a wire saying he missed her. She finds him wonderful and such a difference to be thought of instead of being neglected by Hugh. However they find Paris very dull and flat after Egypt and even buying a nightie, stockings, gloves, an evening bag and eau de cologne and lunching at Pruniers off delicious 'sole au four' does not stop Mother and Cesca wishing they were leaving sooner. Tuesday 27 March they leave Paris and have a splendid crossing and are met by Dad with Hogben, delighted to see them again motors them home arriving at 6.30. 'Everything quiet and peaceful and comfy, only I am not the same and feel out of place'. Two days later Cesca is sent the most marvellously long letter from Bill followed by a huge box of pink and white tulips! Letters fly back and forth from Egypt and Cesca sends Bill two ties. Wednesday 4 April feeling fed up, Cesca travels up to town with Mother who gives her a marvellous evening dress from Gray's for 17 guineas. Cesca has now arranged to meet Hugh for lunch in London on Saturday 14 April. She feels frightened to death and thinks it will be fearful to have to explain everything.

Saturday 14 April

Went up to London by 10.07. Very cold so wore fur coat and brown hat. Went to Debenhams and Fortnums in morning. Then to see Vi whose engagement is announced in today's *Times* to Robert Henriques. He is very young. Priceless! Then to Mayfair at 1.00 and found Hughie waiting for me. It was awful and after eating my lunch, I told him everything. Poor dear Hugh was awfully upset and miserable and made it worse by saying nothing. Home by 3.30. I can think only of Hugh and Bill and my future and don't know what to.

Wednesday 18 April

Mother in town. Dad's gout is very bad and he is very grumpy. Had a very charming letter from Mrs Lunn, Bill's Mother in the evening. She is sending me Bill's photograph. [This arrives the following day].

Friday 4 May is a lovely day as Bill sends Cesca some beautiful lilies. She never ceases to miss him and wish he was not so far away in the terrible heat of Egypt.

Cesca goes up to the Skinners Ball where she sees Pat and dances with him. She is relieved to get the inevitable meeting over with. Cesca's Mother has given her another £500 of investments and in June they spend an hour in Frogmorton Avenue discussing her finances with a Mr Lawford.

On Monday 11 June Cesca is invited to join Lady Anderson's party staying at Eastcote, for the Caledonian Ball where it is impossible to dance as there are over 2,000 guests dancing in uniform or kilts. A wonderful sight. Peggy and Blanche come over for lunch on Thursday and they watch the cricket, quite exciting as Kent declared after making 519 runs for six wickets against Warwick. Cesca is one of the bridesmaids for Norah William's wedding on Saturday 16 June. The dresses are most attractive and the reception was great fun, over 400 there. She comes home about 5.30 in the best man's Chrysler to change and returns to a dinner for 40 in the evening followed by dancing. Lots of tennis parties most afternoons followed by dinner parties throughout June. Dad also is playing tennis. Norah and Rowland return from their honeymoon of a week, 'Norah looking terribly ill and is to have an operation for tonsils'. Cesca wishes she was at Henley and Eton v Harrow and feels lonely at home and cuts out a nightie.

Cesca goes to stay at Boxley House with the Styles. A lovely old Elizabethan house where they all play tennis and the next day she and Betty go out in the pony cart and Cesca rides a funny old white Iceland pony. She then goes to stay for the weekend of 14-15 July with Uncle Alfred and Barbara and is collected by Barbara in the new Rolls at Slough. On Sunday they have a run in the car to Harmondsworth and Cesca sees the church where her Mother was married and the vicarage where Uncle John lived for such a long time. In London on her way home Cesca has lunch with Mary Richards, now Wilson, in her house in Ovington Square. She is to have a baby in November. 'We had a long talk about Hugh and she agrees that his behaviour is most odd'. The Tunbridge Wells Agricultural Show is held over two days at the end of July and Cesca and Blanche go down in the car with Hogben and enjoy themselves. Lots of friends there and the Prince of Wales arrived at 2.30 and stayed for about two hours watching the jumping.

Monday 29 July

Mum and I decided to go to the Exhibition of Antiques at Olympia so left home at 9.50 and went straight there. We were disappointed as it was rather a muddle and a lot of fakes. However the Loan exhibits are wonderful. A lot lent by Mrs Levy and Lord Bearsted and Stuart Montagu. After lunch at Marshalls, Mum bought me a lovely diamond watch for my birthday present.

Tuesday 31 July

Peggy came to lunch and she, Mum and I went to Muriel William's Wedding to David Jennings at the Catholic church which was crammed. Muriel looked nice and the bridesmaids wore very pretty pink frocks. Went to the reception at Shernfold, everyone there. Lovely presents. Blanche and Ian came to dinner and we dined simply as Lily left this afternoon for her holiday. Went up to Frant in the car and enjoyed the evening more than Norah's wedding party. Danced with Gerald, Peter, Jim, Harry, Ian, Eddie etc. Home at 3.15am.

Cesca, Jim & Hugh Scotland 1926

Dr Bisshopp & Hugh Lang 1927
'Neat not gaudy, gaudy not neat'

Panmure Hotel Edzell 1925

Bill & Cesca Mena House February 1928

Bill 1928

Dr B., Cesca, Bill Scotland 1928

Bill & Cesca & Sunbeam Scotland 1928

Cesca goes over to Maidstone in the car with Hogben the following evening for the Styles dance. 'Wore blue dress and arrived about 9.30. About 200 people there and very well done. At first as I knew no one thought it was going to be awful but everyone introduced and I enjoyed it thoroughly. Danced with two Air Force fellows. One rather lost his heart'! A letter arrives the next morning from Bill which made Cesca much happier. Dad leaves for Scotland on Wednesday 8 August with Hogben and Nigger by the 7.20 from Euston arriving in Carrbridge tomorrow. Hogben very excited.

Wednesday 15 August

Today Bill begins his leave and departs Port Said by the Cheshire. I can't believe it. Dad shot 19 brace on the 12th! Had our first grouse sent by Dad this evening.

Cesca goes down by train to stay in Mrs Levy's house party, Craigwell, Bognor for a long weekend. Lots of tennis and dancing and trips to the coast where Cesca watches everyone else bathe. [She never learned to swim]. Lady Swaythling who has a house nearby comes over bringing six more house guests to join the fun. Cesca leaves on Tuesday by train from Brighton to Tunbridge Wells. That evening Bill rings up! Cesca cannot believe it was him speaking to her. They plan to see each other the next day in London.

Wednesday 22 August

Have seen Bill and still feel I must be dreaming. Went to town by 9.58. Went to Times Book Club before meeting Bill at 12.00 at the Berkeley. He looked so nice and my heart beat 20 times faster than usual. We went for a walk in Green Park after the first exciting few minutes and then lunched at the Berkeley. Then we went to see 'Plunder' at the Aldwych, a wonderful show and we laughed and laughed. Bill saw me off on my train home. He looks wonderful but very tired.

Bill is coming down on Saturday. Cesca longs to see him and it seems ages to wait till he comes down in his new Vauxhall.

Saturday 25 August

Went over to Southborough to meet Bill and found him waiting for me at the Hand and Sceptre in a lovely Vauxhall 30-98. Lovely car and he took me home. I feel so in love with him. Went for a drive in the car to Crowborough to see if there would be a dance there. Went for a long walk. In the evening went with the Williams in their boxes to 'Hit the Deck'. Very good show. Came home and had a wonderful hour with Bill.

Sunday 26 August

Feel so very happy, 24 today. Bill and I had our early tea in Mum's room. Bill has given me a lovely cut glass scent bottle and Alkinson Eau de Colgne. £10 from Dad and the diamond watch from Mum. Trevor Cripps could not come over as he had crashed his car, the Styles could not come either so just Peg joined us for lunch and bridge. After dinner went up to Shernfold and danced.

Monday 17 August

Bill and I went up to London in his car, a lovely drive and we went to their home in Regents Park where I saw his Mother whom I quite liked but felt rather frightened of. She is very good looking like Bill with lovely eyes. Hoped that she would like me. We then had lunch at the Mayfair and did some shopping. Came home here by 5.15. The train full of hop-pickers.

Wednesday 29 August

Bill arrived just as we had finished breakfast at 9.00 having left London at 7.30. He bought me a big box of chocolates. In afternoon went over to the Sale at Goudhurst. Enjoyed it and bought stool for £1.12.6 and Mother bought the old Georgian chairs for £2! She did not mean to buy them. We brought them all home in the back of the Vauxhall. Do love him desperately.

Saturday 1 September

Bill and I took his 30-98 over to Hadlow to see Peg but she was out cubbing so left a message for her. Went over to the Podmore's tennis party in the afternoon, awful party and Bill must have been bored. After dinner he and I went over to Wadhurst Castle to dance there.

Sunday 2 September

Went to King Charles in the morning with Mother and Bill. After lunch we set off in the car leaving it at Holtye Common then walked across country to Withyham and had tea at the Dorset Arms then walked back to the car. Very hot day and walked about 9 miles. Slept on Bill's shoulder after dinner.

Monday 3 September

After lunch Bill and I went up to London in the car. I went to Millie's to have my hair washed and bought some stockings. Arrived about 5.30 at Ulster Terrace and unpacked. Pat Pearson-Rogers arrived and talked to me for half an hour before Bill arrived. Dined with Bill's Mother who I think is charming and George Lunn, a funny old thing! Then we changed and went and danced and had supper at the Berkeley.

Tuesday 4 September

Felt very sleepy when Mrs Lunn came to say goodbye at 8.30. After they had gone, Bill came in had breakfast with me and then we went out shopping to Bond Street and tried on rings!! But did not like any. After lunching together at the Piccadilly Grill, I came home in time for tea with Mum.

Friday 7 September

Very busy packing for Scotland with Nellie. Mum saw me off on the 6.00 train to London and Bill met me at Charing Cross and took me to 1 Ulster Terrace. We went to the theatre and saw 'Alibi' at the Haymarket, a very good show with Bill and his two sisters and little brother Peter. I felt terribly tired and seedy. Had cold supper when we got in at 11.30.

Saturday 8 September

Left London after breakfast at 9.00 seen off by Peter and Elizabeth. Bill and I motored to Grantham where we had lunch and a rest for two hours. Then on to York by 5.00 sooner than we expected and met Mother's train at 5.40 and spent the night at the Station Hotel. Horrid hotel and poor food.

Sunday 9 September

Left York at 9.30 leaving Mother to come on by train. Went to the George Hotel at Penrith for lunch and then on to Carlisle, Lockerbie and Moffat arriving at Edinburgh about 6.00. Spent the night at the North British Hotel, a first class hotel. Mother arrived at 8.40 and we all had dinner together at 9.00. Lovely weather and no rain since leaving London.

Monday 10 September

Left Edinburgh with Bill and Mother and motored to Queensferry and had to wait there for an hour before crossing to North Queensferry. Thirteen cars on the ferry. We then motored through Kinross, Perth and then to Pitlochry, Blair Athol where we had tea and saw Mrs Jewell and Godfrey. Then on to Newtonmore, Aviemore arriving here, Carrbridge, at teatime. Found Dad very seedy with gout. He does not seem to care for Bill much so felt rather miserable.

Tuesday 11 September

Dad in bed for the morning so Bill went and talked to him about our Engagement and got it over. After lunch we motored Mother and Dad into Inverary for the afternoon and Bill had his hair cut. Roads lovely all the way and back in time for dinner.

Wednesday 12 September

Had day on the moor. Dad and Mother stayed till lunch and then came home. Bill, the Fawcetts, Sinclair and the Ghillie stayed till 4.30 but had a poor day. Just one brace grouse, two brace partridge, four hares and a rabbit.

The warm, dry weather continues and Cesca and Bill enjoy being together in Scotland shooting and walking. On Saturday 15 September they motor to Grantown and Bill gives Cesca a motoring lesson on the Nairn road. Three letters arrive from Bill's Mother for all of them congratulating them on their engagement. On Wednesday Bill and Cesca raced some cars along the road after tea. Bill is at last winning at bridge. On their last day Bill takes them all over to Inverness for the Northern Meeting Games. Cesca found them rather dull and the Station Hotel where they had tea full of awful people.

Friday 21 September

Left Carrbridge at 10.30 and very sad to leave as it has been such a happy time and all of us have enjoyed it so. Mother came with us and we motored through Aviemore, Blair Atholl, Perth and had lunch at Gleneagles. Perfect weather and a very good lunch. Then on through Falkirk arriving North British Hotel, Edinburgh at 6.00 and had lovely rooms and a good dinner there.

They left Edinburgh at 10.00 and lunched at the George at Penrith at 12.30. They then drive on via Scotch Corner and Ripon and arrive for tea at Harrogate at 4.15. They spent the night at the Majestic, expensive and danced at the dreadful Saturday night dance there. The next morning Bill has trouble with the car as the man who washed it got water in the carburettor so they were delayed for nearly two hours. However they arrive at the George at Stamford only 40 minutes late and are joined by Dick Atcherley who is to be their best man, for lunch. He is Bill's best friend and is charming. Bill and he go off to camp at Wittering for an hour. They motor on arriving in London, Park Lane Hotel at 7.00 and Bill dines with them. Cesca and Bill then go over to the Berkeley and dance there till midnight.

Monday 24 September

Had breakfast in bed and then packed. Bill arrived at 10.00 looking very smart. Mother left us and went home with the luggage. Bill and I went to Shaplands and he bought me the most lovely engagement ring, emeralds and diamonds set in platinum. Much too expensive. I bought him a gold cigarette case, engine turned, £17. Then we felt quite exhausted and returned to Park Lane. Had lunch at Ulster Terrace where we saw Mrs G. Lunn, Pat and Peter. I then had my hair washed and came home. Bill rang up at 7.30.

Dad arrives home the following day having had a bad journey. Mother busy writing to Aunt Edie etc. When Cesca told Hogben she would be living in Egypt he was very upset and his wife in tears. Nellie too. Very emotional. Bill rang up after dinner. Wednesday Aunt Edie rings to condole with Mother and Cesca is busy writing to friends about her engagement.

Thursday 27 September

Went up to town and Bill met me at Charing Cross with the car. We went to the *Times* office and left the announcement of our engagement, cost £5. Then to Yevonde's to have our photographs taken. Then lunched with Bill's grandmother, Mrs Richard Currie at her flat in Hampstead. Elizabeth was there too and we took her afterwards back to her studio. Then saw dear Aunt Edie who was delighted with us both and loved Bill. Then we motored home and were showered with congratulations from Hogben and Nellie.

Saturday 29 September

In afternoon motored down to Hove to see Bill's guardian, Clement Davies and had tea with him. I liked him very much. Home to dinner and played bridge.

Monday 1 October

Our Engagement announced today in the *Times* and the *Morning Post*. Had many letters from Mrs Levy, Vi, Pat, Joannie etc. Bill and I went out for a long walk to avoid all the callers and letters and wires. Lovely walk and perfect weather. I am so happy. Went over in afternoon to Hadlow to see Peggy and Mabel who had returned from hunting.

Shoals of letters of congratulation continue to pour in and also masses of advertisements of all sorts, photographers etc. Bill and Cesca motor up to London on Wednesday where they check on the photographs and take Cesca's ring to be altered. They visit Mrs Levy who gives Cesca a lovely diamond and pearl brooch and seems to like Bill. They also go to Ulster Terrace and find Mum there having tea with Mrs Lunn, George and Elizabeth. Cesca feels very tired and done up and stays in bed for breakfast most mornings that week and then tackles all her correspondence which keep on coming by every post. On Saturday 6 October Bill and Cesca, after early breakfast in the car, motor up the Great North Road through Stamford, Newark and Doncaster, having tea at the Three Arrows at Boroughbridge and finally arrive at Spennithorne House, Bedale to stay with Aunt Freda (Mrs Van Straubenzee) who was charming, Aunt Ruth and Mrs Lyon. Cesca finds the house most attractive, with rambling passages and a lovely view over the Dales. They enjoyed the peace and quiet and the kindness shown to her and Bill. They enjoyed their visit and motored home and on the way had exciting races with two cars south of Stamford. A Packard and a Voisin beating them both and did from Stamford to Biggleswade in under an hour, averaging 45mph!!

Thursday 11 October

Bill and I motored up to London in the Vauxhall at 10.00. I changed into black coat and skirt at Ulster Terrace and we motored to lunch in Hampstead with Bill's grandmother, Mrs Currie, known as Dandy. She was so sweet to us. Then I joined Mum and went to the Synagogue to Vi's wedding. Enjoyed the wedding very much, everyone there. Then after dinner we went on to the Berkeley and danced and saw lots of the bridesmaids and friends there too.

Friday 19 October

Had dreadful night owing to noisy room. Then Bill and I, Mother, and Elizabeth motored down to Marlborough, the car went very badly and Bill was livid. But we arrived in time for lunch and his brother Peter joined us. Bill and he played squash together in the afternoon.

The weekend is spent at Marlborough, walking in Savernake Forest, watching a rugger match, School v Harlequins then Peter and two friends dined with them and played games. On Sunday they go to Chapel and then walk round the College. After lunch motored back to London, Mum and Bill in front and me and Elizabeth behind. Then after meeting Dick Atcherley they motored back home together.

On Wednesday 24 October Cesca receives a letter congratulating her from Hugh that rather shakes her. Bill spent the night with his guardian. On Thursday 25 October Bill and Cesca went to St Margaret's Westminster and booked the Church for 11 February for their Wedding. The next day they went to his lawyers and Bill signed his Will and then lunched with an aunt of Bill's, sister of his Father. [Unfortunately her name is not given as Bill's past is rather shrouded in mystery]. On Sunday 28 October Dad, Mum, Bill and Cesca all went to church at King Charles and listened to a dreadful sermon preached by some miserable fellow. Bill roared with laughter throughout! On 5 November Bill and Cesca return from several days spent at Townhill and after tea let off some marvellous fireworks and rockets. Cesca is dreading Bill leaving on Thursday.

Tuesday 6 November

Packed up and Bill said goodbye to Parham House. Motored to London, our last trip in the dear Vauxhall and arrived Langham at 12.30. Had lunch there with Mother who came up by train. Afterwards Bill went home and packed and Mother and I went to see James Winter's Exhibition and ordered some linen for me. Bill dined at home, then we went and danced at the Berkeley till 1.00.

Wednesday 7 November

Woke up feeling desperately sad that this is our last day together. Bill took the dear dirty '98 back to the shop and came for me at 10.30. We shopped together, going to Picketts, the bank and office about his Income Tax which is unpaid. Then joined Dad and Mum at the Piccadilly Grill for lunch and then went to 'The Return Journey' at St James, very well acted but most depressing. Bill had to dine at home but came for me at 9.30 and we danced at the Berkeley until 12 .30. Desperate.

Thursday's entry is blank. On Friday 9 November she feels so unhappy when she awoke realising Bill was far away. She had a sweet letter from him written yesterday at lunchtime and she writes to him. Later that day Cesca goes over to see how Jessie is getting on with her trousseau. The next day she receives a wire from Bill from Venice.

Sunday 11 November

A miserable cold day and listened to services broadcast from the Cenotaph. Then Mother and I made out a list of friends to invite to our Wedding. Total came to 685 without any of Bill's.

Wednesday 14 November

Mother and I went to London by 10.00 train and went to Golanski to see about the grey squirrel coat that Mother is giving me as a Wedding present. [A useful present for living in Egypt!]. Then to Scott's for a chest for my silver and lunched at the Piccadilly Grill. After lunch I bought half a dozen lovely linen hankies and bought a princess petticoat in satin. Had a letter from Bill when I got home, from Brindisi.

Cesca's first wedding present arrives on Friday 16 November from Mr and Mrs Ainslie, a black and gold lacquer table. On Saturday the first consignment of linen arrived from Laurencekirk. On Wednesday 21 November Cesca goes to look at wedding dresses at Miss Gray's. A parcel of lovely green and gold coffee cups arrive from Shirley. Cesca stays with Aunt Edie for two days and has fittings and shops in Bond Street and Fortnum & Mason. She also chooses a dinner service at Harrods which Aunt Edie is giving her. On Wednesday 28 November Cesca went to Joannie Horden's wedding at St Mark's, North Audley Street and did not care for Joannie's dress or the bridesmaids dresses. [Joannie was an old flame of Bill's during the summer of 1925 and her brother Edmund an ardent admirer of Cesca]. Bill's leave is confirmed so all is well.

Friday 30 November
Mother and I went up to London and had a very busy day. We went to Miss Gray's and settled on my dress and on Mother's for the wedding. Mine to be white tulle with silver lame train and Mother's to be black and white. The bridesmaids to be in white chiffon. Then Mum and I went together to St Margaret's and settled on the day to be the 12 February, a Tuesday. Went to Yevonde's, the photographer and recovered my lost brooch and came home by the 5.15.

Dr Richardson comes to the house on Monday 3 December and vaccinates Cesca. Her leg becomes very painful during the next few days. Jim has agreed to be an usher but Gerald is unable to be there. Mother is ill in bed for her birthday on Saturday 8 December and the next day but decides to accompany Cesca to London on Monday to Miss Gray's where she gives Cesca lovely black faille dress with pink bow at the base of the back for 19 guineas. Absolutely lovely. Then they lunch with Mrs Levy who is most helpful. [Mrs Levy gave her home, 54 Lowndes Square for the reception]. Then they spent two hours with the family solicitor, Hughes, followed by tea at Gunters and home by 6.00 train. Long letters arrive from Bill and are replied to by return. Cesca tries on veils and orange blossom and has a fitting for her wedding dress and shops and shops.

Saturday 15 December

Dr Richardson came at 10.00 and inoculated me for typhoid. Stayed in bed all day and in evening felt very seedy with temperature of 100 and felt rather sick.

Friday 21 December

Busy morning packing up parcels. A Christmas present from Mrs Lunn and best of all three letters from Bill and a wire from him which did cheer me up so. Took parcels to Peggy in afternoon and stayed to tea with her.

Saturday 22 December

Bill sent me the most lovely diamond badge RAF brooch today. He means it for me for Christmas but I shall keep it as a wedding present. Ordered biscuits for Mrs Lunn and called to see Mrs Cartwright. Sent Bill a wire and in the evening wrote to Bill and to Mrs Levy who sent me a little present.

Sunday 23 December

We all went to church at King Charles. Mother's cough very bad. Spent the afternoon writing out invitations to the wedding. Such fun.

Both Christmas Eve and Christmas Day vanish beneath the piles of invitations being written by Cesca and her Mother. No mention of presents received or given. Just lots of letters for Cesca and two from Bill. Even Dr Richardson appears on Christmas Day at 10.00 to inoculate Cesca for a second time. Cesca finishes writing the invitations in the afternoon and goes to bed after tea with a temperature.

On Friday 28 December Cesca went over to the Styles at Maidstone who host a dinner for twelve for a dance given by the Mayor of Maidstone at the Old Palace. Cesca enjoys it as much as she could enjoy a dance without Bill and stayed till 3.30. Canon Oliver signs Cesca's passports.

The last day of 1928 is spent with Mother in London having a fitting for her wedding dress and shopping all afternoon.

The Pearson-Rogers Family

My grandfather's name was Henry William Pearson-Rogers, known as Bill. And according to both of his obituaries he was born in Staffordshire but one states the date as 18 March 1906. The other two years earlier in1904. And to add to the confusion I have in my possession a birth certificate that states he was born in Johannesburg 18 March 1906 at 76, Park Lane, Parkstown. Bill's father is recorded as being Henry Rogers, Director of General Companies, born in the Cape Colony. His Mother, May (nee Currie), was born in Natal and they were married at Hilton Road, Natal. May added "Pearson" as she thought it looked grander. The Currie family owned the Premier Milling Company in Johannesburg. It is alleged that Henry committed suicide owing to his wife's many affairs. The word amongst the family is that Bill's father was in fact Lord Bagot. May, known as Pattie, was tall, about five foot ten inches, dark and glamorous. The official story after the suicide was that Henry had been shot and killed by a black man. Not surprisingly it has been impossible to verify this story in South Africa or here in the U.K.
Bill was extremely good looking and quite unlike his siblings. Allegedly Lord Bagot paid for his education at Marlborough College. Bill's younger brother Peter was also educated at Marlborough.

Bill had two sisters and two brothers, Patricia, Elizabeth, Peter and Richard. Patricia, the eldest, was born in Guildford on 22 September 1901, and died unmarried at her home 12, Brook Street, Woodbridge Suffolk on the 25th October 1982. Elizabeth married a naval officer named Arthur Gordon Voules Hubback in 1930. They lived near Ringwood in Hampshire. They had a son Richard born in 1939.

Peter and Richard both were younger than Bill. Richard died whilst still a child. Peter was killed tragically aged 22 as reported here by the Air Ministry.

'The Air Ministry regrets to announce that F/O Peter John Pearson Rogers lost his life and Sub-Lt. Philip Alexander Roby Bremridge RN Flying officer, RAF was injured as the result of a collision in the air which occurred off Malta on February 12 1935 between two "Nimrod" aircraft of No. 800 (Fleet Fighter) Squadron. F/O Pearson-Rogers and Sub-Lt Brembridge were the pilots and sole occupants of their respective aircraft".

This fatal flying accident did nothing to allay Cesca's fears every time Bill returned to flying after his leave. Her fears increased after the outbreak of WWII.

Elizabeth was lonely and unhappy as her husband was away constantly with the Navy. He was having an affair and when her son went away to boarding school, she made an attempt to kill herself on the railway line near Tostock. Cesca managed to avert this attempt but sadly Elizabeth succeeded on the second occasion gassing herself in 1949. Her husband promptly remarried the same year, a Mary Roberton. Arthur rose to the rank of Vice Admiral in 1954 and was decorated, C.B, CBE, MID, Croix de Guerre and Knighted. The family did not care for him and blamed him for Elizabeth's tragic death.

Pattie (May) Pearson-Rogers, after her husband's death, married George Lunn, then a wealthy man, whose brother was the tour operator, Alfred Lunn. The announcement on a South African website, states they were married on 22 October 1918 at All Saint's Church, Branksome Park, Bournmouth. George is described as Captain George Whitton Lunn, A.S.C. youngest son of Mr Henry Lunn, The Firs, Horncastle, Lincolnshire. Pattie only daughter of Mr and Mrs Richard Currie of Johannesburg and widow of Mr

H.P. Rogers, Redmere, Branksome Park, Bournemouth. George was 42 years old, born in 1876, and Pattie two years younger. They lived for a while in a large house near Regent's Park, 1 Ulster Terrace and later 2, Park Crescent, London. They were both heavy drinkers and enjoyed a rather tempestuous relationship that involved hurling decanters at each other.

This upset Bill greatly and consequently he never drank much himself. George Lunn became bankrupt and he and Pattie then moved about the country renting cottages. In Somerset, during 1940/41 at Cesca's invitation they stayed in the cottage next to Pardlestone House in Kilve, then Greenbanks, Nether Stowey, Rendham and finally Walberswick Suffolk.

Bill was educated at a prep school called The Golden Parsonage at Hemel Hempstead from 1914-1919. The head master was a Mr G Tylecote and the house, a fine Georgian building owned by the Halsey family, was a school from 1875-1935. His education continued at Marlborough College from Michaelmas 1919 until December 1923. His boarding house was Littlefield House and the Housemaster a Mr J.P. Prior. Bill was awarded his 3rd XV Rugby colours cap in his last term. He also played for his House 1st Rugby XV in his final term, he played in the forwards and was a hooker. His best position in the class was the Lent term 1921 where he finished 3rd out of 21 boys. For the most part he remained an average scholar.

Bill joined the RAF at the age of 18 and joined as a cadet at RAF Cranwell near Sleaford on the 18 January 1924. RAF Cranwell was originally known as HMS Daedalus and accommodation for the men in 1915 comprised three cottages and the outbuildings of the original farmhouse. By 1917 RNAS Cranwell was the Royal Navy's nerve centre for aviation training. It had developed into a complex training establishment able to train pilots, observers, wireless operators, mechanics and engineers. It also had the Lighter-than-air section (Airships). Prior to the building of College Hall, the College had been housed in adapted wartime huts, where 'many pleasant and useful traditions, associated with a democratic and independent spirit where formed.' These huts were located on the south side of the public Sleaford to Newark road (now Cranwell Avenue). They were later demolished.

Bill continued to play Rugger for Cranwell and is described in the RAF Cadet College Magasine as a fastish forward who has greatly improved this season. Good in the loose, but does not use his height in the line out.
December 1925 Bill passed out from RAF Cranwell as an Under Officer, a photograph from the 1926-27 Journal, shows his year seated outside the now demolished building with snow on the ground. By his own admission he found that time 'Tough'. His passing out report labelled him: "Apt to be foolhardy and too confident"

The new College was first used by cadets in the autumn of 1933 and was officially opened on the 11th October 1934 by AM HRH Edward, Prince of Wales. Bill would not have enjoyed the comforts of the current impressive College building until he returned as Station Commander in 1946.

It is perhaps worth mentioning that, housed in the extensive Library, is The Lawrence Room, named after Col T.E. Lawrence (AC2 T.E. Shaw) or more famously as Lawrence of Arabia. T.E. Lawrence was stationed at RAF Cranwell as AC2 T.E. Shaw from 1925-1926 so my grandfather and Lawrence of Arabia may well have known each other! Of course Lawrence was his senior by 18 years. They both had a passion for motorcycles. However tragically Lawrence was fatally injured in May 1935, having swerved to avoid two boys on bicycles near his home in Dorset.

During 1941-42 when Bill was desk bound attached to the Chief of Air Staff's Department in London he would relieve his frustration by tearing between London and Suffolk on his racing motor bike, a 350cc Manx TT Norton. These motor bicycles demanded a running start! There is no mention of motor bicycles journeys in Cesca's diaries. However 1943,1946 and 1947 are all missing.

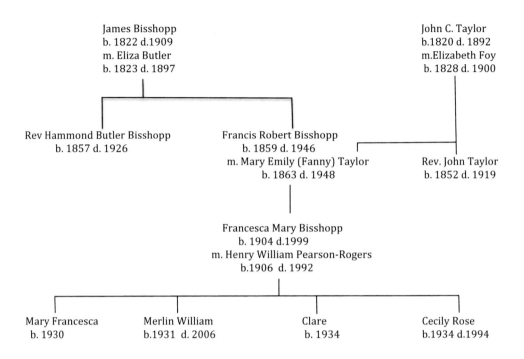

James Bisshopp
b. 1822 d.1909
m. Eliza Butler
b. 1823 d. 1897

John C. Taylor
b.1820 d. 1892
m.Elizabeth Foy
b. 1828 d. 1900

Rev Hammond Butler Bisshopp
b. 1857 d. 1926

Francis Robert Bisshopp
b. 1859 d. 1946
m. Mary Emily (Fanny) Taylor
b. 1863 d. 1948

Rev. John Taylor
b. 1852 d. 1919

Francesca Mary Bisshopp
b. 1904 d.1999
m. Henry William Pearson-Rogers
b.1906 d. 1992

Mary Francesca
b. 1930

Merlin William
b.1931 d. 2006

Clare
b. 1934

Cecily Rose
b.1934 d.1994

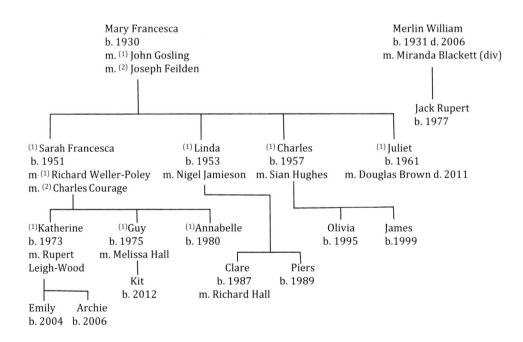

Mary Francesca
b. 1930
m. (1) John Gosling
m. (2) Joseph Feilden

Merlin William
b. 1931 d. 2006
m. Miranda Blackett (div)

Jack Rupert
b. 1977

(1) Sarah Francesca
b. 1951
m (1) Richard Weller-Poley
m. (2) Charles Courage

(1) Linda
b. 1953
m. Nigel Jamieson

(1) Charles
b. 1957
m. Sian Hughes

(1) Juliet
b. 1961
m. Douglas Brown d. 2011

(1)Katherine
b. 1973
m. Rupert
Leigh-Wood

(1)Guy
b. 1975
m. Melissa Hall

(1)Annabelle
b. 1980

Olivia
b. 1995

James
b.1999

Kit
b. 2012

Clare
b. 1987
m. Richard Hall

Piers
b. 1989

Emily
b. 2004

Archie
b. 2006

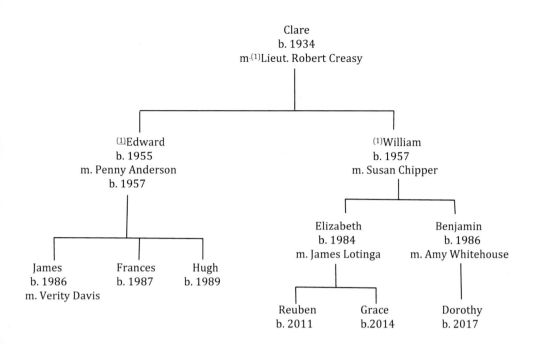

Clare
b. 1934
m.(1)Lieut. Robert Creasy

(1)Edward
b. 1955
m. Penny Anderson
b. 1957

(1)William
b. 1957
m. Susan Chipper

James
b. 1986
m. Verity Davis

Frances
b. 1987

Hugh
b. 1989

Elizabeth
b. 1984
m. James Lotinga

Benjamin
b. 1986
m. Amy Whitehouse

Reuben
b. 2011

Grace
b.2014

Dorothy
b. 2017

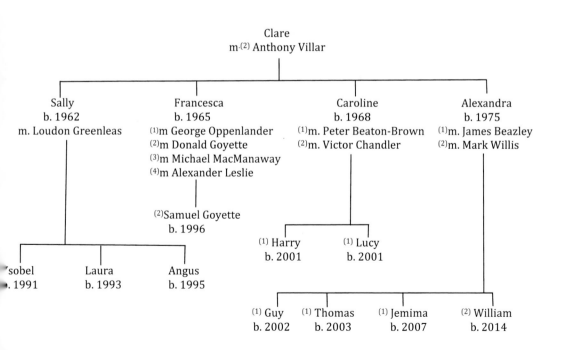

Clare
m.(2) Anthony Villar

Sally
b. 1962
m. Loudon Greenleas

Francesca
b. 1965
(1)m George Oppenlander
(2)m Donald Goyette
(3)m Michael MacManaway
(4)m Alexander Leslie

Caroline
b. 1968
(1)m. Peter Beaton-Brown
(2)m. Victor Chandler

Alexandra
b. 1975
(1)m. James Beazley
(2)m. Mark Willis

(2)Samuel Goyette
b. 1996

(1) Harry
b. 2001

(1) Lucy
b. 2001

'sobel
. 1991

Laura
b. 1993

Angus
b. 1995

(1) Guy
b. 2002

(1) Thomas
b. 2003

(1) Jemima
b. 2007

(2) William
b. 2014

Bill's Family

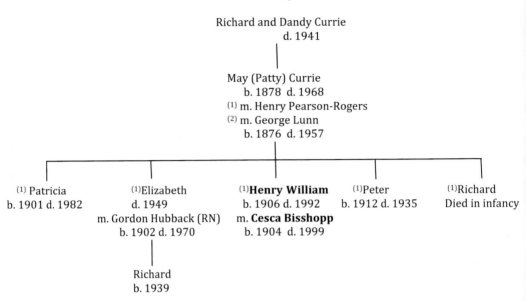

Richard and Dandy Currie
d. 1941

May (Patty) Currie
b. 1878 d. 1968
[1] m. Henry Pearson-Rogers
[2] m. George Lunn
b. 1876 d. 1957

[1] Patricia
b. 1901 d. 1982

[1]Elizabeth
d. 1949
m. Gordon Hubback (RN)
b. 1902 d. 1970

[1]**Henry William**
b. 1906 d. 1992
m. **Cesca Bisshopp**
b. 1904 d. 1999

[1]Peter
b. 1912 d. 1935

[1]Richard
Died in infancy

Richard
b. 1939

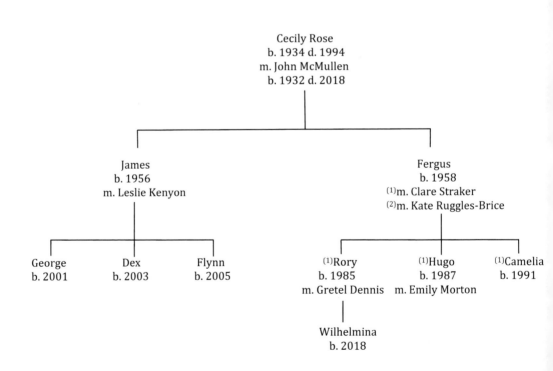

Cecily Rose
b. 1934 d. 1994
m. John McMullen
b. 1932 d. 2018

James
b. 1956
m. Leslie Kenyon

Fergus
b. 1958
[1]m. Clare Straker
[2]m. Kate Ruggles-Brice

George
b. 2001

Dex
b. 2003

Flynn
b. 2005

[1]Rory
b. 1985
m. Gretel Dennis

[1]Hugo
b. 1987
m. Emily Morton

[1]Camelia
b. 1991

Wilhelmina
b. 2018

Littlefield House, Marlborough College, House Master Mr. J.P. Prior
with his wife and a Pomeranian dog on her knee. Summer 1923

Marlborough Rugby Team 1922

Bill

The Passing-Out Term Cranwell 1925 Bill sitting third from left.

115

1930

V PITTS-BROWNS

(B.3)

LOST 0-2

V NEWMANS

(C.2)

WON 5-3

V SPRECKLEYS

(C.3)

WON 4-0

V CORNWALLS

(B.2)

WON 4-0

J.S.HARRISON. C.E.HARBINSON. G.H.HUGHES ESQ. C.R.SEYMOUR. R.H.E.GLADSTONE.

P.H.YEATES. G.J.F.MACKAY. R.M.CHAPMAN. J.A.R.STANIFORTH. R.M.HUGO.

P.J.P.ROGERS   R.W.ASQUITH.

Peter Pearson-Rogers Hockey Marlborough 1930

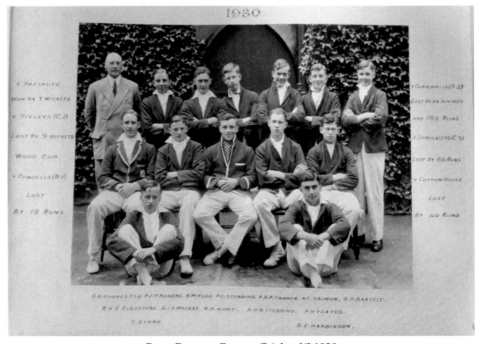

V PRESHUTE

WON BY 7 WICKETS

V TITLEYS (C.1)

LOST BY 9 WICKETS

WOOD CUP

V DOWDELLS (B.1)

LOST

BY 15 RUNS

V CORNWALLS (B.2)

LOST BY AN INNINGS

AND 186 RUNS

V SPRECKLEYS (C.3)

LOST BY 86 RUNS

V COTTON HOUSE

LOST

BY 40 RUNS

G.H.HUGHES ESQ. P.J.P.ROGERS. R.M.HUGO. P.C.STEBBING. A.D.P.TANNER. A.F.SALMON. G.P.BARTELT.

R.H.E.GLADSTONE. G.J.F.MACKAY. R.H.HUNT. A.M.R.STEBBING. P.H.YEATES.

T.STONE   G.E.HARBINSON.

Peter Pearson-Rogers Cricket XI 1930

1929
Frank Smythson's featherweight diary.

Bill is stationed in Egypt at Flying Training School as an Instructor having passed in 1926. A huge number of wedding presents pour in from the 850 guests invited to Bill and Cesca's wedding at St Margaret's Westminster in February. Their departure for Egypt and Cesca's unexpected return to Parham House, England after only four months of wedded bliss.

Tuesday 1 January
Mother and I in London and went to Aunt Edie's New Year's Lunch Party. Sir John and Lady Ramsay amongst others were there. Went to Bradleys and Golanski and then home on 6.00. Very cold.

Wednesday 2 January
Saw Peggy, her first visitor. Busy taking Wedding notes. Had present from Jim Reed a silver entrée dish.

Thursday 3 January
Went and saw Peggy again, found her very well. Four letters from Bill which I answered and a letter from Mrs Lunn.

Friday 4 January
Went to London by 9.00 train and went to Golanski and Debenhams and ordered blouses. Met Dad at Goldsmiths and chose Bill's watch and my wedding present, a diamond bow brooch. Then met Blanche for lunch. Home by 5.00. Lots of letters.

Saturday 5 January
Very cold. At 10.15 Dad gave me gas and Mr Pedrick took a tooth out. Harold and Ursula came to lunch and stayed on for tea. Still on crutches and looking very seedy.

Monday 7 January and Tuesday 8 January
Very busy writing letters of thanks for presents received. Had two letters from Bill. In evening wonderful present from Uncle Arthur

and Barbara arrived. Silver tea service, tray and rose bowl. Mum and I busy with wedding arrangements.

Thursday 10 January

Mother still seedy but went to London together and stayed at Hans Crescent. Mother went to see Mrs Currie [Bill's grandmother]. I shopped busily all the afternoon. Went to Lady Swaythling for dinner.

Saturday 12 January

Mother in bed all day with bad chill after her two days in London. Spent very busy day writing about 30 letters.

Sunday 13 January

Mother in bed all day, very seedy. My Banns read at Holy Trinity this morning. Did not go however, stayed with Mum. Wrote to Bill. In evening went up and saw Peggy.

Monday 14 January

Mother in bed all day but better and had a good night. Lots of presents, wrote and thanked them all. Letters from Bill, Mrs Lunn and Elizabeth.

Monday 15 January

Felt seedy so stayed in bed for breakfast with Mother. Maids left suddenly in morning. Nellie better after her inoculation.

Wednesday 16 January

Very cold with heavy fall of snow in morning. Mother is in bed for breakfast, lots of presents. Silver coffee tray from Mrs Davis. Silver salver from Simpsons, writing case from Lady Louche.

Thursday 17 January

Went up to London and had busy day shopping. Lunched with Blanche. Came home and found letter from Bill.

Friday 18 January

Felt very seedy and am afraid I am starting a cold. Stayed in bed trying to get rid of it without success. Parcels and presents coming all day long.

Saturday 19 January

Mother and I terribly busy sorting out the presents and getting them all ready to display for bridesmaids to see tomorrow and to take out to Egypt. More presents and a lot of letters to write.

Sunday 20 January

Lady Swaythling and Joyce came to lunch also Elizabeth Pearson-Rogers, Peggy, Blanche and Ian. After lunch Mrs Sandeman and Betty and Muriel came in and later Miss Williams, Maurice Simpson and Cartwrights. Elizabeth left at 6.00. Dislike her very much.

Monday 21 January

Felt seedy. Whole lot of people came in to see presents in the afternoon. Afterwards put them all away which was a fearful business.

Tuesday 22 January

Stayed in bed all day to try and get rid of this cold and by evening it felt better. Twelve presents came today, very busy writing letters all day.

The diary lapses until:

Wednesday 6 February

Went to Folkestone in the car to meet Bill. Boat came in at 1.00. Lunched together at Pavilion. Everything marvellous. Terribly happy. Motored back to Parham.

Thursday 7 January

Spent day in London shopping. Saw Hughes [family solicitor] in afternoon. Home to dinner.

Friday 8 February

Very busy writing letters of thanks all day. Mum in London. Presents are arriving all the time. Terribly happy.

Saturday 9 February

Not so well. Stayed in bed all day. Bill in London. Came home early and spent afternoon with me. Terribly busy. Suzanne arrived from Brussels [governess].

Sunday 10 February

Peggy came to lunch, also Hughes and Suzanne. In afternoon all Marriage Settlements took place. Very cold still. Bill and I are terribly happy.

Monday 11 February

Went up to London in afternoon with Mother and Bill. Stayed at 54 Lowndes Square. Had my hair done at Millie's. Bill came to dinner and Dick came to see us. Both left together at 10.30.

Tuesday 12 February Cesca and Bill's Wedding Day

Woke up early. Fearfully excited. Dressed and had lunch. Lydia and assistants from Miss Gray's came to help. Felt a little sad at leaving Mum. Wedding at 2.15 at St Margaret's Westminster. Bill wonderful. Reception was a blur. Left at 5.00 for Hyde Park Hotel, terribly happy.

The *Courier* stated Mrs Pearson-Rogers travelling in a grey squirrel fur coat trimmed with grey fox (wedding present from her mother) and a dress of printed satin in shades of green with a green felt hat to match.

Wednesday 13 February

Bill and I went shopping in Bond Street. Lunched at Hatchetts. Mum came and had tea with us. Rang up Aunt Edie. Mum and Dad dined with us at Hyde Park and went to Chinese Bungalow! Hated saying goodbye to them.

Thursday 14 February

Had lunch at Hyde Park and left London by 2 o'clock boat train for Egypt.

Amongst the hundreds of wedding presents a few are worth mentioning. Mrs Hugh Lang a glass ice pail, Brigadier General and Mrs Stanley-Clarke a pair of cut glass decanters, Mr Clement Davies (Bill's guardian) silver sweet basket and

Bill & Cesca, Dick Atcherley and bridesmaids 12-2-1929

Bill & Cesca leaving St Margaret's Westminster 12-2-1929

Bill Egypt 1929   Bill & Cesca Lake Timsah Egypt 1929

The Fiat Egypt 1929

a cheque, the Hon Mrs Walter Levy seed pearl and ruby necklace and Pat Ainslie a motoring rug.

The diary lapses until:

Wednesday 20 February
Arrived Port Said late in evening and travelled by 6.20 train to Cairo arriving midnight Mena at 1.00 Wonderful room. Terribly happy but very tired.

Another month goes by

Sunday 24 March
I left Ismailia for Cairo. Abdul came too with the luggage. Bill saw me off. Arrived 4.20 and Mother arrived with Nellie at the Semiramis at 6.00 [first hotel to be built on the Nile in 1907 and bathed in beauty from the outset]. Lovely to see her again and we talked and talked.

Monday 25 March
Busy shopping in Cairo buying groceries etc. with Mum. Left by 5.30 train to return to Ismailia. Bill met us at the platform. Lovely to have Mum to stay.

Friday 5 April
Arrived at Mena House with Bill and Abdul by car. Mother and Nellie by train. Very hot day. Had very comfortable rooms next door to each other.

They all stayed at Mena for 12 days

Wednesday 17 April
Left Mena at 10.00. Mother and Nellie by train and Bill and I by car. Lovely run but had 2 punctures arriving teatime. Very tired.

Wednesday 24 April

Mother left 1.30. Felt very, very sad. Saw her off on platform to Alexandria. Bill and I rested and then went for a drive in the evening.

Saturday 27 April

Bill back at work. Stayed in bed all morning feeling very seedy.

The diary resumes after over another month.

Monday 3 June

Bill had whole holiday but had to go to camp in the morning. I went with him. Rested in afternoon. Very worried about Nellie. [Nellie is pregnant]. Went to the Point for Bill's bathe.

Thursday 6 June and Friday 7 June

Busy packing up the flat and all my things. Terribly sad. Bill back for lunch at 1.00. Rested. Out to the Point for his bathe and said goodbye to the little car. [This was a Fiat Tipo 509 Tourer.] Left Ismailia at 8.30 in Pullman for Port Said. Stayed at Casino Palace.

Saturday 8 June

Hotel quite comfortable. Went to Cooks and learnt that *Osterley* not due to leave till Monday. Danced in evening for short time. Both feeling very unhappy.

Sunday 9 June

Breakfast in bed. Spent morning reading on the terrace and went for a walk. Bill bathed in afternoon. Dined in evening. Bill met some RAF friends. We were both miserable. Cannot bear this dreadful parting.

Monday 10 June

Felt absolutely miserable at leaving my beloved husband. [This separation is decided on because of Cesca's pregnancy in the intense heat during June, July and August.] Spent morning at Cooks and shopping. Went aboard *Osterley* at 12.00 and had lunch together on board. Secured First Class cabin for Nellie. Bill left me at 5.30....It was awful. I went straight to bed.

Tuesday 11 June

In bed all day. Feeling very seedy and miserable. Wire from Bill.

Wednesday 12 June

Wire from Bill. Have been married 4 months today. Sent him a signal. Got up and sat on deck. Awful people everywhere.

Thursday 13 June

In evening arrived at Naples and posted letters to Bill and also sent wire. Had letter from Mum who meets me at Toulon.

Saturday 15 June

Arrived Toulon 1.00 am. Woke at 4.00 and up by 6.30. Left boat at 9.00. Officer helped me. Met darling Mum on quay. Lunched at her hotel. Travelled to Paris in couchettes leaving 5.30.

Sunday 16 June

Arrived Paris 9.30 after dreadful night on hard couchettes. Very uncomfortable. Stayed with Lottie and dined with Lottie. Letter and wire from Bill.

Monday 17 June

Left Paris 10.00. Very comfortable journey. Calais 1.15 Dover 3.00. Train to Tonbridge arrived 6.00. Left Nellie. Dad and Hogben met us. Home 6.30. Letters from Bill.

Tuesday 18 June

Unpacking. Mrs Jewell came to see me and brought roses. She is so sweet. Harold and Ursula came to tea. Wire from Bill.

Wednesday 19 June

Wrote to Bill. Met Mr Jewell who took me for drive in his new Vauxhall 20/80 in evening.

Thursday 20 June

Mrs Jewell came to see me and brought me strawberries, sweet of her. Had long letter from Bill and wire to say he may get leave sooner. Wonderful! So happy all day.

Friday 21 June

Went to London by 10.00 train with Mother. Enjoyed it very much. Called on Blanche and had fitting at Miss Gray's and went to Fortnum & Masons. Lovely day. Home at 7.00. Very tired.

Monday 24 June

Met Peggy and went over in the car to lunch with her and spent afternoon at Hadlow Down. Motored home in evening. Busy packing for London.

Tuesday 25 June

Left home by 10.00 train with luggage. Mother came up later. Went up with Peg and Mabel with flowers to Albany and had hair washed. Lunch Hans Crescent with Mother.

Wednesday 26 June

Busy shopping. Aunt Edie came to lunch at Hans Crescent. Rested in afternoon and shopped after tea. In evening dined with the Reeds at Chelsea.

Thursday 27 June

Morning shopping and lunch Piccadilly. Hogben came up bringing letters from Bill who is ill and being invalided home. Very worried. Dressed for Court and had hair done. Felt miserable. Long wait in the Mall. Did not enjoy it much.

Friday 28 June

Busy packing. Had wire of congratulations from Bill who is pleased and delighted. [Due to her appearance at Court. It was customary to be presented at court following one's marriage.] Called Buckingham Palace and came home by train to Tunbridge Wells.

Saturday 29 June

Busy at home getting straight after London. Letter from Bill who is delayed.

Monday 1 July

Mrs Currie and Patricia came down for the afternoon and were very pleasant arriving at 3.00 and left at 6.00. Wire from Bill who leaves on Thursday. Interviewed maid.

Thursday 4 July

Pouring wet day. Went to London in the car, leaving here 9.00 am. Changed a lot of wedding presents with Mum and lunched together at Piccadilly Grill. Home at 6.00.

Friday 5 July

Had wire from Mrs Lunn about Bill and another in afternoon. Replied to both. In afternoon went to tea with Nellie and saw her baby. [Only 17 days after returning from Egypt! No wonder Cesca was worried about her]. Peggy came to dinner and we both went to the Cripps dance. Was rather bored.

Sunday 7 July

Listened to Thanksgiving Service in Abbey on wireless. [This was a special day of thanksgiving observed in churches across the British Empire to express gratitude for the recovery of King George V from his lengthy illness.] Heard that Dick Atcherley [Bill's best man] has won the King's Cup for Air Race. Went over to the Jewells in the afternoon.

Tuesday 9 July

Went to Folkestone to meet Bill who arrived at 1.00 looking very ill and done in, poor darling. Lunched at Burlington and home to tea. So very happy.

This diary is a complete blank for the rest of the year. The need for Cesca to pour out her feelings and thoughts to her diary seems to be removed by Bill's presence. There are however, a few photographs in an album that throw a little light on Bill and Cesca's whereabouts. There is one of Cesca in July sitting in the drawing room at Parham and another of Bill leaning against the Vauxhall Sunbeam on the moor between Brough and Scotch Corner in August. Bill was stationed at Northolt with No 24 Squadron (King's Flight) from September 1929 to October 1930 with the responsibility of flying the Prince of Wales.

Cesca Parham drawing room August 1929

The Sunbeam & Bill on the moor August 1929

Cesca unable to reverse! August 1929

Walton Place 1930

Enter the Standard June 1931

Harrods bus Grantchester to Tunbridge Wells
1.9.1932

1930

2 Walton Place.

This tiny diary, only 10x7 cm., is incomplete. Cesca is pregnant with her first child, due in February. She and Bill are living at 2 Walton Place, Chelsea SW3 most convenient for Harrods, Harvey Nichols and Bond Street. Bill was based at Northolt with No 24 Squadron, Kings Flight with special responsibility for HRH the Prince of Wales.

Wednesday 1 January
Went off early to Italian Exhibition at Burlington House and stayed an hour and a half. Shopping in Bond Street, E. Arden and Steinmann for some baby things. Came in and changed before going to Aunt Edie's for her New Year's lunch party. Sir John and Lady Ramsay, Col and Mrs Stewart amongst others there. Bill home early from seeing his Mother, Mrs Lunn. Bill gave me some lovely flowers.

Friday 3 January
Very busy morning shopping. Walked a long way to see Mr Richardson at 10 Wimpole Street at 12.30 He kept me waiting half an hour. He seemed very pleased with me and said I might do more or less as I liked. Changed books at Harrods. Maud cooked very good dinner.

Saturday 4 January
Met Mrs Carter at greengrocers and she asked us to dinner tonight. Bill at camp all day and playing rugger. Had a rest all afternoon and did not feel very well. Had bath and tea in my room. Went to dine at 7.30. Rather dull, just Mrs Cartwright and a friend of hers there. Very good dinner. Glad to get to bed.

Sunday 5 January
Stayed in bed till 11.00 and had good rest. Bill and I went for a walk in the Park and felt very cold. Went out in the car to take birthday present to Aunt Edie. Leave the car at Shrimptons, the

new garage which is cheaper than Landaus. Bill worked for his exam until bedtime.

Monday 6 January

Mother came up for the day bringing me some baby things, also some jasmine and some earth for the garden. Went out together after lunch for her inoculation and then to Debenhams where we saw the sweetest cot for the baby and I bought some clothes for the poor mite. Changed my book at Times Book Club and home at 4.15. Bill home at 5.00 and Mum left at 5.30. Col and Mrs Ian Smith came to dine as their cook had left suddenly.

Wednesday 8 January

Had my hair washed at Millie's. Very cold and came home with neuralgia so rested all the afternoon in bed and tea in my room. Bill came home very tired and wet and dirty from rugger. Went to dinner at Dandy's in the car. She was very nice and pleased to see us and gave us a good dinner.

Thursday 9 January

Bill off to work as usual at 8.10 and I busy shopping early. Dad came up and brought a pheasant. Mrs Lunn came to call while he was here so only stayed 10 minutes and left some lovely tulips. Went shopping with Dad and he ordered us 3 bottles each of whisky and port from Justerini and Brookes. Home to lunch. Went to dine at Gabriel and Jim's.

Saturday 11 January

After breakfast in the dining room, busy ordering. Mum and I went to the Italian Exhibition together and then went shopping with her. Mr and Mrs Ormond came to tea and said such nice things about the house. Went to Peter Pan at St James Theatre which I enjoyed very much. Had excellent seats. Home 11.30

Sunday 12 January

Most awful wet and cold day. Mum and I went to church at Wellington Barracks Chapel and enjoyed the service. In afternoon went to see new talkie with Harold Lloyd, "Welcome Danger" at the Carlton. Did not think it very good.

Monday 13 January

Mother sick in night and not feeling well. Made her rest till 11.00. Bill starts his week's leave today and works for his promotion exam on 4 Feb. After lunch Mother had another inoculation and left after tea for home. Dick Atcherley and Father William came for dinner.

Wednesday 15 January

Heard from Mum that a delivery of my things was coming this morning so stayed in and was busy arranging them. Bill went to Northolt for Rugger and returned at 4.30 very tired and filthy dirty. Both had dinner and to bed early.

Thursday 16 January

Bill busy moving all the books for me from top of the house downstairs so the nursery can be cleaned. Home to lunch after shopping in the car and visiting Bill's Mother. Peg arrived for tea and stayed the night. Loved having her. She is such a dear girl.

Friday 17 January

Peggy's birthday and she went off shopping. Bill and I went to Northolt in the car where he had a few things to do and I watched the flying. Home for lunch and Peggy left for Tunbridge Wells. Mum came in on her way back from Winchester.

Saturday 18 January

Bill working so I went shopping in Bond Street. Read quietly till teatime then decided we would get tickets for The Private Secretary. I rested while Bill went and collected the tickets and we had an early dinner. Then went to the Criterion at 8.30 but was disappointed. Walked home as far as Hyde Park Corner.

Monday 20 January

Bill hard at work. Mum arrived at 12.30 bringing me sheets , blankets, flowers and no end of nice things for the house. Barbara came to tea, I like her so much. Went to bed early in preparation for Bill and Mum's long day tomorrow. Do not feel very well.

Tuesday 21 January

Felt seedy so stayed in bed. Mum and Bill started off at 8.30 in the car but returned after a short while due to very thick fog. Horrible dark and gloomy day. Felt seedy and was sick in morning. Felt better after lunch so went with Bill and Mum to hear Sir Henry Wood's orchestra. Wonderful.

Wednesday 22 January

Bill and Mother out in car all day. Went out later shopping at Peter Jones.Mum and Bill home at teatime and Mum dashed off to catch her train. Auntie Fan called.

Thursday 23 January

Bill at work again. Blanche and Mary Wilson came to lunch. Poor Bill had his all alone upstairs. Went to Mrs Busse's and looked at cot and patterns. Dined alone together.

Friday 24 January

Bill and I out in car to Mortimer St and Surgical Supplies. Came home via Bond St and Jermyn St where we shopped. Bill rather cross and grumpy.Bill worked in afternoon and then rang up Ulster Terrace as Elizabeth has to have an operation for mastoid [ear op]. Bill joined me at dinner at Lowndes Sq. after the operation was successfully over.

Saturday 25 January

Bill went up to Ulster Terrace first thing and rang me to say Elizabeth doing well. The divan bed was delivered. Pat came to lunch, very worried about Elizabeth. Bill took her to Ulster Terrace in the car. She came back for dinner.

Monday 27 January

Mother came for the day and helped me interview 2 nurses in the morning. Both quite useless. Mother went off for her last inoculation.

Wednesday 29 January

Bill went up to Ulster Terrace in afternoon and found all well. Tried to get a young housemaid in Victoria Street. Early to bed very tired.

Thursday 30 January

After very bad night with indigestion stayed in bed feeling so rotten. In afternoon to Harrods and then tea with Mary Wilson. She has such a sweet baby and is so nice. Bill came and collected me.

Friday 31 January

Felt very seedy with heartburn and neuralgia. A young housemaid came to see me at lunchtime. Dad came looking very ill, I thought, so blue and cold.

Saturday 1 February

Bill had to go to camp and I did some ordering, then went to Harrods and changed my books. I got some fruit for Elizabeth which he took up to her in the afternoon. Neuralgia very bad so sat by the fire and read.

Monday 3 February

Had very bad night and thought I might need the doctor. Mother came up and brought me some medicine from Dad which I took and felt immediately better. Saw a nurse I liked this afternoon. Bill at camp for the night before his exam. Mrs Lang came to see me for tea and asked to bring Hugh, I said no {former boyfriend now engaged to be married]. She was very full of the wedding and losing Hugh etc.!

Wednesday 5 February

Busy shopping in morning with Mother. Bill back for tea after having had exams all day, poor darling and was rather depressed about them.

Saturday 8 February

Bill took me in the car to collect the cot and then we shopped in Bond Street. Bill went off to Waterloo to meet the Ian Smiths and go with them to the RAF v RN match at Twickenham.

Monday 10 February

Bill went off to camp until Wednesday as orderly officer. Miss him very much. Mum came up to stay. Mary Wilson joined us for tea. We talked of babies!

Tuesday 11 February

Mum and I went shopping at Harrods in the morning and got some lovely baby things. Mum is good to me. Peggy came to see me.

Wednesday 12 February

Woke up feeling seedy. Rang Bill to wish him Happy Wedding Anniversary. He wrote to me and sent me most lovely flowers. Lots of letters. Stayed in bed till lunchtime. Then went to Hugh Lang's wedding at St Margaret's Westminster with Bill and Mother. Enjoyed it very much and saw lots of friends. Came home while Mum and Bill went to the reception at the Rembrandt. Then Dad came up and dined here and we went to Bitter Sweet at His Majesty. Disappointing.

Thursday, Friday, Saturday and **Sunday** stayed in bed feeling rotten.

Monday 17 February

Had a very busy day washing out net curtains. Dad came up to see me and brought me some medicine.

Wednesday 10 February

Mum came up and stayed the night. Lovely to have her here and we talked and talked.

Friday 21 February

Nurse Manning arrived at lunchtime. Nellie turned out nursery and we got it already. Housemaid came in afternoon. Feel so relieved that everything is getting settled.

Saturday 22 February

Nurse and I went to Bond Street and I had my hair washed and waved. Nurse collected me. Bill went to rugger match with Ralph Millais.

Monday 24 February

Felt terribly depressed so rang Mother and got her to come up at once. She arrived at 12.00. We went to see a pram at 9 Ovington Gardens and then tea with Gabriel and saw her sweet baby just 4 weeks old. Bill away for the night.

Tuesday 25 February

Baby due today. No sign yet. Maud the cook gave notice this morning which rather upset me. Dad came up for lunch and we all went to matinee at St Martin's, Honours Easy. I enjoyed it most awfully. Bill got back early with some new gramophone records.

Wednesday 26 February

Stayed in bed for breakfast as Dr Richardson came at 9.30. Looked at my tummy and said baby should be induced on Friday so am to take pills. Went to see Aunt Edie with Mother. Bill home and rang up for theatre tickets for tonight. Pains started at 3.30 pm. Told nurse, Mum and Bill. Went to theatre and home by 11.30.

Thursday 27 February

Baby born at 3.10 am. Did not have a bad time and was very quick at the end. Mr Richardson sent for at 2.15 am and arrived just before 3.00. Dr Shelley came just after she was born, a small girl weighing 6½lbs. Bill, followed by Mum came in immediately afterwards. Felt so glad it was all over. Dad came up to see me and Mary, and flowers from everyone. So happy.

Friday 28 February

Tried to feed my little girl but she would not get on. She is perfectly sweet. Very fair and blue eyes and like Bill a bit. Lovely flowers, presents and congratulations all day. Announcement in *Times* and *Courier*. Bill on leave. Very busy writing letters and answering telephone. Nurse so nice and kind and everyone so good to me. Dr Shelley came to see me.

Saturday 1 March

Dad came up for the day. Dr Richardson came to see me in the morning. Mary Wilson came to see me in the evening. Feeling really very well.

Sunday 2 March

Mother returned to T.W. for the day. Mrs Lunn and George came to see the baby. Bill showed them the house. Nurse awfully kind and so nice to me. Slept all the afternoon. Simply adore my little girl and still can't believe it's true and all over and she is really here.

Monday 3 March

More flowers, letters and telephone messages. Dr Shelley came to see me. Aunt Edie and Blanche came to see the baby. Each day seems to fly by and I am busy feeding Mary, writing or being washed and tidied or eating or sleeping. It's such a lovely life. Peg's wedding to Vernon today at Rusthall, Dad attending. Bill and I sent a wire.

Tuesday 4 March

Mother terribly busy arranging flowers that come continually.

Monday 10 March

Miss Davy the masseuse came in the morning. Then Ursula and Mary Wilson came to tea bringing violets and a toy dog. Bill home for tea.

Wednesday 12 March

Mum terribly busy for me today. So many came to tea to see the baby including Mrs Ian Smith who brought me some sweet peas. Mrs Currie came and brought me some flowers. Felt rather tired when they had all gone.

Friday 14 March

Mother went back to Parham for the day. Miss Davy came in the morning and gave me some new exercises to do. Bill home at 5.00.

Saturday 15 March

Bill went off to the International with Dad who came to see me first. Mum went to theatre then we had tea together. Bill back for dinner before returning to camp, as orderly officer for the weekend.

Sunday 16 March

Mother went to church at Holy Trinity Brompton and enjoyed the service. Mum and I left in charge of Mary as nurse went out. Mary cried a lot. I miss Bill very much.

Monday 17 March

Dr Richardson came to see me. I told him I was going away on Monday.

Tuesday 18 March

Bill's birthday, 24 years today. I gave him 2 pairs of silk socks and am giving him a suit at Brinkmans. This afternoon I got up for the first time, sat in the armchair in my room and had tea. Such fun being up again.

Wednesday 19 March

I did my exercises and then slept after lunch. Then got up and dressed for tea. Felt a bit shaky but better than yesterday.

Thursday 20 March

First day down. Mother took me in the big Daimler to Northolt where we saw Bill. Stayed only a short time then motored back to London for lunch. Rested in afternoon and down to tea. Bill and Mum came up and talked to me in evening. Had the sweep and spring-clean in the drawing room.

Friday 21 March

Mum returned today to prepare for our visit to Parham on Monday. Bill at the camp until teatime. I went to Millie's to have my hair washed and then for fittings for my coats and skirts and came home by taxi for lunch.

Saturday 22 March

Bill took me out in the car and we went to Bond Street to Brinkmans Tailor. Then he went on to Ulster Terrace and I to hat shop in Sloane Street. After my rest I went to tea with Mary Wilson. Bill had Turkish Bath.

Monday 24 March

Mr Richardson came and examined me for the last time. Very busy shutting up the house and packing. Bill's first day of leave. Left Walton Place with Mum, Mary and nurse in the car at 2.30. Bill left to see the servants off and to come on in the Morris. Arrived Parham. Felt very tired and went to bed after tea and had dinner in bed.

Tuesday 25 March

In bed till 10.00. Went out with Bill in the town. Mary in the pram in the garden enjoying the sun. Rested in afternoon and later went out with Bill.

Wednesday 26 March

Bill and I went over in the car to Best Beech Hill to the Meet there. Lovely morning. Met Peg and Vernon and saw all the Eridge people. Home for lunch and my rest. Am enjoying the rest down here enormously and feel better.

Thursday 27 March

Decided to have Mary christened on Sunday at King Charles the Martyr church. Rang Ursula and asked her to be godmother and Harold to christen her. Went to Shirley and got Peg to come on Sunday. Played bridge in evening.

Friday 28 March

Very busy making arrangements for the christening on Sunday. Went to interview a maid and engaged one to come in on Monday.

Saturday 29 March

Heard from Mrs Lunn that they cannot come to Mary's christening. Bill rang Dandy and asked her and Pat to motor down. Went to the Meet at Old Buckhurst with Bill. Talked to Peggy and Vernon and the Jewells etc. Rested in afternoon. Heard from Blanche and Ursula, godmothers both coming tomorrow.

Sunday 30 March

Mary's Christening.

Lovely day and Bill and I went out for a run in the car before lunch. Ralph Millais arrived by train and Ursula and Harold by car. No sign of Dick Atcherley till we met him at the church at 3.00pm for the christening. Godmothers, Blanche Ferguson, Peggy Williams, Ursula Taylor. Ralph Millais, and Dick Atcherley her Godfathers. Harold baptised her, Mary Francesca. Nurse, Mother, Dad, Hogben and Mrs Hogben, Vernon Williams were there and all came back for tea.

Monday 31 March

Bill and Mum went off to London early, Bill by car with the luggage and Mother by train to get the house ready for me. Nurse, Mary and I went up to London by 2.45 train in reserved First class carriage to ourselves. Bill met me at Charing Cross with big Rolls and we got back at teatime. Dad rang up after Mother had left to say that Mrs Dwyer was not coming. So now no cook. Rushed round to Mrs Webb and succeeded in getting her to come tomorrow.

Tuesday 1 April

Bill off to work again. Lunatic parlourmaid arrived late last night. Got along somehow with her, Ivy and Mrs Webb.

Wednesday 2 April

Mrs Lugg new temporary cook arrived at 9.30 so now all goes well again. Mrs Webb here, also window cleaner. Continue to feed baby and nurse is a great help and so good to me.

Thursday 4 April

Went to tea with Mary Wilson, Peggy there too and Mrs Richards. Home to Bill at 5.30. Pat came to tea with him to discuss their brother Peter's future. Peter came to dinner at 7.00.

Sunday 6 April

John Wilson rang to say Mary had safely had another son this morning. Bill and I went for a walk in the Park.

Monday 7 April

Bought some flowers for Mary and took them round to her in the evening. She is going on well. I spend all my time feeding Mary and looking after her.

Thursday 10 April

Nurse Nice arrived early this morning to get into routine before Nurse Manning leaves. Nurse left during the afternoon, felt rather miserable but like new nannie very much. Had a tea party, Mrs Pontifex, Aunt Ruth and Mrs Smith came. Had Barbara Ware and Peter to dinner, both left early. Felt very tired.

Saturday 12 April

Bill on leave so went to Bond Street and shopped. Bought new satin blouse. Peter came to tea with Bill who played squash with him at RAF Club. Have been married 14 months today.

Sunday 13 April

Bill rang up his Mother and asked her over this afternoon. I went to tea with Mrs Rawlinson and found Mr and Mrs Lunn here to see Mary when I got back.

Monday 14 April

Asked Elizabeth to dine and then rang Pat. She rang back later and accepted. Then Elizabeth asked if Gordon Hubback might come too. So we were 5. Had soup, sole, fillets of beef with tomatoes and spinach, charlotte russe and savoury. It meant a lot of work. Mrs Currie came to tea and brought Lena. Evening party went off well and I enjoyed it. They all came up to see Mary.

Tuesday 15 April

Bill left for two nights, orderly officer tonight and tomorrow at Lossiemouth. Mum came to lunch. I went for fitting at Miss Gray's. Had quiet afternoon after the rush of yesterday.

Wednesday 16 April

Bill leaves with Heslop and the PM Ramsay MacDonald today from Hendon for Lossiemouth. Lunched with Dad at Gunter's, saw Clement Davies there, Bill's guardian. Then went to tea with Mary Wilson. Saw her baby John and gave him a little coat.

Friday 18 April: Good Friday

Bill and I went in the car to church at Wellington Barracks.

Saturday 19 April

Letter from Dad enclosing a cheque for £5 as Easter present. Decided to go to the Berkeley tonight. Had a message from Don saying Bill might have to go up to Lossiemouth to fetch aeroplane. However a false alarm, so we went to the Berkeley and thoroughly enjoyed ourselves.

Sunday 20 April: Easter Day

Had breakfast in bed with Bill. Then after Mary's 10.00 feed went to Holy Communion at Holy Trinity Brompton. A wet miserable day.

Monday 21 April

Bill went to Northolt to see Don and get maps ready for tomorrow's trip to France. Mary flourishing and getting fatter every day.

Tuesday 22 April

Bill went to York House to see General Trotter to fetch letter from the Queen for the Prince of Wales. Then to Air Ministry. Bill brought Wing Commander Maltby to lunch, a very nice man. Bill and he left at 1.30. Bill flies to Paris this afternoon en route to Marseilles to fetch the Prince of Wales home with Don. Mum came to stay in the afternoon.

Wednesday 23 April

Bill rang up from Paris. Mother and I went to Harrods and bought newspapers with news of the Prince's return journey. Bill's name in the papers. Had early lunch and fed Mary before going with Mother to matinee at the Globe, a Naval play well acted. Wire from Bill in evening from Lyon.

Thursday 24 April

Had letter from Bill from Paris. Mum and I busy shopping. Chose a dress for myself. After feeding Mary, went to Blanche's wedding at St Margaret's. She looked lovely and the bridesmaids charming.

Friday 25 April

News in all the papers of the Prince of Wales flight home today. Felt very thrilled about it. Met Mum and Dad at Hotel Splendid for lunch at 1.00. Came back home to feed Mary. Dad thought her splendid. Bill got in at 6.15, very tired. Lovely to have him home, he has had a wonderful trip.

Saturday 26 April

Bill on leave today so had breakfast in bed. Then Bill took me to a fitting at Bradleys. Pat came to tea and stayed to dinner. Saw Graf

Zeppelin fly over. [German built and operated passenger carrying rigid airship.] Then after dinner changed into wedding dress and went to Berkeley to meet Don and Heslop. Had an amusing evening celebrating the trip and enjoyed it and liked Bill's CO.

Sunday 27 April

Felt rather tired so stayed in bed till 11.00. After lunch Bill and I took the car down to Twickenham. Took car back to Shrimptons and then home to feed Mary.

Tuesday 29 April

Mum came up for the day and planted some antirrhinums for me.

Thursday 1 May

Mrs Levy invited me to a concert this afternoon in Park Lane. Accepted and invited Mum to come and join me which she did. So we went together to Sir Philip Sassoon's house. Paul Robeson and Marjorie Clark.

Friday 2 May

Mary Wilson sent me tickets for Private View of Royal Academy to which I went to this afternoon. Busy shopping for dinner party on Monday. Bill home late.

Saturday 3 May

Spent morning shopping with Bill. In afternoon Bill played squash then brought Pilot Officer Bishop back for bath and dinner. Pat came to dine too and stayed very late. Felt very tired out.

Monday 5 May

Very busy preparing for dinner party. Mum and Dad came and took me to lunch at Rembrandts. In afternoon went to Selfridges for servant's dresses, caps and aprons. Came home by bus. Mary and John Wilson, and Dorothy Harvey came to dinner.

The rest of the week goes by with the usual shopping, feeding Mary, and Bill playing squash. On Sunday Cesca writes that 'she visited a friend, saw her baby who is very fat and big and not pretty at all'.

Tuesday 13 May

Dad came up to lunch and we went to the Academy together. Then met Dorothy Harvey for tea at Park Lane. Came home to find Bill back. Had dinner party, Mr and Mrs Stemp and Harold and Ursula. They stayed terribly late and I was worn out but all went very well.

Friday 16 May

Dad came to tea at 4.30. Very worried about poor Mum who is very seedy still. She sent me some lovely flowers from Parham. Mr and Mrs Cartwright came to dinner and we went on afterwards to the Skinners Ball which I enjoyed very much. Very well done but our party was dull.

Sunday 18 May

Bill on duty so missed him terribly when I woke up. Mum came up for the day so I met her at Charing Cross at 11.00. Such fun having her here all day. She left at 8.30.

Wednesday 21 May

Mum came up for the day and we had lunch here. Bill in Cardiff with the Prince of Wales. In afternoon went with Mum to Finnigans to choose a wedding present for Elizabeth and then home to tea. Bill home very late.

Thursday 22 May

Went with Mrs Carter to the Chelsea Flower Show. Wonderful displays, especially of carnations, tulips, sweet peas and vegetables. But it was very wet and cold. Had lunch at Searcy's and came home to rest. Jim and Gabriel came to dinner. Afterwards we played bridge, then went on to the Sandeman's dance after Mary's feed. Terribly crowded so we left early.

Saturday 24 May

Went shopping in Bond Street with Bill in the morning. In the evening Bill played squash and then we went down to dine with Harold and Ursula at Cheam School which we enjoyed very much.

The days pass by filled with visitors for tea and dinners and balls and Cesca recovering from being sick and too little sleep.

Friday 30 May
Felt much better but still shaky having had nothing to eat. Mary had a bottle of Cow & Gate again. I went to the Sports at Northolt with Bill. It poured with rain and was a dreadful show. I was brought home by Squadron Leader Huskisson as Bill ran out of petrol and I had to get back to feed Mary.

Saturday 31 May
Very busy packing up go to Tunbridge Wells. Nannie and I left London with Ivy and Dad who came up to fetch me at 2.30. I was met by Mum, Hogben and Bogey at 4.00. Bill arrived later.

Tuesday 3 June
Bill returned after lunch as it is the King's Birthday. Don rang to say HRH wished us to go to his Birthday at the Derby tomorrow, so have been busy making preparations. An awful bore.

Wednesday 4 June
Bill went up to London to get his clothes from Walton Place and his tickets from the club. I went up by 10.14 arriving at Waterloo at 11.30 and we then both went to Epsom by train arriving at 12.00. Had excellent box with Sir Phillip Sassoon, Admiral Sir Lionel Halsey and a golfer from the American team. HRH was in next box. Home by 6.00 very tired.

Thursday 5 June
Went together to London by train then we lunched at Mayfair. Saw Hubback and his best man there. Bill took me to the club where I waited till 2.00 for Dick Atcherley but as he did not turn up I went alone to Elizabeth's wedding at St Mark's, North Audley Street. I wore my new black which looked nice. Elizabeth looked quite pretty. Bill and I came home together.

Friday and Saturday filled with tea parties and dinner parties at Parham. Bill arrives back from Cardiff where he had escorted the Prince of Wales. Cesca is unwell on Tuesday, very sick and had diarrhoea and unable to sleep. Bill in Scotland on Wednesday to fetch home HRH from Edinburgh on Thursday.

Thursday 12 June
Had a very bad night and felt so seedy. Busy packing to return to London. Mum and Ivy went off at 10.15 with part of the luggage and a lot of flowers. However by the time nurse and I got to London Ivy had cleared up the house and everything going well. Bill home at 9.00 from Edinburgh.

Monday 16 June
Darling Mum off to Mont Dore [a thermal resort] today for her cure which I pray will do her good. Mary flourishing and if only I was not feeding her I would go with Mum. Aunt Edie came for tea and was very dull poor dear!

The rest of the week is filled with yet more lunches and dinners and dress fittings.

Saturday 21 June
Bill had to go to Wing Commander Smythie's funeral. In the afternoon Bill played squash, then came home, changed and together we went down to Harold and Ursula at Cheam where we watched the cricket match. Eton Rambers v Harold's X1 and stayed to dinner. Bill bathed and we came home having very much enjoyed our day.

Sunday 22 June
In the afternoon we went down to Northolt to see the aeroplanes and got into Bill's. Then had a picnic tea at Beaconsfield and then home for dinner at 7.30.

The diary lapses until Monday 15 July.

Tuesday 15 July
Dad's Birthday. Rang him up. Had fearful upset with housemaid Joan Donovan who I cleared out of the house eventually. Felt quite

ill afterwards and retired to bed for the rest of the day. Bill was supposed to dine in the Mess but came home.

Thursday 17 July

Lunched with Mum and Dad at the Piccadilly at 1.30 and then went to see The Swan at the St James which we much enjoyed. Came home and Bill got in at 8.15 having flown Lord de la Warr [Secretary to the Ministry of Agriculture and Fisheries] to Hull Agricultural Show.

Saturday 19 July

Bill on leave. Went together to Whitehall and shopped. Bill played squash all afternoon. Mrs Greaves and Norah came to tea and were excessively dull.

Sunday 20 July

Lovely morning. Bill and I motored down to Sittingbourne House, Dorking to lunch with the Ainslies. Eustace, Audrey and Pat [ex fiancee] were there. It poured with rain so we played bridge until teatime. Played more bridge after dinner and motored home through pouring rain.

Tuesday 22 July

In evening went to a dinner party and dance with the Blunts at the Savoy. Excellent dinner and danced a good deal. Came home by 1.30 as Bill rather tired. A very enjoyable evening.

Wednesday 23 July

Mother arrived at 11.30. Bill came home to lunch and afterwards came shopping with us at Aspreys. Came home to tea and as it was so bitterly cold had a fire.

Thursday 24 July

Bill and I dined with Mr and Mrs Ionides before going to the Woolwich Tattoo which we enjoyed. Prince Henry was there.

Monday 28 July

Had a very busy day getting straight after the weekend. Mary five months old today and is too sweet for words. Bill is off to Antwerp with the Prince of Wales tomorrow.

Tuesday 29 July

Bill left for Antwerp and I felt rather sad. Sent him two letters, one to Northolt and one to Brussels. Peter called to see me and told me all about his love affairs. Had a wire from Bill saying he had safely arrived at Brussels.

Wednesday 30 July

Met Mum and Dad for lunch at Gunter's after they had seen a nose and throat specialist. He said there was nothing wrong with Mother so she had meat for lunch for the first time since she has dieted and loved it. We went to see Cynara at the Playhouse with Gladys Cooper and Celia Johnson. It was excellent. Came home to a desolate house.

Thursday 31 July

A letter from Bill. He is due home late tonight. Went to Millie's to have my hair washed. Mrs Lang and Margaret came to tea to see Mary. Peter came to dine and we went together to Joan Belcher's dance at her studio. Rather arty party, all artists and odd people there. Peter loved it and when Bill rang up I left him enjoying it and came home to Bill who had just returned from Northolt having landed in the dark.

Friday 1 August

Peter came to lunch with us to see Bill who had the day off. In the afternoon we went to Hornchurch to see what sort of place it was. Never saw such a ghastly before in all my life. Could have cried. Had rather a depressing picnic tea there and were thankful to get home again.

Peter is constantly dropping in on Cesca and Bill much to their annoyance. Bill flies up to Cranwell for a week 9 August and Cesca is busy packing up to go down 12 August to Brockenhurst in Hampshire on the edge of the New Forest. The pram is packed up and a bus arrives to take Cesca, Nannie and Mary to Waterloo where they meet Dad and Mum and travel down by First Class carriage to Brockenhurst. Very comfortable rooms, a suite with sitting rooms awaits them. Cesca's 26 birthday, Tuesday 26 August, and she is given a cheque for £100 from Mum and £20 from Dad. Bill gives her scent and lilies.

Mary suffers from an upset tummy for a week and Bill painful toothache which results in a trip to the dentist on a Sunday afternoon. Dad goes with him to give him gas and Mum to hold Cesca's hand. The tooth is successfully removed though a return visit 2 days later is required to staunch the bleeding!
By 1 September having tried various potions in vain, Cesca resigns herself to her fate. Her second child is on the way! Bill is posted to Duxford No 19 Squadron and flies up there via Northolt Thursday 11 September. A letter arrives for Bill saying there is £247 unclaimed in South Africa but Bill must establish a claim. The diary lapses for 2 months.

Tuesday 11 November: Armistice Day

Went out with Nannie and Mary in morning and listened to silence at Albert Gate. Bill on leave as it is Armistice Day and came to lunch. Twelve guineas per week are offered by D.B. Gray for Walton Place.

Thursday 13 November

After ordering food and lunching at Searcy's went to D.B. Gray and said I would take thirteen and a half guineas for the house.

The diary lapses for the rest of 1930.

Dr Bisshopp & Mary 1931

Cesca and Mary

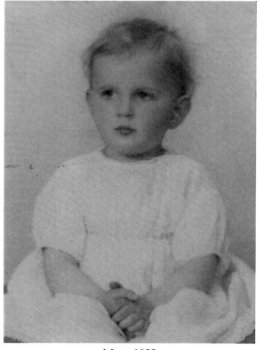

Mary 1932

Cesca Mary and Merlin, vaccinated and cross 1931

Merlin and Mary

1931
2 Walton Place

A baby brother for Mary and a constant flow of cooks and nannies keep Cesca busy when she is not shopping with Bill in Bond Street. A six week summer break in a comfortable house at Kingswear, Devon is much enjoyed by all the family. Both Merlin and Cesca have a narrow escape from injury after a fall in November. Bill replaces the Morris with a new Standard Avon Special and motors many miles back and forth from Duxford.

Thursday 1 January

Very cold day. Bill took me in the car to Registry Office and then to the Air Ministry after some shopping. Went together to Aunt Edie's New Year's Lunch for ten including Sir John and Lady Ramsay. Home for tea and rested till dinnertime.

Friday 2 January

Bill left for Duxford at 5.30 am, a lovely cold morning and no fog. Heard from Harold that they had had a smash in the car and Ursula very much shaken. Engaged a parlour maid before leaving by train for Tunbridge Wells. Met by Dad and Hogben and arrived to find Mum with the 'little miss'. Everyone very cheerful and well.

Cesca spent Saturday and Sunday sewing and making things for Mary and the baby. Bill rang and wanted her to return to Walton Place Sunday evening so she caught the 6 o'clock to Charing Cross. Bill was there but they missed each other and Cesca's taxi skidded avoiding a woman and she was flung from side to side hitting her head and very shaken on arriving home.

Tuesday 6 January

Letter from Bill and one from Mother to say Mary is coming back this morning. Met the train but had to wait 35 minutes owing to thick fog in the country. Mary looking very well and nurse very pleasant and affable on her return. Called on Mrs Busse re nursery and saw Hugh Lang driving yellow three litre Sunbeam. Nurse

Manning came to tea and we talked about her coming in April when the new baby arrives. New parlour maid came in evening.

A constant stream of cooks come and go and Mary has a visit from the doctor as is unwell with a sore throat. Cesca and her Mother take the train down to Cheam and lunch with Harold and Ursula who is very seedy and thin after her car crash.

Saturday 17 January
Had most upsetting morning as nurse gave in her notice on a piece of paper. I did feel altogether rather upset especially as Mary not well. Bill and I got seats for the theatre as we feel must be cheered up. Dined at 7.00 and went to see Marry the Girl at the Aldwych which was quite amusing.

Sunday 18 January
Awful day! Mary refusing all food since yesterday. Rang up Doctor Morcom and he came to see her. Said she was teething. Mother came up by 11.00 train and Bill met her. Felt very upset and wept as Mary's incessant crying is so awful. Dad came up by 1.40 and stayed to tea. Then nurse was very rude to us all especially Mother and I threatened to clear her out of the house. Altogether a terrible day and felt worn out! Bill very sweet to me.

Monday 19 January
Mary better but still crying. Gave her all meals myself as after yesterday feel I cannot trust nurse although I do not think she would ever neglect or be unkind to Mary. Hope to get a new nannie as soon as possible, as everything is very unpleasant. Went out to dinner but home in time to give Mary her last feed. Have gone back to bottles till she is quite well. Wrote to four nurses.

Tuesday 20 January
Mary, thank heavens is quite herself again. Had breakfast in bed as have such horrid pains in my thighs the same as last time.

The search for another nannie continues until the following Monday when nurse Hubbard is engaged to come on Saturday 31 January. Meanwhile Mary has put on 13 oz. so regaining the weight she lost.

Saturday 31 January

Bill and I went out shopping in the morning, then he told his Mother about me having another baby! Apparently Peter had guessed and told her. [By now Cesca was 6 months pregnant]. Then the afternoon I had so much dreaded went off quite well, much better than I expected. Nurse Nice departed sometime after lunch, we do not know when as she never said goodbye to any of us! Nurse Hubbard arrived and there were very few tears at bedtime.

Sunday 1 February

Bill and I spent day together. I spent most of it rushing up and down stairs to see how nurse was dealing with Mary. I gave her most of her meals and by the end of the day felt quite worn out.

Monday 2 February

Bill went off very early and I spent the day settling the new nurse into my routine. Feel she is very incompetent after Nurse Nice but I am much more sure of myself and able to cope now. Rang up Mum to say goodbye as she leaves for Mentone with Ursula tomorrow. I wished I was going with her but I should have hated the crossing.

Wednesday 4 February

Feeling much happier about Mary. Saw Dr Richardson and he was very pleased with me and said I need not see him again till mid-March.

Saturday 7 February

Heard from Mum and Ursula both sounding depressed after their journey. Spent a lot of time with Mary who grows sweeter and more attractive every day.

Wednesday 11 February

Mum and Ursula sent me lovely flowers from Mentone for my Wedding Anniversary tomorrow. Dad and Mum have each given us a cheque for £50.

Very happy and Bill and I had dinner together.

Thursday 12 February

Bill left for work at 6.00 so we are not to be together for our second Wedding Anniversary, alas! Bill sent me an exact replica of my wedding bouquet of lilies of the valley and carnations. Mrs Lunn and Pat also sent flowers.

Saturday 14 February

We both went to see Mr Hughes about Mary's settlement and the Power of Attorney. Bill home after rugger match with Stuart Swaythling [Montagu].

Sunday 15 February

Bill had to return to Duxford for Church Parade which was annoying. Dandy and Pat arrived for lunch and stayed till 3.00. Felt it was a fiasco as Dandy scarcely ate anything then Mary who came down after lunch yelled all the time and obviously loathed Dandy. Then Dandy said Mary and all small babies were like monkeys! After they left I felt seedy and had a slight show. This worried me. Bill came down and stayed the night.

Monday 16 February

Rang up Dad and told him. He arrived suddenly at 3.00 and insisted on my going to bed and ringing up Dr Richardson. He was away on a case. Dad told nurse I must be most careful and she must not go out. Wrote to Bill and told him everything, but am not saying a word to Mum.

Cesca is careful for the next few days staying in bed until lunchtime on Wednesday. Bill arrives for lunch looking ill. He went off to see the Attorney and returns looking very ill. He has a temperature of 103 and Cesca puts him to bed. Flu is diagnosed. Visits from Dad and Doctor Morcon and a wire sent to Mother on Thursday. Bill still ill on Friday and Dad and Dr Morcon advise that a nurse should be engaged as Cesca is doing too much. Nurse arrives at midday and sponges Bill reducing his temperature. A new pair of pyjamas are purchased at Harrods and nurse returns in the evening.

Saturday 21 February
Dad came up again like the dear he is and Dr Morcon also came. Bill seems a little better but nurse told Squadron Leader Keary when he rang that Bill would not be fit for work for some days. Tried to rest in the drawing room with a rug over me but felt seedy and cold and shivery. Letter from Mum, who has received my wire, but is not returning home. Nurse came again.

The next day Cesca has a temperature of 100 and although Bill is better, panic sets in and a wire is sent to Mother requesting her return. Mary too has a temperature of 100 and is coughing. To Cesca's and Dad's great relief Mum arrives at Victoria station the following evening. The nurse is still coming morning and evening.

Friday 27 February
Mary's 1st Birthday.
Bill improving but is easily tired. Mum came round at 9.30 and we went out to get Dad's present for Mary, a lovely quilted silk dressing gown from Debenhams. Mary better and receiving lots of presents. Boxes of bricks were given by Mrs Lunn, Patricia, and Mary Wilson! Also silk coats and pink shoes, a yellow duck, from Nannie and a sweet dress from Mum embroidered with lambs from Mentone. Mum and Dad took us to lunch at Mayfair before returning to Tunbridge Wells.

Sunday and Monday bitterly cold with snow and Bill busy moving snow from the doorstep and kitchen roof. The next week is filled with visits to the theatre and searching for a house for the summer. Bill's birthday on Wednesday 18 March. Presents of cheques from his Mother and Cesca's, cigarettes from Dad and pyjamas from Cesca. Peter gave him a pair of silk socks. A visit to Dr Richardson on Monday 30 March upsets Cesca as he tells her she will not have an easy time owing to the position of the baby. Mary now has six teeth.

Monday 6 April: Easter Monday

Letter from Dad enclosing cheque for £5 for Easter. Heard from Nurse Manning that she is coming on Tuesday instead of Wednesday so Mary will have to go down to Tunbridge Wells tomorrow with nurse. Arranged for station bus from Charing Cross to take her and nurse catching the 2.18.

Bill and I went to see St Joan at the Haymarket after dinner and enjoyed it most awfully.

Tuesday 7 April

Bill left at 6.00. Very busy morning shopping and packing up dear little Mary. Saw her and nurse off and felt very unhappy and miss her terribly. Nurse Manning arrived from Cheshire. Feel so relieved nurse is here.

The clocks go forward at midnight on Saturday 18 April and Cesca becomes increasingly fed up and bored that there is still no sign of the baby, known as the Bonbon. No names have been mentioned.

Friday 24 April

Woke up at 2.15 am with pain and lay awake for more which came and so woke Bill and then went up to nurse who got up. Wandered about till 4.00 then had very hot bath and an enema. Nurse rang up Mr Richardson at 6.00 and Bill tried to telephone family but no reply. Pains worse after 6.00 and Mr Richardson arrived at 8.00 having been called again at 7.00.

SON BORN AT 8.40.

Bill came in afterwards and we were both so happy. Baby lovely and weighs 7 lbs 2 oz. Mum arrived at 10.00. Bill and Mum went out and bought baskets of flowers for me. Flowers poured in all day and Dr Morcon and Mr Richardson came to see me in the evening.

Saturday 25 April

Feel awfully well and happy and the little Bon is a darling. Dad and Mum both gave me rather a sermon in the evening so that I felt very miserable.

[This perhaps was about the consequences and risks of not avoiding being pregnant again so quickly].

The following week Cesca is uncomfortable as her breasts fill up with milk and then cannot sleep for pains in her tummy, a headache and a temperature. Mr Richardson prescribes pills from John Bell and Croyden. Mother and nurse are worried about her. By Friday 1 May Cesca is better and Mother returns to Tunbridge Wells. The baby has only lost an ounce and Dr Richardson came and arranged for him to be circumcised the following Tuesday. Cesca writes to Mrs Lunn suggesting she should give a pram for the two babies.
Mrs Lunn comes to inspect the new baby and approves of him as she thought him like her babies and Bill. The new double pram duly arrives from Milsoms and a little chair for Mary.
Having heard from Nurse Hubbard, who is looking after Mary, saying she is handing in her notice on return, Cesca is very worried and is occupied interviewing nurses for the next ten days and feeding the Bon. Still no names suggested for him yet. The Christening is fixed for Wednesday 27 May.

Tuesday 19 May
Interviewing Nannies again. Engaged Nurse Castle who was with Japanese people in Walton Street. Hope she will be satisfactory. Bill's legacy arrived which I was delighted about and sent it off to him express and registered. Dad came up and very sweetly gave me a cheque for £50 to help us with expenses. He saw the baby and checked his navel which is not yet healed. Sent invitations for the Christening, asked over 50 people. Baby putting on weight, 9 oz this week!

Sunday 24 May
Bill and I walked in the Park after breakfast and then went to St Saviours and after the morning service arranged about the Christening.

Tuesday 26 May
Nurse Castle arrived at 9.30 and Nurse Searle left at 11.00. Went out shopping with Gabriel and did a lot of ordering for the Christening tomorrow. Did not feel well so had to rest in afternoon. Dear Mum came up by 4.00 train and brought me all the

flowers, arranged them all, had tea and talked over the party for tomorrow. New Nannie seems nice and efficient.

Wednesday 27 May

Terribly hot day. Breakfast in bed. House looking so nice. Went in taxi to Miss Gold's and got my chiffon dress and then put notice in *Times* about today's Christening. {This cutting still survives]. Lunched at Rembrandt and then Merlin William was christened at St Saviour's Walton Street at 3.30 by Rev Prebendary Osborne. The godparents were Flt. Lieut. J.H. Hutchinson, Mr C.W. Reed [Jim], Dr W.G. Roger (by proxy) and Lady Wilson. Mrs Lunn, Mrs Currie, Aunt Edie, Auntie Cassie, Patricia, John Wilson, Mrs Richards all came to tea afterwards at Walton Place. Bill left for Wittering at 9.00pm.

Thursday and Friday are both filled with packing up the house, sending off laundry, and paying servants and accounts in readiness for the departure to Tunbridge Wells on Saturday. Merlin's photograph was taken on Friday afternoon. And Mr Richardson paid his last visit seeing Cesca and checking Merlin's navel. Cesca feels worn out by the time she, Nannie and Merlin get on the train arriving at Tunbridge Wells at 4.20 pm. 'Dad met us. I tore up to see my little girl who I have missed so much all this time away from her and hardly recognised her as she has grown so much and is so sweet. Mum very good to me'.

Sunday 31 May

Had splendid night and feel very well. Mary woke early and she and the baby woke each other alternately which is tiresome. Spent morning in bed and then finished unpacking and settling in. Wrote to Bill. Lovely being with both my babies and Mum and Dad. Mary is very attractive.

Monday 1 June

Very busy with laundry, babies and getting nurse into routine. Mary had a fearful upset this afternoon, about nothing really, but is jealous of Merlin.

'Boy' as she calls him! Rested in afternoon. Miss Bill very much and wrote to him.

Wednesday 3 June

Whole holiday for Bill as it is the King's Birthday so he arrived at lunchtime having motored from Duxford to London and then train here. Spent afternoon together in my room. Had long talk and felt very happy having not seen each other for a week. After dinner saw him off at the station where he will stay the night in London with Jim and Gabriel.

Thursday 4 June

Fetched the baby early as Mary and he were both yelling and poor Mum had a bad night. A present came for Merlin from Pat, a table napkin ring with his initials.

Friday 5 June

A parcel arrived from Dandy with two blue blankets for Merlin. Bill arrived very tired after a long drive from Duxford via London. Mary is in our room again.

Mary is teething and won't sleep. Everyone is exhausted. Bill returns to Duxford and Dad attends a Guy's Hospital Dinner in London. The following day Dad returns very cross and gouty. He went off to the cricket at Tonbridge by himself in the pouring rain. Mother away looking at houses. Merlin is vaccinated on Wednesday 10 June and Cesca can't bear it so took Mary out in the pram.

Friday 12 June

Up to London by 2.45. Had hair washed at Andre Hugo's 8/- Very dear. Met Bill at 6.30 and dined at Park Lane Hotel then collected fur coat from Walton Place before motoring home at 9.30. Very tired.

Sunday 14 June

Had another bad night with the baby and felt wretched. I had to go to church and felt so tired and ill. Came home and felt hysterical and was cross with Bill and Mother. Had a sleep in afternoon and felt better. Bill left for London at 6.00 where he leaves the dear little Morris at Shrimptons and on Wednesday has delivered the new Standard Avon we have ordered. Merlin's arm more swollen.

Friday 19 June

Merlin's arm much better and Mary very well. Both weighed today. Mary weighs 22lbs 8oz and Merlin 10lbs 6oz at 8 weeks.

Saturday 20 June

Bill arrived about 6.00 in the new motor which is divine. Went off out with him in it at once and motored round Penshurst. I think it is a dream and goes beautifully. It is a Standard Avon Special 16hp and cost £350.

Monday 22 June

Went up to London by 11.00 train and went to Walton Place but found I had forgotten keys so had my fitting with Miss Gold down in the area! Very annoying. Lunched with Mrs Durham and then bought gloves, corsets etc. from Harvey Nicholls. Home on 4.15 very hot and tired.

Tuesday 23 June

Lovely day again. In afternoon Norah and her baby came to tea. Norah was looking awful and child worse, poor mite. Mary, very sweet, and Merlin came down and both were very good and I felt very proud of my family.

Saturday 27 June

Bill and I out shopping in the morning and then I had my hair washed locally. They did it very badly. I rested all afternoon, then we changed and motored up to London to dine at the Berkeley which was such fun. They had the most amusing Gali Gali man there. [My mother explained they are a kind of magician producing hen's eggs out of your ears etc.]. Lovely run back afterwards.

Sunday 28 June

Motored over to Westerham with Billy in the morning, a lovely drive, but our reception here on being 10 minutes late for lunch spoilt the whole day for me. Mum gets so difficult and makes it so hard for Bill and me.

On Sunday 5 July Cesca and Bill went out after dinner to Hastings Road and watched the traffic! This entry surprised me.

Monday 6 July

Up at 5.30 and fed Merlin and had hot tea and biscuits and motored up to London with Bill in the car leaving at 6.00 and arriving at 7.00. Left me at Basil St. Hotel for breakfast which is charmingly furnished and very comfy. Then I saw Mary Wilson before arriving at Harrods sale at 9.00. Bought lots of things in the Men's dept. for Bill and also a lot in Baby Dept. and household and linen etc. Came home by train from Charing Cross arriving for lunch at 1.30.

Tuesday 7 July

Went to London again with Mum. Went shopping all morning and had fitting with Miss Gold at Walton Place and then met Mum for lunch at Gunters. Then went to Oxford and Cambridge Cricket at Lords and had tea with Harold and Ursula at Free Foresters Tent. Dull party and as did not feel well did not enjoy it much. Home by 7.00. Dad very cross and grumpy.

Thursday 9 July

Dad is very cross and does not speak to me or Mum.

Monday 13 July

Bill and I went off to London arriving at 7.00. I went into the house to find water pouring down the stairs and the carpets and bathroom flooded. Bill went on to Duxford and left me to wrestle with it. Had Busset and Co there, their men and Southcott came. Shopped and had fitting with Miss Gold. Feel very upset. Lunched with Mrs Ian Smith and came home by 4.18. Bill rang up in evening re house insurance.

Wednesday 15 July

Dad's birthday. Gave him four spotted foulard ties. Bill and I went off to London by 9.50 to Cannon Street in pouring rain. Went to Golanski and saw silver fox furs which we thought were poor. Then to Hughes re insurance policy and then to Westminster Fire Office, Covent Garden about our claim for the insurance. We then

lunched at Boulestin, very good but expensive, before going to
Harrods and Harvey Nicholls returning home for tea.

Sunday 19 July

In the afternoon Hutch and a friend of his came to tea and ate the
most terrific meal finishing up all the raspberries and cream.
Merlin and Mary came down and were very good and Mary much
admired. They left about 6.00 and nurse went to church. Merlin
shrieked and shrieked and was very naughty but I got them both
to sleep.

Monday 20 July

Bill left early for Northolt, I wished I was going with him. Spent
the day packing and paying bills and helping Mother. All ready by
the evening.

Tuesday 21 July

Up early helping Nurse to do up cots, pen and all children's
luggage. Left the house at 9.30 in the car, all heavy luggage having
gone off in advance. Discovered as the train left T.W. that nurse
had left the bag with all children's food behind. Was in a terrible
state of worry and got out at Cannon St. and tore off in taxi to a
dairy and to Gamages where I bought a spirit stove, saucepan and
methylated spirits. Arrived after the bus had taken nurse, children,
Mother, Mrs Knight, Kitty and Dorothy to the station and was met
by Bill who had come to see us off. Dad turned up with the
missing bag! Nurse and Mary both sick in train and we arrived at
Kingswear at 4.10 and met by the bus. I like the house awfully.
Had busy time getting the babies to bed and unpacking.

Wednesday 22 July

Woke up to a glorious morning. Think this place is fascinating. It
faces Dartmouth one side and the river and open sea the other and
the views are lovely. It's a very big comfy country house with
pretty garden sheltered and facing south. Mum and I fearfully
busy shopping and ordering. Unpacked and then went to meet
Dad at the station at 4.10. He likes this place too and his attitude
seems to have quite changed. Servants all very difficult.

Friday 24 July

Get two letters a day from Bill but miss him and won't see him now until the dance on 31st. Sent some cream to Aunt Edie.

Saturday 25 July

Woken up by Bill who had motored all night from Duxford [a journey of some 250 miles] to come to me for the weekend. Was so surprised and delighted! Had baths together and then went out to Dartmouth by ferry. Bill very thrilled and delighted with the place too. So lovely to have him here. He slept all afternoon in the Billiard room. Sent cream to Mrs Lunn.

Sunday 26 July

Went to church at Kingswear. Went for long walk after lunch to end of cliff with Bill. Nurse out and I put babies to bed. Mum came up and started to suggest things and interfere which made me very cross and the result was a row. Bill backed me up and I went to bed, miserable and cried.

Monday 27 July

Felt awfully upset at Bill having to leave early this morning. Went into Mum's room, she was as cross as ever. But later I saw her in the sitting room and we had a talk and made it up. Wired to Bill that storm was blowing over.

Friday 31 July

Mum and Dad saw me off to London by 11.20. Good journey but very hot and awful people from Paignton to London. Bill met me in the car at Paddington and took me to Basil St Hotel where I found Miss Gold with my dresses. Had my hair washed at Hugo's. Wore my black dress. Went off after dinner in the car and motored to Duxford for the Air Force Dance which I enjoyed and danced mostly with Bill. Came home at 4.00, lovely drive back in dark.

Saturday 1 August

Had breakfast at 10.00 and Miss Gold came at 11.00 for another fitting. Looked at poor Walton Place and spoke to the insurance people about it.

Had lunch at Basil St and paid the bill. Very expensive. Left at 2.45 and got on so well decided to come all the way. Had tea near Basingstoke and another stop at Salisbury. Telephoned Mum from Exeter. Arrived at 11.00 very tired.

The prospect of a month's leave here with Bill is divine.

Friday 7 August

Bill took me out in a rowing boat in the morning and frightened me out of my life, but I survived it and he had a very nice bathe at Dartmouth Castle but it was hard work getting the boat back against the tide. He blistered his hands and was very tired.

Their days are spent visiting Dartmouth and the surrounding countryside and playing bridge most evenings. Mary was weighed in Dartmouth with clothes on, 24 lbs, clothes weighed 14 ozs. The car was left at Torquay to be decarbonised and Bill and Cesca return by bus. They are all invited to join the Drewes in their motor boat for the Torquay Regatta. But a gale and rain got up and the Regatta was washed out. Cesca had never seen such waves and sea. Four people were drowned at Torquay. On her 27th birthday, Cesca became increasingly nervous that she was expecting another baby and spent the next four days unable to sleep for worry, taking Ergot and Femergen. Both she and Bill are miserable and her parents very sweet but equally upset. However with only two doses left, huge relief all round and Cesca and Bill leave early for London on Sunday 30 August. The car went like a dream via Exeter, Ilchester, Amesbury (lunch stop), Basingstoke arriving at the Rembrandt at 4.30pm. Then visited Walton Place, very depressing, dined together at the Rembrandt and Bill departed for Duxford having seen Cesca into bed.

Monday 31 August

Fearfully busy day that I had mapped out beforehand. Went off to shops and house early and then met Mrs Webb. Then to agencies re. servants. Then the manager of the Rembrandt gave me a private first floor sitting room and there I interviewed one parlour maid and three cooks and after lunch two more parlour maids and one more cook. Saw Miss Gold as well and then left London by 3.30 train arriving Kingswear 8.15 after a good dinner on the train. Mum and Dad met me.

Tuesday 1 September

Felt rather tired after yesterday. Wrote to Bill and servants. Mary and Merlin both very well and very good. Mary very pleased to see me again. Two letters from Bill. I miss him very much. I have been elected member of the Harrods Ladies Club. The Drewes came to tea and were very thrilled with the babies especially Mary and came and saw her in her bath.

Wednesday 9 September

My last day at Riversea. Don't want to go back to London one bit and feel depressed at the thought of housekeeping again. Went up the Dart by steamer with Mother.

Thursday 10 September

Said goodbye to the babies and felt very sad. Gave Mrs Knight £1 and Kitty and Dorothy 10/- each. Mum and Dad saw me off with my luggage at the station. Crowds got in at Torquay into my First class carriage so it was not a very comfy journey. Arrived at the house and found Mrs Webb hard at work. Mrs Flynn, cook, and two maids arrived at 5.30. Bill came down from Duxford and we dined at the Rembrandt.

Saturday 12 September

Shopping with Bill all morning in the car. Miss the babies awfully. Let the servants go to floodlighting at Buckingham Palace and was furious when they were late in. Bill and I waiting up for them.

Sunday13 September

Went for a walk with Jim and Gabriel along the Embankment. In afternoon went to Golden Parsonage, Bill's private school at Hemel Hempstead.

Tuesday 15 September

Went to John Lewis and bought myself a new felt hat for 12/9 very cheap! Then to meet the babies at Paddington. Mum very sad and tired. Nannie and Mary had been sick on the train but Merlin very well. Hurried my lot home to comfy tea in their own nursery. Wrote to Mum and Dad for their 40th Wedding Anniversary tomorrow.

Thursday 17 September

Had talk to Nannie as I heard her being cross with Mary unnecessarily and saying 'shut up'. Mary came down in my bed and was very good.

Saturday 19 September

Went off at 10.00 to Marlborough for the day with Bill in the motor. Had a glorious run and arrived there at 1.00 and took our lunch hamper up on the downs and had our picnic. Then Bill interviewed his housemaster and the head master about the Air Force liaison business. Left for London at 3.30 arriving at 6.30 after tea on the way. Jim and Gabriel came to dine at 8.00.

Tuesday 22 September

Took Mary to be weighed at Harrods, 26 lbs. Bill brought me a big basket of vegetables from Duxford. Had row with nurse about several things and she wept and so did Mary. Mum came up for the day.

Wednesday 7 October

Bill down for lunch. Mrs Lunn came to tea to see Mary and Merlin. Merlin was of course naughty and Mary did not care for her much but was better later on. Mrs Lunn brought us fruit and toys and book for Mary and was very nice altogether. As Merlin has been so naughty at night, Dr Morcom suggested Sunshine Glaxo so we are trying it tonight.

Saturday 17 October

Left London with Bill in the car to Duxford. Hated leaving my sweet babies. Had lodgings at 'Pines'. Big double bed and comfy bedroom and nice sitting room with big fire. Had lunch and tea at Mess then dined with Sqd. Leader and Mrs Sanderson at Orchard Cottage. Nice cottage but cold.

Sunday 18 October

Bill had to take Church Parade so went with him and enjoyed the short service. Went for long walk in afternoon and got some pretty berries. Came home by 6.17 from Royston and home by 8.30.

Monday 19 October

Mrs Durham brought Jane to tea and she and Mary were perfectly sweet together and loved each other. [My Mother does not remember loving Jane!].

Sunday 25 October

Went to tea with Gabriel and Jim and Bill walked each other's legs off in Richmond Park. Bill looked quite white and exhausted. Motored to supper at Cheam. Poor food and felt frozen. Ursula and Harold and all the Masters there. House like a refrigerator. Motored home to our warm little nest.

Tuesday 27 October

Great Day of Election. Everyone very excited but a thick yellow fog prevented most people from going out.Bill and I amused the babies until teatime and had nursery tea. Dined at the Durhams and played bridge losing 2/- and then listened to the wireless for Election results which as they came through made us very excited all being Conservative victories and a wiping of Labour.

Wednesday 28 October

Great excitement. National Government getting enormous majority, 400, and Labour hardly any seats at all and all Labour leaders out of it too. Felt most cheered. Dad came up and took Bill and me to lunch at the Piccadilly Grill and then to the theatre.

Wednesday 4 November

Waited in for cook till 11.00 and then went to bank to cash cheque. Then to Hugo's where I had my hair washed and set. Enjoyed it and felt clean and lovely. Bought some setting lotion for 4/6. Bill arrived after lunch and loved my hair done in the middle. Made love all the afternoon and then went to my club! Went to bed early after a vile dinner badly cooked by Mrs Flynn.

Thursday 5 November

Busy morning. Went to Woodhouse, dentist, at 11.00 and had fiendish time until 12.30. Felt like a rag and pain intense and my jaw ached terribly. Had to come home and rest. Aunt Edie came to tea and saw Mary and Merlin who did not like her and cried!

Monday 9 November

Went off to Woodhouse at 10.00 and had another frightful time for half an hour. Mary rang and asked me to dine. After nice dinner a deux (John ill in bed) in walked Hugh Lang! [An old boyfriend]. Most amusing as he was so very embarrassed, poor dear. Brought me home at 10.00.

Wednesday 11 November

Went to see Mary Wilson after breakfast and discussed Hugh's visit the other evening. Bill's car still being repaired at Shrimptons.

Saturday 14 November

A lovely morning. Put on shooting clothes and went off with Bill, Mr Cripps and Betty to Chasewood at Frant near Tonbridge. Bill had an excellent days shooting, much enjoyed himself and shot very well and got three lovely high birds to end the day. Dinner of seven, very rich courses with champagne etc. Rather too much. Felt very tired and went to bed as soon as I could get away from Mrs Cripps incessant talk!

Sunday 15 November

Left early after bad and uncomfortable night. Betty and Mr and Mrs Cripps charming and we came away with a brace of pheasants and a bunch of chrysanthemums. Home for lunch. Cold and foggy. Bill went back to Duxford in evening fearing a foggy morning.

Monday 16 November

Nurse out with babies till teatime. Then I took them. Gave them their tea and then as I was taking Merlin to his bath, fell all the way down top flight of stairs with him. Fortunately he was not hurt, only frightened. Cut ankle and bruised all my leg and felt very shaken and upset. Had brandy and soda and then felt better and got babies to bed. And then attended to my leg. Wrote to Mum about it and went to bed as soon as nurse came in.

Tuesday 17 November

Leg very bad, swollen and inflamed and painful. Stayed in bed till lunchtime and rested it on the sofa all afternoon. Bill came down late and we went to dine at the Seligmanns in Kensington Palace

Gardens. Lovely house and good dinner. 14 of us dining. Home at 12.00, tired and leg very painful.

Friday 20 November

My leg better, managed to walk as far as Montpelier Street this morning and had lunch with Mary Wilson. Mum came up and stayed till Bill came home.

Saturday 21 November

Mrs Flynn left in morning and new cook Dorothy Lake arrived. Went out to lunch with Gabriel and Bill. Had vile lunch and came home cross. New cook cooked dinner quite well. Letter from Hugh accepting invitation for dinner.

Wednesday 25 November

Lovely having Bill on leave. He went off shopping and I had flowers to get and things to order for tonight's dinner party. Bill had to go and see his Mother who has sold her house and is taking a flat in Marylebone Road. In evening Hugh and his wife Maydee came to dine. Hugh is still the same and very nice. Disliked her very much as she is so grand and pretentious.

Thursday 26 November

Mary came in to see me and hear all about last evening. Mum came up by train bringing me 2 rabbits, also medicine and a darling cameo brooch.

Merlin rather fretty and cross with teeth coming.

Friday 27 November

Lovely morning. Went in Isobel's Sunbeam to Duxford. Had very good run arriving for lunch. In afternoon watched flying in the rain, and went over the hangars and saw Vickers Gun being fired. Then came home in pouring rain arriving 5.30. Felt worried as Isobel told me her nurse says nannie is unkind to Mary in Park.

Wednesday 2 December

Went shopping with Bill to Fortnum & Masons and met Mum by chance and she bought me a new dress there, most attractive dark brown model for four and a half guineas. Mum arrived with flowers for my tea party and then we went out in the afternoon.

She bought me a fascinating new lamp shade for my room which I love and makes the room simply lovely.

Saturday 5 December

Went out Christmas shopping at Debenhams etc. Merlin and Mary both had their new coats fitted by Miss Gold. Went down to Parham House at 11.30 arriving for lunch with Mum and Dad. Bought some biscuits and sausages and home in time to see babies before they went to bed.

Sunday 6 December

Went to church at St Saviours and then after a walk had quiet afternoon in preparation for evening party. Went in car to Arts Theatre Club where we dined with Mr and Mrs Ionides and then went on with them to The Green Room Rag Show at Shaftesbury which we both enjoyed enormously.

Monday 7 December

Bill left early. Nurse went out in afternoon and evening so had Mary and Merlin to look after. Was furious to find Marlin frightfully constipated. Rang up Dad who advised castor oil and by 10.00 he had slight action. Worried all night and beat up nurse.

Tuesday 9 December

Gave nurse a good talking to, she wept all morning.

Wednesday 9 December

Bill arrived for lunch. We spent afternoon shopping together. Letter from Mrs Lunn saying I was to buy things to value of 30/- each for babies. Went to Harrods and chose dressing gown for Merlin and material for dresses for Mary.

Friday 11 December

Busy preparing for dinner party tonight. Squadron Leader and Mrs Sanderson came. Had tomato cream, turbot, hollandaise sauce, fillets of grilled steak with mushrooms, tomatoes and cauliflower and Plum pudding and Devonshire cream and orange soufflé, coffee and dessert.

Still cannot get over Mrs Lunn's quite impossible letter which arrived yesterday evening.

Saturday 12 December

Rested all afternoon. Went out to dine at 8.00 with Colonel and Mrs Ian Smith then went on to dance at the Malmaison and danced till 2.00 and enjoyed it awfully.

Monday 14 December

Mum arrived and had lunch here and was horrified by Mrs Lunn's letter and behaviour. Later nurse told me she would have to leave as it was all too much for her. I said I would discuss it whilst we were at Tunbridge Wells and not before.

Tuesday 13 December

Made final arrangements for children to Tunbridge Wells. Nurse and Elsie and the babies left by 2.00 train. Saw them off safely and finally dispatched the pram. Came home feeling rather lonely and sad. Did my nails, altered my dress and went to bed early.

Wednesday 16 December

Had excellent night sleeping till 7.30 and had breakfast in bed. Met Mary and Peg who told me that Hugh's wife loathes me! Had my hair washed and set at Hugo's. Went to Ivy Hudsons for hat fittings. Bill arrived looking very well. Changed and wore my black lace dress and went in the car to the Lang's at 5 Chesham Place, an awful boarding house. Maydee made it as awkward as possible for me.

Thursday 17 December

Mary Wilson came round to hear about last night before Bill and I left for Cranwell at 10.30. Had an excellent run up. Saw Peter who came with us to Sleaford and had tea. Had bath and nice rest and big fire in my room. Wore my new white chiffon and dined at 7.30. Bill and Peter in uniform. Went to Cranwell by taxi and quite enjoyed big cadet dance. Love being with Bill. To bed at 2.00.

Friday 18 December

Most uncomfortable bed and slept badly. Hotel charged us a frightful packet, £4 for one night. Left after Inspection and Drill at Cranwell which was excellent and Bill most impressed. Motored home via lunch at Stamford but once we reached the bypass road we came into thick fog and had to crawl all along past Hendon to Finchley Road. Perishing cold too with windscreen wide open and Bill and I peering out. Arrived home to hot baths and comfy fires and felt better after a good dinner.

Saturday 19 December

Had busy morning packing up house and shopping in Bond Street with Bill. Took Dorothy (cook) to Charing Cross in taxi as Mother wrote urgent letter to say her cook had decamped! Shut up the house and left at noon, fog coming down again so decided to get out of London. Stopped at horrid wayside inn and had vile plateful of steak and kidney pudding costing 5/-. Arrived at 3.00 and found Mum and the babies flourishing, also cook and Elsie all right too. To bed very early. No news from Mrs Lunn.

The days pass in a flurry of parcel wrapping and posting, tea parties and lunches and a Nativity Play at the village hall. A local shoot at Hurst Green with Bill and Dad, getting eight pheasants and six rabbits. Home after lunch in the car with Mum, both very cold.

Thursday 24 December

Nurse gave in her notice to leave on January 25. She has been very tiresome lately. Merlin has a first tooth. Parcels and cards arriving all day. I drove the car in the morning very badly. Bill and Mother not getting on well which ended after dinner just before we went to bed with frightful row. Bill rude at bridge and Mother was furious and very rude to him about Mrs Lunn's letter to me. All misery and most upsetting.

Friday 25 December: Christmas Day

That upheaval over but now a fresh upset. Heard nurse being unkind and saying beastly things to Mary at 5.30. Bill and I went in in a fury and wanted to turn her out. Opened all our parcels with Mary and Merlin. Went to church in car with Bill and had good short service. Bill gave me a box of powder, two bottles of scent and a lovely Squadron brooch. Mum a new dress, bath salts, Dad £25 and Aunt Edie tablemats. Babies have had lovely presents too.

Saturday 26 December

Bill and I went out in the car for my driving lesson. Went out to tea in the afternoon with Blanche and saw her baby John who looks pale and delicate and has an awful squint. Played bridge in evening till 10.00

Tuesday 29 December

Snow falling all morning and very cold. Went to bank and paid nurse (very disagreeable). Spent all afternoon sewing and making new dress for Mary by enormous fire. A letter came from Bill about going to London on Thursday, New Years Eve, to the Circus. Merlin has another tooth.

Wednesday 30 December

Letters from more nurses and two letters from Bill. Nurse more pleasant and babies both well.

Thursday 31 December: New Year's Eve

Had some sandwiches and soup before leaving by train for London. Shopped all afternoon at Debenhams, Goldsmiths, and to Fortnum & Mason. Went to the Club at 6.00 and met Bill. Then dined at Club at 7.00. Went to Circus at Olympia which we both enjoyed very much and came home in the car arriving back at the stroke of midnight. To bed before a big fire. Very cold but very happy.

1933
Herschel House and Walton Place
1932 diary is missing

At the beginning of the year Cesca and Bill received an offer of eight guineas per week for 2 Walton Place. They made an offer of nine guineas a week, including the gardener Blunts's wages, for Herschel House in Cambridge. Cesca is preoccupied with her recovery from a motor accident at a crossroads in Cambridge the previous year. Her forehead bore the scar for the rest of her life. Hughes, the family solicitor, is involved. She is hopeful of receiving a large sum for damages. She and Bill met with the assessor, Mr Prime – 'a funny little man, but was recommended and apparently knows his job from A to Z'. A week later, Herschel House rental is confirmed for £9 per week. They are due to arrive on 23 January.
A visit on 14 January by 1st class train to Herschel House found 'all satisfactory, charming house but coke consumption seems heavy'. The next week is taken up by packing up and worrying about Mary who has been ill with coughs, colds and flu since the beginning of the month.

Monday 23 January.
Ghastly day, thick fog and bitterly cold. Bus arrived 9.30 and Mum soon after. All packed in. Two children, Mum, Nurse, Elsie and Dorothy, looking ill. Said goodbye to Bill and left at 10.30 arriving at Herschel House at 2.00. No lunch, just as busy as can be. Dined at Varsity Arms and home in bitter cold. Could not get water hot. Dorothy and Nannie both ill, with temperatures of 102 with flu. I had both children to sleep with me.

Tuesday 24 January
Another awful day. Up at dawn after no sleep, Merlin ill. Dressed children and gave them breakfast, cooked by Elsie who looked equally ill, and then off out in car to summon panel doctor, own doctor for Merlin and temporary cook and two temporary maids for cleaning the filthy house. Gave babies their lunch and spent afternoon with them. Felt worn out. Nurse better and Doctor said she could get to work and have the babies back. Elsie succumbed and she and Dorothy in night nursery.

Wednesday 25 January

Elsie's temperature of 105 thoroughly frightened me. Mum and I summoned Dr Budd and the panel doctor and together they succeeded in getting her a bed in the Isolation Hospital and fetched in an ambulance. Dorothy better. The old cook useless but the two girls are good and getting the house cleaner. Dr Budd to see Merlin, Mary ill now and is in bed. Dad arrived to check on babies and on Elsie in Hospital.

Thursday 26 January

Mother has been an angel in helping me so much, but today is returning home, as she looks ill and is worn out. Felt about done in myself.

Friday 27 January

Still having girls for cleaning and it all is going to be very expensive. Worried about the expense and trouble the central heating and hot water system are giving us.

Wednesday 1 February

Elsie came to get her money and departed for Norfolk looking better but rather white. Milder, and children are out for first time. No writing paper from Harrods which is tiresome. Bill home for tea and is agitated about the bomb that Blunt found under the house in the cellar. According to experts it is a live one.

By 11 February Cesca thinks she is having another baby. On the 12th, they celebrate their fourth wedding anniversary, 'four years of great happiness and I could never wish to have a better or sweeter husband or such sweet children'. They were both overjoyed to discover that Cesca was not pregnant. It was a false alarm. Whilst Bill is stationed at Duxford he is able to see his family frequently. Mother is a regular visitor bringing with her presents and on the 17 February 'a whole lot of silver from Dad as it had all belonged to Uncle Harold'. Cesca went to church with Bill at Duxford, 'church bitter and a miserable service for the poor troops ending with a useless sermon from the wretched old priest'.

Monday 27 February

My little girl's third birthday. Mary very thrilled with all her presents. Mum and Dad bought Mary sweet frocks as well as a cake and books galore. Mother and Dad rather difficult which made us feel rather depressed and miserable. Mary loved her day however and was as good as gold.

Saturday 18 March.

Bill's cufflinks arrived [it was his 27th birthday] and he had handkies from Dandy [his grandmother], shaving soap, soap, and two ties from Mrs Lunn and chocolates from the babies. Mother, who was very difficult and trying, ended up leaving by the 6.00 pm train in tears. We were both worried by this. More unsuccessful letters and communications about the accident, unlikely to get anything by proceeding with it, felt miserable and depressed.

Saturday 15 April

Went in the car with Bill to stay at Parham House for Easter having left Cambridge after lunch, had tea with Dandy in London 3.30 and arrived with Mum and Dad at 6.15 leaving the babies at Herschel House. Dad gave us each £5 [£250 today]. All went to church at King Charles. Attended the Conservative Ball at the Pump Rooms on Easter Monday.

On 18 April Cesca is off early to London to stay with Aunt Edie.

...enjoy staying there, comfy room. Saw dressmakers and a new tailor, shopped at Harrods and then the following day with Bill's voucher got a first class fare for the price of third from Waterloo to Lyme Regis. Stayed at the Alexandra Hotel, dull but clean. Next day after paying her bill of 15/- she saw two useless houses for her mother. Swift journey home to Cambridge by fast taxi from Liverpool St arriving two hours early! Lovely being with Bill and the babies.

Monday April 24 Merlin's 2nd birthday.

Met Mother and Dad at the station at 1.15. They bought Merlin a lovely cake with icing, also £1 for his bank account. We had lunch and then discussed the business of the cruise and it was decided I must go to take Ursula's place owing to her illness. Hate and loathe the thought of it and leaving Bill and the babies.

Wednesday and Thursday that week are taken up by trips to London, to find clothes for the cruise.
Then to "Pierre", Harrods, Selfridges, Ivy Hudson for hats, Raynes for shoes, feeling tired and miserable and Bill sad and cross. She saw Hughes re the accident who seemed more hopeful. Bought sweets and rubber buckets for the children. Only two more days at home. Last day at home spent with the babies and Nannie, shopping and paying bills. Cesca longs now to get off and have it over with and get home again.

Saturday 29 April
So tired and miserable. Hate to leave them, they are so sweet. Bill took me to the station and I could not stop crying. It is awful to have to leave him. 1st class to London, met Mum at Waterloo, had nice seats on special train with lunch on board. Awful looking people going on their fortnight's cruise on the *Homeric*. Arrived Southampton, went aboard. [Bill had sent pink tulips to her cabin.] Miss him so. Mum and I watched the land slipping by from the rail.

Sunday 30 April
Felt better after a good night but still unhappy. People on this cruise are too awful, men dreadful cads and women appalling – and the clothes! About 450 aboard. The boat is lovely and beautifully appointed, not good food so far. However we have a lovely cabin and perfect bathroom of our own which is delightful. Rather rough and cold.

The following day was quite choppy, very cold and they both were muffled up in fur coats!

Mum not feeling well. Gala dinner which was too awful. Everyone blowing trumpets and wearing paper hats. Got rougher, most unpleasant and a gale getting up. Bad night. The boat going every which way. Ate nothing and both stayed in bed feeling very sick. Miserable and loathe it all.

Wednesday 3 May Arrived at Gibraltar

Calm so had slept well. Went ashore early by tender and took a cab around the town. Sat on top deck and read in peace and quiet in warm sunshine.

A woman in the next cabin kept them awake till past 1.00 am 'with her infernal gramophone'. Next morning Cesca went straight to the Captain 'and spoke about vile woman and gramophone. He said he will see it is stopped.'

Hottest day so far and everyone is bathing and sunbathing with almost nothing on. Don't think it is pretty especially the elderly people with awful figures!

Friday 5 May

Arrived at Palma, hot morning, wore thin things. We decided not to be herded with Cook's tourists and go ashore in our own tender. Cathedral impressed me with its pinky yellow stone and a service going on around a corpse. Lovely to go to other side of the island but could not find lunch so took perilous drive by another route. We were both frightened but managed to return in time for a good tea!

Letters are received and sent to Bill throughout the trip. The day out resulted in severe sunburn, at sea all day until 5.00 pm when they arrived at Monaco.

Had excellent dinner in the Hotel de Paris but had to wait two hours to be collected by the tender. That woman is playing that gramophone again.

On Sunday she writes 'this time next week I shall be home.'

Monday 8 May Arrival at Barcelona

…very rough so do not go ashore until afternoon and were terrified as the seas were enormous! And nothing much to see either. A dreadful place, unfinished and horrid.

She is not impressed by Tangier either, 'awful place, filthy dirty and full of Arabs and awful smells'. She observes that most of Cook's tourists are on donkeys. It was rough that evening and all the next day. Cesca writes '...shall be thankful when it's over now.'

Thursday 11 May
Everyone in fancy dress tonight for the last Gala Dinner and Dance and judging of costumes.

The next day was calmer. They toured the kitchens and pantries and were impressed by all they saw.

Saturday 13 May
Woke up feeling very excited and this whirly, wild feeling continued all day until the climax of being with Bill again. Just heaven…. Very cold and raining as we watched Southampton draw closer. We docked at 2.15 and were through customs and away by 3.35. Mother hated the tipping, managed to do it all for £5. Arrived in London at 5.00. Bill and Dad to meet us. One rush and I was in Bill's arms. Marvellous to be together again. Said goodbye to dear Mum. They rushed for their train and we for ours. Arrived at 7.00. Marvellous to be home, so happy!

Sunday 14 May
So glad to be home again. Spent all day close to Bill and the babies who are both well and look so wonderful. So proud of them and my dear family and home. The next few days spent getting straight, writing letters and shopping and organising everything for weekend party of guests. Also played tennis with Bill.

Saturday 20 May
Weekend party seems to be going well. Except Peter [Bill's younger brother] rather tiresome, taking it all for granted which I do hate so and smoking ceaselessly, our cigarettes too! On Sunday after lovely service at Kings, Bill asked me to tackle Peter on the walk back about too frequent visits to town, extravagance, debts, truthfulness and many other difficult subjects. Not a success as he

resents our interfering and is a spoilt boy. Cannot make him out and dislike him very much at times.

Tuesday 23 May

Lovely having Mother here today, sad she has to go back to Dad tonight. Bill and I agreed that these casual young people are not worth having to stay. They eat your food, smoke your cigarettes, live in luxury and leave your house, rooms, bathrooms all a mess. Even ask you to pay their tips to your maids. Mother a perfect guest and never 'de trop'. That weekend, without wines cost us £4.8.10 for food and lemonades. A rude letter from Peter arrived. The last time I have him to stay, little horror!

Wednesday 31 May

Had early lunch with Bill and then set off for Thorpeness and Aldeburgh. A most lovely drive through wonderfully, pretty country. Suffolk is beautiful. Went through Newmarket, Bury, Stowmarket, Needham Market and Wickham Market. Aldeburgh a sweet spot. Found charming cottage on front called Swiss Cottage that we like. Then we looked at hotels, poor, and then over to Thorpeness which is not so nice. Back to Bury for dinner at the Angel, quite good. Home to bed 10.00. Paid maids wages, £15 for the month.

Thursday 2 June

Bill is on leave until next Tuesday. Busy preparing for Mum and Dad's visit. So hot. Met Mum at 6.00 from station. Played tennis till dinner time. Hotter and hotter. Dad's foot is better and he looks very well. We all went to Kings for Whitsunday service, Dad wearing MD [Doctor of Medicine] hood and very pleased and happy. The weather becomes hotter, 86F, both babies in white bathing costumes and looked so sweet.

Thursday 8 June

A letter from Hughes announcing I am to receive £68.10.0 for my special damages for the accident claim. [£4,000 today.] It does not cover my expenses, the devils! However I am glad to get it.

Sunday 11 June
Cold wet morning finds another member of Bill's family arriving to stay. Pat, one of his sisters, whom Cesca found:

...trying and difficult but not as bad as Peter. She is well dressed and quite good looking too, though very 'Airforce'. Start getting ready for the move and wrote to the Captain telling him of our departure to the sea.
A few days later
Bill receives a letter from the Captain which makes us both quite furious and fed up. Final shopping and will be sad to leave Herschel House on Monday.

Monday 19 June
Frightful day. We were up very early and left at 8.15 in two taxis. Left Rose to tidy up and Bill there to tip Blunt, £3. A tiresome journey with two changes, at Ipswich and Saxmundham. I seemed to spend pounds on porters, taxis, and tipping guards but we got a carriage to ourselves all the way to Aldeburgh and arrived at 11.45. [Aldeburgh station was closed in 1966]. Cottage is sweet and by evening we had it straight and cosy with a fire, all unpacked and food ordered and children to bed as usual. The next day was cold and wet. The children not very thrilled with the sea.

Wednesday 21 June
Found cards of Swiss Cottage which I sent to Dad, Aunt Edie and Suzanne. Met Mum at the station. Thrilled to have her to stay. She thinks the cottage and the place quite charming and loves it all. Talked about Scotland where Dad has taken Lord Shaw's shoot and the fun we shall have there. Watched babies on the beach and received letter from Bill. He is now at Hendon practising for the Air Pageant. Spent the next day with Mum with a picnic at Thorpeness on the sands.

Friday 23 June
Went up to town by 8.50 train with Mum, a through carriage to Liverpool St. arriving at 11.20. Mum went home to see Dad off to Scotland and I had dress fitting, shopped for lunch at Harrods for

tomorrow including strawberries and cream. Had hair washed and set and then went to Bond St for shoes and toothbrushes. Light lunch at Searcy's and tea with Mrs Richards. Bill arrived looking very tired. Dined and played bridge until 11.00. Period late, wondered why. [In fact Cesca was pregnant this time.]

Saturday 24 June RAF Air Pageant Hendon

Woke to wet and misty morning. Bill upset and worried. Tore off to Harrods to hurry them up with the lunch and bought myself a new white macintosh, 32/6. Then back to Sloane St. where our party of nine were assembling. All left at 10.20 in two cars in formation for Hendon arriving at 10.45 but could only get in 3rd row. Rain held off till lunch time when it came down in sheets and soaked us all. Saw Pat, Elisabeth and Peter and many others. Got awfully worried over Bill's effort but it was cut short by the AOC. He then had to fly back to Duxford and come on by train joining us at the Savoy at 11.00pm.

Sunday 25 June

So much enjoyed last night's party. Said goodbye to the Richards who have been so good to us. Lovely to think have two more whole days with my Bill. Left for Aldeburgh and had lunch at Witham at the Spread Eagle, quite good and enjoyed the drive but felt very tired. Arrived in time for tea with our darlings who were waiting for us on the corner and looking so sweet.

Monday 26 June

A welcome cheque arrives from Hughes from General Transport and Co for my accident for £68.11.0 at last. Spent a lovely quiet day with my three darlings. Bill left on Tuesday in the car at 9.15. Paddled in the afternoon. Little Mary very frightened of big waves but Merlin does not mind a bit.

On Wednesday Bill flies over with Wing Commander Waller and motors in his car from Martlesham.

Thursday 29 June

Bill off at 8.30 with the Wing Commander. [Cesca gets to the sale at Alde End early and stays all day.] On the whole things fetched big prices but I managed to get a set of nice glass for £2.10.0, also some nice fireproof dishes, egg poachers, set of plates and salad plates to match my own at home. A man brought me home in his car.

Friday 30 June

Lovely day out on the beach with the babies. Bill arrived at the Wallers with the Wing Commander and Mrs Waller fetched us all in her car and we all went to tea there.

Saturday 1 July

Lovely hot day. Spent most of it on the beach. Bill, Merlin and Mary bathed.

The next day, I walked into an iron bar coming up from the beach which was extremely painful and made me quite hysterical for a bit. Bill left after dinner with the Commander. Felt terribly sad.

The following Wednesday Cesca travels up to London by train with the glass case and trunk containing all the household requirements. She took a taxi to Ormonde Gate where she is staying with Jim and Gabriel. The next morning she is off early by taxi to Walton Place with trunk and luggage, to meet Mr Dugdale, 'quite the most unpleasant man and so rude. I however gave him as good as I got and told him had I known what he was like I should never have let the house to him'. The next day spent shopping, selling some frocks at the Dress Circle in exhausting heat, sweat running off her in rivers.

Returned home, very full train but travelled 1st class so all right. Nannie upset about Merlin falling out of his cot and Mary with a cold.

Monday 10 July

…woke up feeling rather sick but had to get up and bustle about as Mrs Lunn had sent wire to say she and Elisabeth were coming for the day. Pouring rain so lit fire and ordered food. They enjoyed an excellent lunch cooked by Dorothy of scrambled eggs, tomatoes, roast chicken, sausages and peas, new potatoes. Raspberry tart, cream and strawberries.

There was great excitement on their last day as three rockets went off and the lifeboat went out. They rushed to the front and watched it go out to a tiny sailing boat whose main mast had broken. They packed up to leave early next day.

Tuesday 10 July
To station in the bus, quite a business with so much luggage, went First class and the babies slept all the way to town. Met by Mum. So tired, slept like a log.

In spite of tiredness Cesca was up in London the next day for more fittings and shopping. Came home very tired but arranged to meet Bill in town next evening at the Club.

Wednesday 12 July
Bill all dressed up and looking so nice in tails and a carnation. Dinner and a play at the Globe and drive home in the car.

The next few days spent quietly at Parham House with the parents who are being difficult. Cesca feels unwell and has pains.

Friday 21 July
Heat intense but off to town to meet Hughes and the inventory man at Walton Place. Mr Dugdale very rude again and a lot of damage done. Arranged for things to be cleaned and interviewed decorators.

On Sunday 23 July Bill and Cesca busy packing for Carbeth in Stirlingshire, heavy luggage going up in advance by train. On Tuesday they left Parham House at 9.15, 'Mum in tears and Dad still very cross. London as hot as hell'. Seeing decorators and then to the hairdressers where she was violently sick, could not eat dinner so left with Bill in the car, felt awful and sick again in Seymour Street. They got as far as Stamford where she was sick again so stayed the night at The George.

Wednesday 26 July

Awoke feeling less sick but rather shaky. Bill so sweet and packed my things for me, felt sure I was having a miscarriage. Had lunch at Barnby Moor, sat in the gardens, lovely and cool and felt wonderful. Stayed at Borough Bridge and felt quite well again in the morning.

They went on to Carlisle and arrived at Carbeth on Thursday 27th. They were staying with Mary and John Wilson for a week. Lots of walking and enjoying the lovely peace and quiet, away from the heat of London. The Wilsons sent them off the following Friday with a lovely hamper full of grapes and an excellent lunch which they ate by the Spittal of Glenshee high up on the mountain side. Cesca was 'longing to see the babies'.

Friday 4 August Arrival at Learney Arms, Torphins near Banchory

Most depressing hotel. Food is abominable and Mum and Dad both bolshy. Babies sweet but rather tired after long, hot journey. Bad night and uncomfortable noisy room at the back of the hotel. Unable to get hot water which upset us all especially Mum. Dad livid as he chose the hotel.

The hotel continues to disappoint on all fronts, poor service and food especially upsetting Mum. They search for another suitable hotel in vain. This culminates in Mum and Dad having a proper row over hotel and its discomforts. They had Mr Journeyman in to complain and said unless everything improved they would go elsewhere. Bill and Cesca inspected Huntley Arms, Aboyne, which was very nice. On their return Dad livid and Mum refusing to come down to dinner, Cesca insisted she came down and everyone had it out and the air cleared. 'Next morning storm over and Dad normal again and both Mother and he on speaking terms, if still a trifle dignified. The food is distinctly better.'

Saturday 12 August

A glorious day's shooting, leaving in two cars, the babies coming up with nannie to see the guns off. They shot seven brace of grouse, 1 blackcock, 2 hares and 2 rabbits. Packed up two brace of grouse for Mrs Lunn and Dandy and sent them off on the night train to Aberdeen.

Cesca, Mary, Merlin, Nannie Shirley. Grantchester 1932

Mary, Merlin, Nannie Shirley 1933

Mary Merlin Aldeburgh 1933

Swiss Cottage Aldeburgh 1933

Torphins The Shoot 1933

The remainder of their stay is spent shooting, watching sheep dog trials and train spotting! Bill, Cesca and Mother went to see the King's 'lovely white train' go through the station.

Thursday 24 August
[Cesca and Bill left after lunch] Sad to say goodbye to Mother and the babies. She has been so sweet to me and both agreed how tiresome and impossible Dad has become. Had tea at Perth, sent shortbread to Dandy and arrived in Edinburgh at 7.30, excellent dinner and comfy room at the Caledonian Hotel. Set off at 10.45 after buying things for a picnic and sending Edinburgh Rock to the babies. Stayed the night at Borough Bridge.

Saturday 26 August Cesca's 29th birthday
Warm again, lunch at Stamford and tea at the Mess, Duxford and arrived home at Walton Place at 6.30. Dorothy and Mary full of smiles and pleased to see us. Mum had sent roses, £50, Dad £20 and Bill a lovely Visitors Book. Very hot again.

Much time was spent looking for housemaids and shopping (smoked salmon and tea from Fortnum & Mason) and seeing friends and going to the theatre. They also collected the remainder of their silver from the bank.

Monday 4 September
Up at 6.00 and went to meet the children at Kings Cross on their return from Scotland. Found Mother [then aged 69] and the babies all rather white, tearful and exhausted after a long and trying night journey. Packed Mum into a taxi to Charing Cross and went home in the car with the babies.

After getting the household resettled, haircuts all round and sharing her 'special news' with friend Gabriel who came to see her, Cesca decided to go down on the train to see how her mother was. She 'found her better and busy doing plums etc'. The search continues for a house for Cesca's parents when they sell Parham House. They looked at 14 Herbert Crescent, a bargain at £2,000 for 30 years, £5 annual ground rent. Upheaval with nurse over the childrens' bowels: 'Merlin frightfully constipated, had to have two suppositories'.

Cesca off to Royston by train and met by Bill in the car, to the Mess where they had lunch then watched a cricket match. They stayed in Trumpington at the Red Lion: 'terribly noisy, could not sleep at all'. They went to look at some houses in Cambridge. The best was Leckhampton House, off Grange Rd. They returned home to Walton Place earlier than planned due to Cesca's 'bad headache'. She felt unwell for the next few days. She wrote: 'Mother came up bringing a brace of grouse, apples and chocolate biscuits with her. We went to a dress show, a very ugly lot of dresses.'

Saturday 16 September

Met Mother at Hughes to try and decide whether to accept offer of £20,100 from Cinema Co. for Parham House.

Bill suddenly turned up for tea and they decided to go to The Café de Paris for dinner and dancing where they saw Peter with an ugly young woman. Bill left for Sutton Bridge on September 18 for three weeks.

Wednesday 20 September

Mother has sold Parham House for £21,000. [£1,460,000 today] Poor dear, she was rather upset and weepy over it. Took the children to the Zoo together and she cheered up.

Thursday 21 September

Woke up to a nasty shock as Dorothy and Mary both gave notice to leave, no reason just bored and wanted a change.

Mother departed that afternoon. Left alone Cesca 'felt upset and depressed over these bloody servants'. Bill returned for the weekend and they went to the Strand and Regent St looking at buying or hiring a wireless.

Thursday 5 October

The wireless the man came to install [it] is much too big and will have to go back. Mum came up bringing a pheasant and a rabbit. Dorothy served up a shocking lunch half cold. Peter rang trying to see us but we were out.

Sunday 8 October

We beetled down through the night to Parham and had nice chat with Mum and Dad before bed. [Next day, Bill and Dad went shooting.] Set off for home with pounds and pounds of apples, mushrooms, eggs, rabbits, biscuits and cakes.

Tuesday 10 October

Dorothy making Christmas puddings that we all stirred. The next day Dad came up to lunch, stewed rabbit and orange soufflé. He bought babies a box of sweets and enjoyed seeing them both.

On Friday Cesca looked at maternity frocks in Bond St, she thought were very dowdy. On the 14th stayed at the Blue Boar in Cambridge having looked at various houses, none of which were any good. After church on Sunday they walked over to Leckhampton House where Bill interviewed the chauffeur. Mother is still looking at a house in Limpsfield. Cesca does not care for it.

Saturday October 21

Paid Dorothy and Mary and they departed after lunch. Felt end of the world had come but daresay I shall get over it. New ones came 4.30, seemed pretty hopeless anyhow in appearance.

Sunday October 22.

Awful black day. Started by servants being completely and utterly useless. Cold scrambled eggs and uncooked bacon, black toast and cold tea sent up at 9.30 instead of 9.00. Raw joint and leaden pastry for lunch, unable to even lay the table, and the cook let the boiler go out. Told them to go tomorrow.

The next day Cesca was up early and 'got the awful servants out of the house by 10.00 with payment of £1.4.0 Cooked lunch with Lily and then took Nannie and children in a taxi to station to Tunbridge Wells. Then went to various agencies for cooks and maids'. This went on for the next few days, very tiring but she felt better after an excellent dinner with Bill at the Mayfair for 8/6 each. On Thursday Cesca packed up the house, and left with Lily, dropping her at the tube station, to go down to join the children at T.W. It was 'cold with a slight snow shower. Met by Mother with Hogben.'

Bill came down on the evening of the 27th and they motored over to stay with friends, the Styles, for dinner and shooting the following day. 'Comfortable and good dinner.' They left for Parham after an excellent lunch and Cesca felt much better for having a change away. They arrived for tea. 'The house an "icewell" and Mum and Dad both rather difficult'. After a good supper they left to return to Walton Place which was cold and depressing. Bill left at 6.00 on Monday 30th. Cesca had a hectic day getting the house and the servants straight.

Tuesday 31 October

… the house really almost straight and Nannie and babies back at 3.52. Poor Mum, all maids have decamped except the cook.

Wednesday 1 November

Temp. cook quite good, Tony and Bill to dinner, roast pheasant, potatoes, and orange salad, caramel pudding with delicious sauce and cheese straws. Bill and Tony split a bottle of Pomerol between them.

Saturday 4 November

Just caught the 10.05 to Cambridge where I interviewed and engaged Doris Higgins as nursery maid to come in January or sooner if I get to Cambridge before then. Viewed a house with Bill, no good, then home by 3.30 to give tea to Dandy and Elizabeth and Gordon Hubback. Terribly tired.

Monday 6 November

Went with Nannie, Mary and Merlin to Harrods Toyfair to spend the 5/- that Ralph Millais [godfather] had given Mary yesterday. Eventually chose a dog on a chain for Mary and an engine for Merlin. Merlin was very naughty afterwards. Temporary cook excellent but new cook who arrived later, lasted no time at all. She said she could not possibly stay as she did not like me or the maids or the house so she left on the spot! Another temporary cook was engaged, Mrs Smith and seems a decent woman in every way.

Thursday 9 November

Dr Phillips came to examine me at 9.30 and said all seemed well and normal. But I seemed rather big and my pelvis not over large. Felt very seedy later and faint. The next day still very seedy, awful pains and discomfort, could hardly hobble.

These fainting fits continued so Cesca went to Bond Street and had a fitting for a proper surgical belt. By the 17th she was feeling so much better since having the new corsets. By 21 November she had finished all her Christmas presents except Bill's, the children's and her mother's.

Wednesday 22 November

Hectic day. Went to Peter Jones and returned home to find Mother here unexpectedly, she stayed to lunch and tea. Long talk over the house at Limpsfield, Dad and the difficulties thereof. Then Bill arrived having got the day off. Then Elizabeth rang to ask if she and Gordon could come and see Bill on urgent business this evening, so after dear Mum left and the babies had gone to bed, in came the entire P-R family. Pat, Peter, Elizabeth and Gordon to discuss the imminent crash of George Lunn and P. Currie [Mrs Lunn]. Bill telephoned for Hughes who came and all seems a frightful mess. Bad night worrying. Another meeting fixed for Friday at 2.30 here. Dear me, I wonder how it will all end.

Friday 24 November

Bill arrived at 1.30 then Pat rang to say they could not get here till 3.00. Hughes arrived first, followed by Gordon, Elizabeth, Patricia and Peter. Peter says he will do nothing more. Long talks till 5.30. We are now out of the Lunn matter and it is in Hughes' and Gordon's hands. They propose putting up £500, maybe more later, but will without doubt lose all. Hughes thinks so too. [George Lunn faces being bankrupt].

An offer for Walton Place of £275 refused. [Two days later they cannot decide whether to accept £335 for 14 months.]

Monday 27 November

Very cold day. Bill went back to Cambridge to see what he could do about Leckhampton House. And I spent the day chasing agents re letting this house. Suddenly had offer of £350 for year from M. Bardossi, 1st Secretary at Hungarian Legation. Rang up Bill who has put in counter offer for eight guineas a week for Leckhampton House. Could not sleep for excitement.

Tuesday 28 November

After most agitating morning, M and Mme Bardossi called and decided to take it furnished for one year, £350. We also heard that Mrs Myers had agreed to let Leckhampton House for 9 guineas. [This news did not go down well with Cesca's mother. She hates them to be far away, as she cannot pop up to see them.] Very busy few days, packing up and getting the agreements signed, and paying wages, nannie £4.15.0. Also rushed down by hire car to Westerham to see Farley Grange for Mother, which is thought very suitable.

Saturday 2 December

Rush up to Cambridge by 10.05 train after ordering food at Harrods en route. Bitterly cold, seem fated to move in cold weather. Lunched with Lady Hope, told us all about the Myers. Then go through the rooms at Leckhampton House before next week's move. Motored home with Bill, enjoying the trip, when suddenly at a crossroads a car ran into us [their Standard motorcar]. I was very frightened and felt the baby might arrive at any minute, most alarming. Went home in a taxi, to bed and Dr Phillips called out.

Next day, despite a very stiff and bruised shoulder and in bitterly cold weather, Cesca was up and about as usual and together they sorted out the drawing room drawers, desk and cupboards. On Monday she lunched with Mary Wilson and ordered more groceries from Harrods and Fortnum & Mason.

Tuesday 5 December

Dad came up to say goodbye, very melancholy and then Mother who wept most of the time. All rather depressing. Had terrible shock and blow at lunch time, call from agents to say could not move into the house. Bill rose nobly to the occasion, dashed round to Mrs Myers, eventually spoke to her on the telephone and all was well. Shall not be happy until all is signed. Met Mrs Myers at a cocktail party that evening.

Wednesday 6 December

Accomplished the move wonderfully well without any of the anticipated difficulties. Bus arrived 9.00 and took one and a half hours to load. Children, nurse, new cook, Lily, Joyce in bus with all luggage, silver, linen, pram, cots, mattresses and blankets. Bill and I behind in the car. At Ware/Royston crossroads, changed over with nannie and the babies who went with Bill to the Mess for lunch, I went on in the bus to direct the maids getting to work straight away. Very tired but nearly straight by bedtime and babies safely into bed.

Thursday 7 December

Very busy getting straight, the house is beautifully warm and clean which is half the battle. Coal and coke consumption will be high, I'm afraid. New nursery maid seems very stupid.

Friday 8 December

Mum's birthday and have ordered her a puppy, Dandie Dinmont, from the Bellmead Kennels. Like the house immensely, maids good but need a lot of chasing. Bill home every day which is lovely. Children's doves arrived, very sweet.

Saturday 9 December

Feel already much better for being in the country and the babies look quite different. The garden is most attractive. Mum is very pleased with her puppy. Doves are a great success with the babies. Sadly the puppy, after a few days, had to go back as he was having fits. The nursery maid's days also seem numbered as so very stupid. Bill and Peel play squash at Grantham and Uxbridge. In evening finish most of the Christmas cards and letters.

On 15 December Doris the nursery maid, was told to leave on the 20th. Cesca was suffering from pressure and indigestion. On Sunday 17th Cesca went to Dullingham to interview a new nursery maid, Irene Edwards, whom she engages. It was very foggy but less cold.

Tuesday 19 December

Dr Budd came and measured and cross questioned me far more than any London doctor ever has! Seems satisfied. Parcels and letters pouring in. The new nursery maid seems satisfactory. The turkey was ordered and rooms prepared for Mum and Dad who are staying for Christmas. Cook is unpleasant and bolshy for no good reason.

Friday 22 December

Went to meet Mother at station to find terrible calamity had befallen her losing her luggage and bag on the train. Bill eventually rescued her suitcase. Lovely to have her here, and babies very excited.

Saturday 23 December

The cook gave notice, wretched woman, felt she might depart at any moment! Rushed into Cambridge to get particulars of three others whom I interviewed that evening. Dad arrived at 4.30 with the Nig. Very cold, and fires lit in all the rooms.

Christmas Eve

To Kings for the Carol Service. Friends came for good lunch of turbot, roast shoulder of lamb, vegetables and Aunt Nelly pudding and stewed plums and cheese etc.

Christmas Day

Children terribly thrilled and excited over Christmas and all their parcels. Busy opening them from 7.00 onwards as nannie went to early service at St Botolphs. Given £30 from Mother, £25 from Dad. We had a Christmas tree in the drawing room with presents for everyone. Went to Kings in morning.

Boxing Day

Great excitement this morning when I saw a pheasant on the lawn and Bill dashed out in his pyjamas and shot it. Nannie tiresome to a degree and so untidy. Lady Hope [Mary calls her Lady Hopeless] came to dinner and talked incessantly.

Wednesday 27 December

Mother, Dad, Elsie and the Nig left this morning to catch the 10.11 for home via London. All went very well except for the scare over the cook and nannie being rather trying. Went to tea with Lady Hope and there met a lot of ghastly females who I suppose will call on me.

The last day of 1933 finds Cesca worrying over the tiresome cook and temporary nurses and the new baby due in February.

Diary 1934 Leckhampton House and Belstead
Car registration number GP 4348

Cesca is heavily pregnant, unaware that twins will be born in February. Still much occupied by the continuing servant problems.
An operation for a lump on her breast in March is traumatic. Cesca and Bill have a frustrating time house hunting for their ever increasing family and also for her parents (having sold Parham House last September, completion came six months later however. The Ritz Cinema is to be built on the site). Bill unexpectedly passes his Staff College exams. In May they all moved from Leckhampton House to Belstead House near Ipswich rented furnished from the Quilters for £400 for 6 months. The end of the year and the search for houses continues and also for a larger motor car.

Monday I January
My sweethearts both came to wish me a happy New Year. Lunched all together with Nannie in the dining room for a special treat. Roast pheasant, potato balls and stewed celery, apple charlotte and cream. Mother and Dad rang to wish us a Happy New Year. Had two doses of green medicine after a bad night.

Wednesday 3 January
Felt very well so Bill and I went to London 1st class on 9.25 to Kings Cross arriving 11.40. Took taxis all day, (extravagant but less tiring) & went to Marian Jacks where I had my corsets altered. Then Nursery Bureau, interviewing temporary nannies to come whilst N. is on holiday. Engaged one after meeting Mother for an excellent lunch at the Welbeck, Mayfair. Taxi to King's Cross after tea at Gunters. Home by train and Cox to meet us. Hot bath, dinner and bed at 9.30.

Thursday 4 January
Parcel of scents and nice things from Elizabeth Arden! Busy writing to all temporary nannies and cooks.

Friday 5 January

Feel rather upset at thought of Nurse's holiday. New nannie Rose arrived this afternoon. The babies went to meet her train at 3.22 with Nannie.

Saturday 6 January

Nannie departed with Bill in the car this morning. No tears from babies and new nurse seems to be quite satisfactory. To bed early but could not sleep.

Sunday 7 January

Everything seems most satisfactory with the new nannie.

Went out in the garden with them this morning. Then after lunch Bill set off for Frensham to stay with the Millais while he works daily for the Staff College exam. Had tea with the babies. Slept much better.

Monday 8 January

Busy morning doing laundry, then shopping in Cambridge. Jennie left 11.30. New cook arrived for a week, Mrs Casson. After lunch rested. Had taxi to meet Mother 4.00 train. Lovely to have her here, though dull for her. Heard from Bill before bedtime. Not much of a dinner from new cook.

Wednesday 10 January

Cold day. New cook is not very good. However I am lucky to have one, I suppose. Babies are very good with temporary nurse.

Thursday 11 January

Mother and I went to Fitzwilliam Museum in afternoon and I enjoyed seeing silver and pictures. It is all beautifully arranged.

Friday 12 January

Mum and I out in morning. Bill turned up for dinner, a lovely surprise as I did not expect him till tomorrow. All had dinner together. To bed early as Bill very tired.

Saturday 13 January

Bill took Mother to the station. Flt Lt and Mrs Broadhurst to dine. Rather ordinary Air Force couple. A good dinner. Grapefruit, fried slip soles, roast saddle of lamb, potatoes, and celery. Charlotte Russe. Ham on toast. They left early.

Sunday 14 January

Bill went to church at St Botolph's. Not feeling very well, as am so troubled with constipation and usual pressure. Lunched with Lady Hope. Frightful upheaval with Lily owing to her sister's visit in the afternoon. Gave in her notice to Bill. Bad night.

Monday 15 January

Spoke to Lily reducing her to tears, poor girl. Sister must be a terror to all accounts! Then after she had decided to stay, Joyce collapsed, more tears and homesickness! Bill on leave, but working hard all day, poor darling.

Tuesday 16 January

New cook came in yesterday. Appears pretty useless, but says she will stay if I engage a kitchen maid. Suppose I shall have to do so rang up Collins. A nice little girl called Frances Greenacre came with her mother to see me whom I have engaged. Bill works from 9.30-1.00, then either 2-4 or after tea and dinner. Do hope he passes this vile exam, poor dear.

Wednesday 17 January

Dad will come on Monday when Bill has to go to Staff College. New cook given notice. Made me furious, so shall now not have kitchen maid till after she leaves.

Friday 19 January

No word from Nannie so sent her a wire. Had hair washed at Sayles. Heard from Nannie so Nurse Rose left at 3.30, Bill taking her to station. I paid her £3 as she was worth it. Felt very seedy with pains and cramp in the evening and could not get up for dinner. Bill worried about me. Nannie returned 10.pm complete with pram! She much enjoyed her holiday.

Sunday 23 January

Very cold. Big fires in my room, dining room and Bill's study, where he departed to after breakfast until lunchtime. Patricia, (Bill's sister), and Mrs Clarkson arrived at 12.45 in the latter's small car. Clara cooked a passable meal of fish soufflé, roast lamb, celery, potatoes. Apple tart with cream and cheese biscuits, celery and coffee. Bitterly cold after lunch all walked in garden. They stayed for tea then Mrs C. put her feet up on the sofa and slept. Do not like her at all.

Monday 22 January

Bill went off early for London, en route for the Staff College Exam at Uxbridge. Dad arrived at 4.15. Babies well and very good. It is nice to have Nannie back again as she is a great help in the household. Dad worried about Parham House.

Wednesday 24 January

Lily off to London for day and due to thick fog she did not get back till 11.30. Nannie and I waited up for her. Felt worried. Dad went to his old haunts and nearly got lost too in the fog.

Thursday 25 January

Joyce went for her day in town leaving 8.45. Dad left and children, Nannie and I went in the car to the station to see him off. Rested in afternoon. Bill back for dinner, very tired and not very happy about the papers these last two days, poor dear. Gave him green medicine.

Friday 26 January

Very depressed letter from Mum about sale of Parham and all the rumours. Bill and I into Cambridge as he has day off which is lovely. Spent afternoon in drawing room resting and reading.

Sunday 28 January

Bill and I are in despair for a cook. Went to see Mrs Chapman, she agreed to come until I get settled. Dandy and Lena arrived at 1.00 from London for the day. She is a wonderful old lady and was very pleasant. Dr and Mrs Hopkinson came to tea. They are Philip's parents who went to the Golden Parsonage (Prep School) with Bill.

Tuesday 30 January

Bill off in a hurry. Busy getting house ready for guests coming this week. Heard about a cook who I must get Bill to interview in

London on Friday. Clara left and Bill brought Mrs Chapman back with him.

Wednesday 31 January

Busy morning. Mrs Lunn came down for the day to see the children and me.

Bill met her and brought her here for lunch. A treat to have meals properly cooked again. Had fried whiting, roast lamb, salsify and potatoes, devonshire apple, cheese and biscuits.

In the afternoon, Bill and I went into Cambridge leaving her with the children. She left soon after 5.00 having enjoyed her visit.

Thursday 1 February

Paid all maids, which now amounts to quite a lot. Mary Wilson arrived and it was lovely for me to have her to gossip with. Mrs Chapman cooked a good lunch of partridges in casserole, apple soufflé and cream.

Friday 2 February

Mary and Bill left in her car for London. Bill driving. Mary to interview the cook for me. Bill to lunch with John Wilson. Mrs C's husband fell off his bike so she had to go back to Whittlesford.

Saturday 3 February

Mrs Chapman returned with Bill arriving at lunch time. Letter from Mrs Lunn saying how much she had enjoyed her day here. Dined with Lady Hope in the evening and had an excellent dinner. Soup, (clear), fish soufflé, veal, orange sponge and cheese straws and coffee.

Sunday 4 February

Had very good night. Woke up feeling very fit and well. Richard and Fay arrived for lunch their car having given them much trouble. Crawled all the way from Royston. Dr Budd came to see me and appeared very pleased. He didn't think it was twins in spite of my size. Arranged about a nurse. Richard and Fay were very nice and left by train as they could not use their car.

Monday 5 February

Felt very tired so rested in bed. Marian came to lunch and was most awfully nice; asked her to be Godmother to the new baby to which she agreed. Mrs Chapman left and Mrs Boland arrived from London and cooked a very nice dinner. Do hope she is a success. Felt seedy, and no good for anything now.

Tuesday 6 February

Felt wretched most of the day, with pressure and pain. Rested in bed all afternoon. Bill home earlier than expected. Very good dinner and new cook seems to be a success so far.

Thursday 8 February

Went into Cambridge, had my hair washed and set. Babies had lunch with me and then went out in garden. Election Day in Cambridge.

Friday 9 February

Up early in preparation for Mum who arrived at 11.30 with suitcase bulging with things for us all.

For children, toffees and wafers, presents for the new baby, old laces and linens for me. Lovely to have her here. We talked and talked. Then Bill came home and took her to the station.

Saturday 10 February

Bill on weekend leave. Went into Cambridge shopping. Mrs Boland cooked excellent dinner of cream of tomato, Turbot and shrimp sauce, and a perfect cheese soufflé.

Sunday 11 February

Elizabeth (Bill's sister) and Gordon, her husband, came down from Blackheath for lunch and tea. Like him but find her very hard to get on with. Mrs Boland again excelled herself at lunch with eggs in cheese sauce, roast beef with spinach, potatoes, rhubarb tart and cream. Went for walk after lunch. Elizabeth and Gordon stayed for tea and then motored home. Very tired.

Monday 12 February

Our 5th Wedding Anniversary. Time seems to have flown. Had very restless night. Piles awful and such pressure. Out in morning with children. Then lovely box of flowers came from Bill. My wedding bouquet again and a big bunch of mixed carnations. Dad sent a cheque for £25, Mother some lovely glass jam jars and a cheque for £100 for the baby.

Tuesday 13 February

Mother rang up to know how I was. Said I felt much better. Lady Hope came to lunch. Grapefruit, chicken soufflé, carrots in cream, potatoes and pancakes as it is Shrove Tuesday. Rested after lunch. Bill home to tea.

Wednesday 14 February

Woke up at 4.00 with waters gone, most difficult to deal with. Bill rushed up to Nannie and I got settled with a macintosh on the bed. Rang up Budd and London Hospital. Felt quite all right till about 7.15 when nurse from local nursing home came with Bill in thick fog. Then at 8.15 Nurse Griffin arrived and at 8.30 Dr Budd. Pains were not too bad until about 9.30. Then a very bad one and I remembered no more, until I came to, I found I had two sweet little twin daughters. Could not believe it. One weighed 6lbs and the other 5lbs! No wonder I had pressure!

Bill and I feel too thrilled for words. Bill telephoning everyone. Mother arrived to see me and the twins at tea time. Nannie thrilled to the marrow! Went happily to sleep. Lovely now it's over.

Thursday 15 February

The twins are too sweet for words. Cannot get over it at all. One looks like Merlin and Bill and the tiny one like me and I think will have reddish hair. Wires, flowers and congratulations pouring in all day. Announcement in the *Times*. Dad arrived to see the twins and me at tea-time and is most proud. Am starting to feed 3 hourly. Two babies will keep me busy.

Friday 16 February

Letters, parcels and wires, flowers and telephones all day and enquiries for self and the twins.

Dr Budd comes daily and I like him awfully, also Nurse who is excellent with me and the babies. Tiny twin not so well tonight, as she was a breach. She was nearly drowned when born and does not seem very full of vitality and cannot suck. Breasts filling up and am to have them pumped so as to give her a feed in bottle.

Saturday 17 February

Worried over the baby who seems very frail. Dr Budd came and said she was to have brandy at night and to be fed from bottle after being pumped from me. Not feeling quite so well. Still a lot of letters and wires and flowers.

Sunday 18 February

Baby better. The other one is splendid and no trouble.

Monday 19 February

Find this everlasting three hourly feeding of two children terrific and very tiring. Felt tired out at the end of the day. Completely exhausted. Day starts 5.30 with feed for one baby and then pumping for the other. Takes an hour then called with tea 6.45. Blanket bath and toilet 7-8. Breakfast 8. Room done 8.30. Babies again 9-10. 10 Bedpan. 10.30-11 Lying on tummy, then the Doctor, then babies 12-1. Lunch 1. Rest 1.30-3. Babies 3-4. Wash at 4.00 Tea 4.30. Big babies 5-5.30. Babies 6-7. Dinner 7.30. Wash 8-9. Bed 10.

Tuesday 20 February

Pretty exhausting day. Felt so tired and done up and weepy that Dr Budd said babies must have 2 bottles of cows milk and water daily, ie: 12pm and 6pm which will be a great help. Slept after lunch.

Wednesday 21 February

Babies weighed. Tiny one much better and has gained 1 ounce, big one lost 2 ounces. Dr Budd came and is pleased with me. Given me a tonic of iron and makes me rest a lot. Feel better.

Thursday 22 February

Can't believe it's all over & such a lovely result. Twins are marvellous. Feel so happy. Mother came down for afternoon and brought me 2 nightgowns for babies. Bill out all day and evening. Had very bad night listening for him to come in.

Friday 23 February
Household runs very smoothly and I am very happy with my large family.

Monday 26 February
Parcels arriving for Mary's birthday, toffee from Aunt Ruth, shoes from Mrs Lunn, books from Dandy. Lovely day, hate being still in bed, but am feeling well. The twins both very well and I am only feeding three times a day now.

Tuesday 27 February
Mary's 4th Birthday. The dear little girl came in early, and opened some of her parcels with me. Books from me and Bill, also a dress from me from Liberty, a picture from Nanny. Mum and Dad arrived full of gifts. Lovely big cake for Mary and socks from Dad. Spent a very happy day. Lovely having Mum and Dad here too. Dr Budd came in the evening. I asked him if I might have a bath.

Wednesday 28 February
Mum stayed last night. Lovely to have her here to talk to. Bill home for lunch. Mother left after tea.

Thursday 1 March
I walked to my bath tonight, but was carried back. Bill home to tea. Dr Budd came.

Friday 2 March
Babies do not seem to be doing so well on me, so am now feeding only twice a day, 9.am and 9pm. Finished all my letters and started wristlets for my sweet twins.

Monday 5 March
Nurse worried that the babies do not seem to be getting sufficient from me. Must ask Dr Budd if I can wean them completely. Sent parcel of snowdrops to Dandy from Mary and Merlin. Up for tea and walking about the house. Babies sweet.

Tuesday 6 March
Bill out at work. Fed big baby at 9, then Nurse rang up Dr Budd and asked him if I could stop nursing. He said I could so this

evening put on Belladonna plasters and was bound up tight with bandages. Not allowed to drink and must take salts. Felt sad.

Wednesday 7 March

Feeling rather uncomfy and worse in evening. Dr Budd said I might go down to dinner, so Bill carried me up and down. I enjoyed being downstairs very much.

Thursday 8 March

Had rather bad night and breasts painful, but felt better when I got about again. Isobel Durham arrived for tea. It was fun seeing her again. She has chosen the tiny twin as her godchild and is very thrilled with them both. After tea went for a drive with Bill. Dr Budd came in the evening to see me.

Friday 9 March

Twins too sweet for words. I love them more and more. Breasts seem better and more or less cleaned up now, but am still plastered and bandaged up. Bill took me over to Thriplow to see a cot at the Rectory. Decided to have it for 15/-.

Saturday 10 March

Dr Budd came to see the babies and said he wanted me to be out as much as possible. Rested after lunch as usual. Then Bill took me out in the car.

Sunday 11 March

Bill took me to Holy Communion with Nurse at St Botolphs and fetched me. Lovely quiet day with Bill, Mary and Merlin and my sweet twins. Wish I could think of names that we both like that suit them, go with Pearson-Rogers and the other two.

Monday 12 March

Bill on leave. Took me for drive to Cambridge, the Gogs and Fulbourn and then home for lunch. Weather lovely so had central heating turned off. Babies all well. Nurse is so good and nice with the babies too. Feel so awfully well and happy.

Tuesday 13 March

Went for drive again with Bill. Poor Mother is having a really awful time leaving Parham. All her time is taken up with removal of furniture and all the miseries of a move.

Thursday 15 March

Bill off to work as usual. Mrs Lunn here for lunch but her train was late. She came bringing grapes, also presents for the babies and seemed to enjoy herself with the twins who she thought were lovely. Bill home to tea. Took her to the station.

Saturday 17 March

Out in the car and went over to the Mess with Bill. Very cold and wet. Had front of car open for air but it was too cold.

Sunday 18 March

Bill's Birthday.

Noticed small red spot with lump underneath on my breast last night. Nurse rang up Dr Budd about this and I had to stay in bed till he came. I gave Bill a macintosh for his birthday, and his mother sent him some hankies. Dandy, a book on the Indian Mutiny. Ursula came to see the twins. Then Richard and Fay came to lunch bringing the twins two sweet pearl brooches.

Monday 19 March

Bill off in great excitement for Pin Pointing, but weather too bad. Quiet day. Fermentations etc to try and get rid of this wretched lump in my breast.

Tuesday 20 March

Not allowed to go to London as must try and get rid of this lump.

Wednesday 21 March Still keeping very quiet. Dr Budd came and saw my breast and still advises antiflogistine and to keep very quiet. Bill had pin pointing again.

Thursday 22 March

Bill heard they are in finals of pin pointing. Breast appears no better. Busy getting Mother's room ready. Nannie in London for the day.

Friday 23 March

Mary and Marian came to spend the day arriving in Marian's car. Mary bought Merlin an awfully nice milk lorry. Mrs Richards sent me two sweet frocks for the twins. They loved the twins and suggested calling them Sara and Anne. Do not care for those names much.

Saturday 24 March

Dr Budd came again. He does not think my breast will improve. Told me to go to bed for 24 hours and if it does not subside Mr Bowen will operate. Miserable outlook. Bill went off at 8.25 to fetch Mother in the car from Parham House. Found Mother in an empty Parham and together they packed all the things into the car and got here at teatime. Sickening being in bed. Dad staying on at Calverley.

Sunday 25 March

Dr Budd came to see me and decided to operate. I had to rest in afternoon, and felt very unhappy about having an operation. At 5.30 Dr B. came and gave me gas then Dr Bowen, Senior Surgeon at Addenbrooks came and cut open my breast. The pain afterwards was too awful and I bled all over the place. At 9.30 they came back again. This time I had a proper anaesthetic and they operated again. I felt so ill and slept all night. Nurse stayed with me and nannie with the twins.

Monday 26 March

Very sick and still feel pretty seedy, but had glucose and black coffee and then chicken jelly. Dr Budd then came twice to see me. Better in the evening. Mother here and very sweet and helpful. Bill home in evening. Feel so weak.

Tuesday 27 March

Dr Budd and Mr Bowen came again to remove packing from my breast and stitch it up. Had gas again but no pain this time and felt all right only still very weak. Mother and Bill with me a lot. Babies flourishing.

Wednesday 28 March

Feeling better but still very weak. Bill home for lunch. Mother in London and worried about completion of sale of Parham House.

Thursday 29 March

Up for tea, just for an hour, but felt so weak had to go back to bed. Mother heard by wire from Hughes the completion of sale was finalised. Rang up Dad to tell him and heard he has Nigger put down. He arrives on Saturday.

Saturday 31 March

Feeling a bit better. Wound healing up now. Lily gave notice after having day off. Went for a walk in garden and a drive in the car to Newmarket with Mother and Bill.

Sunday 1 April

Dr Budd came. Up for lunch, then rested and up again for tea and supper. Mother and Dad went to Kings Chapel. Dad very difficult. He has not said a word to Mother since he came.

Tuesday 3 April

New under nurse Lillian Heard arrived and seems a nice girl, bright and brisk. Sleeping with the children and no tears or upsets.

Saturday 7 April

Dr Budd says I may go to Brighton to see the house Bill likes tomorrow.

Monday 9 April

Off to Brighton by 10 train from here. Arrived Liverpool St 11.30 and Brighton 1.15. Stayed at the Albion and had excellent lunch there. Then Mum and I hired large, comfy Daimler and motored over to see Westergate House, near Arundel [built in 1820's, now a care home]. Were both very disappointed.

Tuesday 10 April

Mother and I went for blow along the front, before returning to town. Enjoyed our little visit to the sea and feel much better for the change. Went to see the agents about the houses and suggested that we concentrate on Norfolk & Suffolk as it is less far to go with twins. Went also to Trollope & John D. Wood. Lunched at Gunters and returned to Cambridge. Felt upset at thought of Nurse leaving tomorrow and hope my twins will be all right.

Wednesday 11 April er

Wept and wept. Feel upset that Nurse is leaving. She left at 10.50. However twins and Nannie seem all right.

Thursday 12 April

Felt much better. Mother and I took children in the car to see Dane End, Little Munden (once home of Lord Gladstone, now Grade 11 listed and used for deaf people). The house itself most attractive, but would not do for summer. Mary very sick all the way home in the car, and Merlin not looking well.

Saturday 14 April

Bill and I spent a delightful day together seeing houses. Went in the car to see Belstead House, nr Ipswich which we liked better than any other house. One great advantage is its distance to the sea. Then to Aldeburgh where both houses were quite hopeless. Then to Finborough Hall, Stowmarket which though a lovely house was too dilapidated for us.

Monday 16 April

Mother and I went off house-hunting. Mother had been told by Lady Hope that Kings Lynn was delightful, so we went there but thought it quite vile! Lunched at Dukes Head. Off after lunch to see Old Hall, Snettisham owned by Sir Peter Strickland whom we remembered from Mena Days, in Egypt. Awful house, tumbledown and depressing, then to Hunstanton where we saw and loved the Hall. Most attractive and feel we must take it. Lovely Tudor house. Home much cheered.

Tuesday 17 April

Busy day getting straight and altering the nurseries. Also preparing for the twin's christening on Saturday.

Wednesday 18 April

Bill and I off to Hunstanton to see the Hall. [Seat of the le Strange family, moated]. Awful wet day and cold. Lunched on arrival at Hunstanton at Golden Bell (poor). Then went over the house and saw the agent Mr Dixon. Bill did not much care for the house which he thinks is spooky. Motored home feeling depressed and cold.

Thursday 19 April

Up early to breakfast with Bill. Caught 8.25 to town and went to Miss Gold for evening dress renovations. Then M. Jacks new corset, Ivy Hudson new hat, Harvey Nicholls new stockings and gloves. And bonnets and new suit for Merlin. Lunched at Gunters. Heard from the Dean of Kings that he will christen the twins on Saturday 12.30- so rang up all godparents.

Friday 20 April

Quiet day. Letter writing and ordering for tomorrow's events. Spoke to Frances and Joyce, both of whom are coming with me to house we take for summer. Mother and Dad off to Hunstanton for day and Dad came back loathing it. However decided to make an offer of £300 guineas for 6 months.

Saturday 21 April

My little girls christening. Busy morning preparing. Took babies, Nannie, Lillian, Mary and Merlin with Mum, Dad, Bill, the Durhams, Fay and Richard, Lady Hope to Kings.

They were christened by the Dean of Kings, the Rev. Eric Milner-White CBE. DSO [military chaplain during WW1], in the Founders Chancel. And are named Clare (big twin) and Cecily Rose (tiny twin). Both babies howled and were very naughty. Back here for lunch. Julie cooked excellent lunch of salmon mayonnaise, lettuce and tomato, chicken creamed with peas & new carrots, potatoes and spinach. Fruit salad, cream and steamed pudding, coffee. The Pecks stayed to tea and the others left early.

Monday 23 April

Our offer of £375 for Hunstanton not accepted. Mother in London. Bill away at Pin Pointing and Attack Competition Finals. Awful crash there and two killed. (This they did not tell me till the morning). The Pellys came to dinner after arriving at Duxford and settling in to 21 Madingley Road. Good dinner- soup, fish soufflé, roast loin of lamb and loganberry cream.

Tuesday 24 April

My little Merlin's 3rd Birthday. Lots of parcels, letters, cards and wires for him. Mother gave him a large Birthday Cake with candles. Merlin had tea party. Jane Pelly, Teddy Wales with their nurses and Lillian, Mother, Mary, Mrs Waller and me in drawing room. W.C. Commander Waller, the Burleighs, John, Dad and Bill in sitting room for tennis.

Wednesday 25 April

Announcement of twins christening in *Times* and *Morning Post*. Went off early in the car to Ipswich to look at houses. Went to Bentley Manor and saw quite a nice house. John, Mother and I had lunch at White Hart at Ipswich. Then saw Belstead and then home for tea. Made offer for Bentley Manor of £350 for 6 months. Dinner, soup, roast lamb, orange cream and cheese soufflé.

Thursday 16 April

John Peel left with Bill and Dad. Mother and I spent morning together. Spent afternoon tidying up and getting straight before Bill's departure for Scotland. Dad home for dinner.

Friday 27 April

Felt as usual utterly miserable at Bill's departure and wept bitterly. He left for 10 days in Scotland. Offer of £350 for the house at Bentley was refused. Made offer for Belstead £275 for 6 months.

Saturday 28 April

Mr Hempson, the house agent, has refused offer for Belstead so I increased to £325. This also he refused so I made final offer of £350 with option of continuing. Out with Mother in morning and in afternoon went to Kings to Dedication of organ by Bishop of Lincoln. Mother with earache so put her to bed after oil in ear, hot bath and a fire.

Monday 30 April

Mother rang up Mr Hempson and made further offer of £400 for 6 months which he submitted. Later we had a wire to say it was accepted. Felt very pleased and relieved.

Tuesday 1 May

Miss Bill very much and it already seems ages since he went away. Sent him a wire to let him know we had Belstead.

Wednesday 2 May

Heard the most staggering and astonishing news that Bill has passed the Staff College. I am delighted and sent him a wire as soon as I had heard from John. Wrote to Bill and feel so happy he has passed.

Thursday 3 May

Mary complaining of feeling sick, poor child. She was sick several times too, poor dear.

I stayed with her all afternoon. Mary sleeping in my room.

Friday 4 May

Mary with temperature and in bed all day. Castor oil was effective, but still very sick, poor child.

Miss Bill terribly. Wrote to him for last time in Scotland. Mary sleeping with Mother, as I have temperature of 100 and am going to bed.

Saturday 5 May

I was afraid I was in for flu yesterday but three aspirins, sleeping in blankets with two hot water bottles has cured it. Mary is still seedy, but no longer sick. Went with Mother to Ipswich, met by Mr Hempson, who took us to Belstead in his car, showed us round the gardens and cottages and we saw Mr R Quilter (owner). We returned by 12.22 and home for late tea.

Monday 7 May

Great excitement when Bill flew over the house in formation just before lunch. Merlin and I went to collect him in the Austin. Lovely to have him home. Had nice dinner.

Tuesday 8 May

Bill and I set off to London early. Stay at the Mayfair and lunched there, then went shopping in Bond Street with Bill and had my hair done at Douglas. Joined Bill for tea at the Mayfair, then rested. Had very bad earache before going to "Reunion in Vienna" which we both enjoyed at the Lyric. Then to Café de Paris where we were joined by Jim and Gabriel for supper.

Wednesday 9 May

Woke about 8.00. Cough and throat bad but earache gone. Love my darling Bill who is so good to me. Morning spent shopping and ordering of dresses. Went to Miss Gray and ordered an evening frock there. Lovely. Lunched with Mary and John, motored back to Cambridge to find Mary better and twins well.

Thursday 10 May

Busy preparing for move all day. Had babies photographed in afternoon as it was such a lovely day. To bed early, cough very bad, so had hot mustard plaster and milk before going to bed.

Saturday 12 May

Very busy finishing off preparations for leaving here. Paid up all the bills at various shops.

Sunday 13 May

Went to church with Bill at Duxford. Then Bill and I then went home. Our last day at Leckhampton which is more sad than I can say. Can hardly believe it possible as it seems only yesterday that we arrived, me so fat and tired with the twins, then their birth and progress ever since.

Monday 14 May

Up very early. Everything done and ready for the bus arriving at 8.30. We had hired a 32 seater coach from Weedon with all but 8 seats removed. At 10.30, it moved off loaded with four maids, three nurses, four children and all luggage. Prams, silver, linen, toys, groceries, ironing boards, cots etc. Bill and I followed in the Standard. Mother and Dad with Smith later in afternoon. Arrived at Belstead at 12.30. Found Mrs Quilter's butler and her gardeners there to help us. Everything in order and we are most thrilled with the house and grounds. Almost straight by evening.

Tuesday 15 May

Bill and I off to Ipswich at 9.00. He returned to Duxford and I busy shopping and ordering all morning in Ipswich. Tried to get servants which seem very scarce, in the hope of being suited before Whitsun. Spent afternoon getting rooms straight; I have a lovely room and Bill a dressing room close to mine. Mother at the end of another wing with bathroom and Dad near her. Dad being difficult and unpleasant over the new house which I think divine.

Wednesday 16 May

Bill away at Cambridge and miss him very much. Dad has engaged chauffeur, P. Sturgeon arriving Friday. Mr Gurney called and is charming.

Thursday 17 May

Sturgeon arrived and is taking top cottage for himself and his wife. Mother and I out for walk in afternoon. Simply love this place.

Friday 18 May

Went to search for maids in Shotley. Car driven by new chauffeur who drove very safely. Bill arrived back at 9.00 Together we went to Hintlesham and engaged Albert (youth I saw this morning) to come to help us over Whitsun. Lily departed tearfully this afternoon. Lovely to have my love back again.

Saturday 19 May

Must make most of this lovely leave with Bill. Took Mary into Ipswich with Mother in the car to have her hair cut. Town very full with trippers about but Belstead is perfect peace and away from it all. Albert the boy seems quite good. Spent a lovely day with Bill and children. The Milbanks called.

Sunday 20 May

Mother went off to early service. The rest of us went at 11.00 and enjoyed a quiet country service at Belstead Church about one and a half miles across the fields. Met the Gurneys there. Home for excellent luncheon. Out for walk with Bill. Love this place as it is so quiet and restful in perfect country, comfy house and lovely big garden.

Tuesday 22 May

Nannie off to London to say goodbye to her Mother, who is going to Australia. Very tiresome, as I am so very busy. And she returned to find me pretty exhausted. Bill, Mother and Dad went to tea at the Gurneys. Very hot day.

Wednesday 23 May

Bill and I went to London to engage servants. Went to Miss Gray for fitting, lunched with Mary Wilson at Gunters in Berkeley Square. Went to Mrs Beauchamps to interview servants. Back very tired to Ipswich on 5.15 Met by Sturgeon.

Thursday 24 May

Went to Ipswich in the car with Bill at 9.45. Car went wrong. A smell of burning rubber but all was well. Stopped at Collins Agency about servants, then on to Cambridge. And to lunch with Margaret Pelly who was charming. Went to Duxford in their car and enjoyed the Pageant. Claud taking part. Bill and I motored home together and had excellent cold supper on our return.

Friday 25 May

After lunch Dr Pretty came and vaccinated my twins. Do not much care for him. Bill and I motored over to Long Melford and then to Bury to see housemaids.

Saturday 26 May

Paid Julie and sent her with her luggage into station. Met Mother and her new Dandy puppy that she has called Pepper and was in a large box. Met the new cook who looks awful and new head housemaid who looks excellent.

Sunday 27 May

Richard and Fay rang to arrange to come over for lunch today. Very pleased to see them again and loved having them here.

Monday 28 May

Had a busy morning looking for cooks as this Mrs Bennet is so impossible. Found no one suitable. Albert, too is tiresome. Went to tea with the Milbanks, they live in a most depressing old house below Belstead, called Belstead Brook. Dad rather difficult and tiresome.

Tuesday 29 May

Went to London by train to Pierre and Miss Gray's for fittings. Then I went to Mrs Beauchamps, Miss Webb and Town and Country Bureau where I saw and engaged Mrs Hunt, a cook. Bought new corsets, belt and bust bodice and a new white jersey. Then home at 6.15 where Bill met me. Then interviewed under-nurse whom I engaged.

Wednesday 30 May

Went to Bury St Edmunds to see another cook in case Mrs Hunt does not materialize. Also interviewed a nursery maid, then to Bardwell where I saw two housemaids and engaged them. Fay and Richard arrived after lunch. Bill and Richard played singles. Fay and Richard stayed to dinner.

Thursday 31 May

This awful cook gets worse and worse and I can't bear Cresswell, the head housemaid and so gave her notice. Babies legs reacting badly to their vaccinations.

Friday 1 June

Poor babies are very seedy, Cecily especially, poor child. Spent quiet day with Bill.

Saturday 2 June

Paid Mrs Bennett and Cresswell who left together thank heaven! Went over in the Austin to Frinton where we all had lunch at the Esplanade. Back for tea after meeting new cook, Mrs Hunt at the station. Thank heaven a good cook at last. She cooked a good dinner and is very clean.

Monday 4 June

Bill's last day. Went into Ipswich and shopped in morning with Mother and Sturgeon. Spent afternoon in garden. Saw Bill off up the drive after dinner on his way back to Duxford. Dad in London, still very difficult.

Wednesday 6 June

We listened to the Derby on wireless after lunch. Went to tea with Mrs Gurney at Stone Lodge and she came back with me to see the babies.

Thursday 7 June

Shopped in Ipswich in the car with Mother and Sturgeon. Met Bill at Martlesham. The Dorries came to tea. She has found me a parlour maid and I hope she will be a success. She is Sturgeon's sister in law. Lovely having Bill here, even for only one night as he is on duty this weekend.

Friday 8 June

Took Nannie, Merlin and Mary with me in the car to Martlesham to see Bill off and watched him fly away and saw the other aeroplanes. Bottled 24 bottles of gooseberries. Mrs Hunt is excellent at this.

Saturday 9 June

Letter from Bill telling me he is not going to Andover in Jan. Felt disappointed. Spent evening with my babies in the garden. Babies photos have arrived and I sent some of them to Dandy, Mrs Lunn and one to Nurse Griffin.

Sunday 10 June

Went over to Cambridge to spend the day with Bill.. Very hot day. Went out to Duxford, walked about the aerodrome with Bill and had lunch in the Mess. Then back to Cambridge and spent the afternoon with the Pellys. Bill and Claude played tennis. After tea Bill took me to the station. He is very disappointed over not going to Andover.

Monday 11 June

Cook making jam and bottling the gooseberries. Pellys came to dinner on their way back from house hunting at Thorpeness.

Tuesday 12 June

Left for 10.00 train to London to stay with Fay and Richard. Took up large basket of roses for Fay and left my luggage there, afterwards going to Miss Gold. Then called at Durhams and invited them down here next week. Went back to the flat and had good dinner. Fay has an excellent cook and seems happily settled.

Wednesday 13 June

Went to Ivy Hudson's, Miss Gray's and Bond Street, then lunched with Aunt Edie. I did not stay long, but hurried back to West End to continue shopping. Had tea at my club, then more shopping before returning to flat to rest. We dined at the RAC before going to Mary Queen of Scots which Richard, Fay and I all thoroughly enjoyed.

Thursday 14 June

Very hot and airless. Went to Miss Gold for fitting and then lunch with Richard and Fay. Then Bill arrived and we changed, but could not wear my new dress from Miss Gray as it was not right, so I wore my black. Dined with Richard and Fay. Then Bill and I went to see Mary and John before going to the Seligman's dance which was extremely well done and quite enjoyable.

Friday 15 June

Woke up very sleepy indeed, could hardly open my eyes. Bill and I packed and left Richard and Fay. I went to Miss Gray's to return my wretched dress, and Bill to Sandons. Then we set off in the little motor and got back to Belstead. Found Margaret Pelly had arrived. Spent busy afternoon preparing for weekend. Reggie arrived at 7.30 by car and Claud about 10.00 in his car.

Saturday 16 June

Most lovely day. Claud, Margaret, Reggie and Mother in Claud's car and Bill and I in ours all went over to bathe at Felixstowe. Mother and I did not bathe, everyone else did, then home to lunch. Tennis after tea. Everyone enjoying themselves. Mrs Hunt cooked quite nicely. Hilda very good and house running smoothly.

Dinner, salmon, (hot), mayonnaise, roast chickens, peas, potatoes. Strawberry ice and angels on horseback.

Sunday 17 June

Absolutely grilling day. Claude, Margaret and Reggie went to Felixstowe to bathe. Turners and Gurneys came to tea and tennis. Almost too hot to play. Mrs Hunt made lovely cakes. Reggie and Claude went off at 5.00. Bill decided to stay the night.

Monday 18 June

Bill left at dawn. Margaret left after breakfast. Mother went off to London; so I had the house to myself to clear up and get straight before fresh visitors arrive tomorrow. Dad and I lunched together. Bombshell! Mrs Hunt gave notice this morning.

Tuesday 19 June

Both Hilda and Kathleen also gave notice. The former to get married. Tiresome women.

Wednesday 20 June

Children are all happy and jolly in the garden. Bill came over for the afternoon and evening. Mother has bought herself a most lovely necklace from Shaplands. It is lovely being such a happy family. Dad went off to Tunbridge Wells yesterday.

Thursday 21 June

Bill left at again at dawn. Twins are sweet, so pretty and good and Mary and Merlin are really model children. Mrs Hunt very trying and inclined to be rude.

Friday 22 June

Mother went to London for the day. So I had the morning to myself with the babies. Left by 12.25 for London taking large box of roses with me for Dandy. Went to Hugo's. Arrived Dandy's at teatime. Bill arrived soon after and we changed. (I wore my new dress from Miss Gray). Then we went in car to the Naval Ball at Greenwich. Dined first with Elizabeth and Gordon at Blackheath. Badly organised dance. Did not much enjoy it.

Saturday 23 June

Feeling very, very sleepy and tired after last night. Could not find my watch or my brooch and felt very worried. Packed up and left after waiting in vain for cook. Dandy packed us a lovely lunch. Then back to Belstead at three. Cook inclined to be rude.

Tuesday 26 June

Mrs Hunt more pleasant so got her to make strawberry and gooseberry jam. Have made 84lbs since we have been here.

Wednesday 27 June

Mrs Hunt absolutely impossible. So rude and insolent and refused to do her work. So after great difficulty turned her out with her wages and was thankful to see the last of her. Spent quiet day with Mother and children. Went over to East Bergholt to see another Cook. Tramp in the evening called at house and later we found he had taken the garage key.

Thursday 28 June

Present of a pound of Earl Grey tea for me from Bill, sweets for children and scent for Mother. Mrs Paton, Scotch cook from Miss Webb came this afternoon.

Friday 29 June

Busy morning seeing the new cook, before leaving for the station and arriving in London 11.30. Then going straight to Fay's where I left flowers and suitcase. Shopping and lunch with Fay then tea with Bill who arrived back from Hendon. Lovely to see him again. He and Richard out to dine at RAF dinner Club. Fay and I dined alone.

Saturday 30 June

I bought a very pretty purple evening dress. Then out to Hendon to the Pageant. Arrived there at 11:30. Bill was on duty as reserve for leader of smoke display but did not have to fly. Display marred by crash when Sqd Leader Collett (Lord Mayors son), was killed. Saw Pat and Peter and Gordon Hubback. Met few other friends. 19 Sqd's smoke display was lovely. Back at seven, changed and went out with Richard, Fay and Bill to Café de Paris for dinner.

Sunday 1 July

Felt very sleepy but back at Belstead, via Epping, Chelmsford and Colchester, the lovely Suffolk air made us feel quite well and fresh again. Mother tiresome over new Cook whom she seems to have upset.

Monday 2 July

Preparations and excitement for Royal Show are tremendous. Paid Nanny, Lillian, Frances, Joyce and Irene. Mrs Paton the new temporary Scotch cook a great success and excellent cook. Ronnie Quilter arrived after tea having motored down from London. Like him very much. He and Bill also seem to get on. Out in the garden after dinner.

Tuesday 3 July

The Royal [this was the Royal Agricultural Show which moved to different venues annually] opened this morning at Chantry Park. Bill and I went up with our season tickets and enjoyed a lovely morning there. Ronnie has also given us seats for the Royal Box and two more complimentary tickets. Ronnie left in evening.

Wednesday 4 July

Went into Ipswich shopping and had frightful job returning as HRH [the Prince of Wales] coming, streets were absolutely packed. A queue stretched from the station to the Showground. Bill and I went up before lunch for an hour. I also sent Nannie. Mary and John arrived having motored down from London. After lunch Mary and Bill went to the Royal Box, the rest of us in stand seats.

Friday 6 July

Went shopping in Ipswich. Bill, Mary and John went to the Show and the children went with Mother this morning. This lovely week of leave seems to be going very fast. Played tennis after tea.

Saturday 7 July

Mary and John left after breakfast to go to Wimbledon. Have so much enjoyed having them here. Then Bill and I went to the Show and again after lunch with the children to watch the jumping and trick riding from the Royal Box. Richard and Fay arrived both very hot after the heat of London.

Sunday 8 July

Bill, Mother and I to Belstead church. Richard and Fay in the garden. The Schreibers all came to tennis. Excellent cakes by Mrs Paton. Richard and Faye left after supper returning to London taking lots of fruit, vegetables and flowers. Bill decided to stay his last night of leave returning in the morning.

Monday 9 July

Bill left for Duxford early. Frying day. Mrs Paton furious with Frances who went away for the night and left her room filthy, chamber pot un-emptied etc. Disgraceful girl.

Thursday 12 July

Very hot and sultry. Mitty and her husband Charles Williams came. She has not improved with time and is definitely old, ugly, very argumentative and bossy. Had a very good dinner white soup fried sole, roast chicken new potatoes and peas. Very well cooked.

Friday 13 July

As I anticipated the parlourmaid gave notice, says she has too much to do. So my search begins again. Mitty's daughter Brenda, aged 18 arrived and is remarkably tall, six foot and not bad looking. Frightful thunderstorm in afternoon that flooded the entire kitchen premises and passage and nearly reached the dining room but Sturgeon, Southgate and Ely swept the water away from the house.

Saturday 14 July

Went into Ipswich shopping with Bill in the car, Dad bringing Mitty, Charles and Brenda. Then Mother took them all to Felixstowe. She returned in a very bad temper before dinner. Bill and I had the afternoon to ourselves. Excellent dinner of rice soup, roast chicken, beans, vanilla ice. Coffee.

Sunday 15 July

Dad's 75th birthday. Good lunch. Forequarter, beans, potatoes, raspberry and blackcurrant tart, cream and a beautiful cheddar cheese sent by John. Play tennis before and after tea till dinner. Bill left after dinner to return to Duxford to Sutton Bridge.

Monday 16 July

The Williams have departed. Thankful to see the back of them as they are without exception the most selfish, tiresome and greedy guests. Dad dropped them at the station then the car returned to take me to the dentist.

Wednesday 18 July

Miss my darling very much, heard from him. Sutton Bridge appears to be pretty foul. Dad and I had lunch together. Francis ran a skewer through the back of her hand. Fortunately got Dad to come and help bandage it up.

Friday 20 July

Have a bad head-ache. To bed in afternoon taking a cachet but still felt very seedy, hot and cold all over. Jim and Gabriel arrived for dinner, Bill soon after. Lovely to see him, but not feeling very well.

Saturday 21 July

Still felt seedy with headache and temperature. Claud and Margaret came to lunch and play tennis with Captain and Mrs Wise. I took aspirins before lunch and two more before going to bed.

Sunday 22 July

Felt much better. Jim, Gabriel, Mother and Dad all went to church. Bill and I stayed at home and did accounts. Very hot. Jim and Gabriel left after dinner. Bill decided to stay the night.

Monday 23 July

Bill left at dawn for Duxford where they have war and night flying for this week. Mrs Davies arrived for tea with her chauffeur at 4:15. Chauffeur to sleep above Mrs Paton and Frances. Mrs Davies very charming and nice in every way.

Tuesday 24 July

Shopped in Ipswich with Mrs Davies and Mother, returning for lunch. Mrs Davies took us all over to Aldeburgh and Thorpeness in her Vauxhall driven by Kirby. Had tea with the Ian Smiths at the Dolphin.

Thursday 2 August

Went to Lord Woodbridge's garden party with the Gurneys. He is an old man of 70 and his daughter is 21, wife in asylum and sons killed in the war.

Friday 3 August

Nurse Griffin came for the day, to see the twins. Took her to the station in the evening and gave her a large parcel of jellies, jams and gooseberries to take to her sister.

Saturday 4 August

To Bury St. Edmunds by train and on to Thetford where my darling Billy met me. We spent a heavenly afternoon together at Brandon and motored slowly from there to Bury where we had tea at the Angel and so to Belstead for dinner. Do love my Bill so very much.

Wednesday 8 August

Nanny away for a day so took her to station in the car. Then the car fused, smoke came out and I, in a panic, got the babies out and left Sturgeon to it, while I, Merlin and Mary returned by bus and was met by Irene in the lane with pram. Sturgeon soon mended it and all was well. Picked peaches after tea.

Tuesday 14 August

Out for long walk with Bill. Mrs Paton gave us an excellent dinner, turbot, shrimp sauce, roast saddle of lamb, roast potatoes, cauliflower. Peach melba and ice.

Wednesday 15 August

Mother and Dad returned from house hunting and have seen a house they like, Newton House. Gave Mrs Paton notice and wrote for reference.

Sunday 26 August

My 30th birthday. Mother gave me a lovely set of beautiful bird plaques. And an attractive dispatch case which will be most useful. Mary and Merlin gave me ribbons and a pincushion with a robin on it. Dad gave me £25 and Bill some very lovely bags. Enjoyed my day. Spent the day with the children and had tea party together.

Monday 27 August

Busy before leaving for London at 9:30 in car, Sturgeon having taken luggage in earlier. Arrived at Euston Hotel which was comfy, if dirty. Lunched at Fortnum & Mason. Had my hair washed, set and eyebrows shaped at Harvey Nichols. Met Bill at Club before dining at Quaglinos, then going to "Family Affairs" at Ambassadors. This made us laugh till we cried.

Tuesday 28 August

Woke up feeling very thrilled at the prospect of our trip to Glasgow. Left by Royal Scot at 10.00 which arrived at Glasgow 5.40 non-stop except changing engines at Carlisle. Lovely carriage all to ourselves. Bought nice papers, books and chocolate and had a delightful day together. Lunch and tea on the train before arriving and met by Peggy Heathcote and Beale. They motored us to Carbeth, most perilously and we arrived half dead with fright at 6:30 to find Mary and John. Mr and Mrs Richards making up the rest of the party. Lovely bedroom, but upset at having twin beds instead of a nice double one.

Wednesday 29 August

Bill went shooting with John. Peggy and I accompanied them on the lower ground and we had a lovely walk together till lunchtime. Played bridge before going to bed.

Thursday 30 August

I went out with guns in afternoon and we had a very pleasant time. Shot snipe, duck, hares and rabbits. Played bridge. Mary's cook is poor, her other maids are good. The house is very comfy.

Saturday 1 September

Lovely day. Out shooting all day with Bill, John and Mr Richards in the morning doing low ground for partridge. Lunch at Carbeth. Had quite a good bag getting 11 ½ brace of partridge, plenty of hares, rabbits and snipe. Bill shooting very well.

Tuesday 4 September

Went over in two cars, Daimler and the Austin to Fort William to inspect Lochaber Power Station and Aluminium Works. Most interesting. Had lunch there and came home by Glencoe. Arrived back at Carbeth in time for late dinner. To bed soon after, felt tired and dizzy from too much motoring.

Wednesday 5 September

Last day in this lovely spot in dear Scotland. Out shooting all afternoon. Packing after tea.

Thursday 6 September

Goodbye to Carbeth. Perilous drive into Glasgow. Caught Royal Scot, had carriage to ourselves and a lovely trip South. Had lunch and tea and arrived at Euston 5.40 then to Liverpool Street and home by 6.39 after changing at Colchester. Met by Sturgeon with the Austin. All well at home except we are without a nursery maid.

Friday 7 September

Getting straight. Bill did desk and accounts. I went into Ipswich shopping, ordering, and also tried to get nursery maid. Excellent dinner by Mrs Paton. Soup, roast partridges, chips, cauliflower and gooseberry fool.

Saturday 8 September

Up early for breakfast and left Belstead 8.15 to motor to Duxford for delightful day's partridge shooting. Had lovely day, very hot. The Wallers have 450 acres. We got 16 brace partridges, 10 hares, 1 duck, in five hours. Good lunch. Motored home for tea. Saw babies who had been to Felixstowe.

Tuesday 11 September

Mother and Dad went to London so Bill and I spent the day together and played tennis in the afternoon. A lovely autumn day.

Wednesday 12 September

Bill and I spent the morning together. Mother rather cross and difficult. Took Ergot as worried about period due soon. Bill left after tea to go to this new station Hornchurch, poor darling. Felt sad and miserable, took more Ergot. (A medication/poison to encourage miscarriage).

Thursday 13 September

Pains and discomfort last night. Off to London and shopped all day. London is so hot and tiring. Got children's undies for winter and shoes. Home by 6.20 tired out, in great pain and but no period yet. Awfully worried.

Friday 14 September

After a ghastly night of worry, misery, heat and pain inside, period came on and I have never felt so absolutely thankful and relieved. Ran down and telephoned Bill at 8:15. Told Mum and Dad, both thankful. Stayed in bed till 11.00.

Saturday 15 September

Bill and I in Ipswich shopping. Mrs Patton very tiresome so is Mother. Had headache so decided to go to the sea with Bill, Mary and Merlin. Home for tea. Richard and Fay arrived soon after. Loved seeing them, both such easy and nice guests.

Sunday 16 September

Mother and Dad's 43rd Wedding Anniversary. Both went to church, Mother rather cross and difficult. Bill returned to Hornchurch after dinner.

Monday 17 September

Went into Ipswich with Richard and Fay in their car. Both looking for antiques. I like Fay and Richard immensely. Mother better tempered. Mrs Paton worse.

Tuesday 18 September

Taking my glucose again. Mrs Paton very difficult. Shall have to get another cook soon as I cannot put up with her much longer. Worried about Bill all alone at Hornchurch which he says is quite vile.

Wednesday 26 September

Went by train to London and went straight to Hotel Meurice where they gave us a very lovely room for the night and every comfort.

Went to Harvey Nichols and had my hair set and bought dresses for the twins. Came back, had dinner and danced at Quaglinos.

Thursday 27 September

Bill and I up early, then he went off to Hornchurch. Home and met by Sturgeon.

Saturday 29 September

Wire from Patricia asking whether she and Peter [Bill's sister and brother] might come up tomorrow.

Sunday 30 September

Pat and Peter arrived together in Peter's brand-new Lagonda which Bill fell in love with. Pat rather tiresome and 'know all'. Bill's new company Squadron leader, Goden, [No19 Fighter Squadron, Duxford] came over in his own aeroplane to lunch.

Wednesday 3 October

Bill rang to let us know he was arriving by air at Martlesham and Sturgeon and I went to meet him. Motored home and had lunch.

Saturday 6 October

Nanny in London. The clocks back an hour. Summer Time over.

Monday 8 October

Bill off to Martlesham and returned to Hornchurch by air. Mrs Paton agitated over her room which she says is cold and damp.

Tuesday 9 October

Went up to London with Mother. Took taxi to Fay's flat with suitcase and box of mushrooms. Went with Bill and Mother to the wedding at St Margaret's Westminster, Ronnie Quilter marrying Doreen Parker. On to reception at Cadogan Gate then Bill and I went to the agents about 2 Walton Place.

Monday 15 October

Mrs Paton says she must leave week after next. Plague! Busy trying to find another cook to take her place.

Tuesday 16 October

Wet morning and cold. New girl came last evening but do not think much of her so far. Arrived minus luggage and with a cold.

Wednesday 17 October

Mother and I went to London to Diana Ferguson's wedding. Lunched with Mum at Gunters then we went to Golanski where Mum gave me the most lovely Chinese Lamb coat with Fox collar. Simply lovely! Then to Diana's wedding. I wore the coat. Deadly people there, on to tea at Mary Wilson's where I met Bill and he took me to Liverpool Street Station.

Thursday 18 October

Descaling of water system being done. Most tiresome and makes everything bitterly cold. No baths.

Friday 19 October

Went off before lunch to spend weekend with the Styles at Boxley. Joined Bill at Romford and had tea there which was nice and then to Boxley. All very jolly. Big bed and comfy room with fire.

Saturday 20 October

Bill out shooting with Mr Styles. Lovely day though cold. I was out all day and enjoyed all except Bill's shooting which was atrocious and depressed me more than I can say. Good bag of 20 brace partridge and about seven brace pheasants.

Monday 22 October

Left Boxley. Went to Harrods who have let 2 Walton Place for us again at 10 guineas a week for three months. Came home, felt seedy and went to bed early. Found Mother in bed with a bad cold and all children too.

Friday 26 October

Mrs Paton left at 12.00. Shall miss her and feel quite sad losing such a good cook. Mrs Marshall arrived. Went with Mother to Lavenham which is a completely unspoiled little Suffolk town

Monday 29 October

Mother and I felt desperate and went up to London on 10 o'clock train. Mother ordered a new evening dress. Went to all agents about houses. Lunched at Gunters returning home by train.

Friday 2 November

Mother and I decided to go and see Abingdon Hall at Cambridge. Went over by train and took a picnic lunch which we ate in the train. Arrived at Abington and saw all over the house which we had seen before, this time last year. Liked it and think it has enormous possibilities. But is of course in very bad condition.

Monday 5 November

Went up to London by train taking Joyce with me. I arrived at 2 Walton Place at 2.00. Inventory taking place. House filthy. Spent nearly all day there except for lunch. I returned to Durhams for dinner. So depressed at finding the house so filthy.

Tuesday 6 November

Have a nice little room and I'm very cosy. Went off to Walton Place again and found Joyce hard at work cleaning, also two chars, Mrs Webb and Mrs Neale. However gradually the house is getting cleaner. Bill came up to dine lovely to see him, but both fell out over the cold bathwater.

Wednesday 7 November

Last morning cleaning up. Inventory men still there. Home after seeing Bill, frightfully weary, Sturgeon met me, very cold.

Saturday 10 November

Dick Atcherley arrived late, after 11.00. Bill gave him his breakfast. Dick has brought a large Great Dane with him called Ben Hur. Mum is rather scared for the poor little Pepper. Gifts showered on Mary by her godfather, a big bad wolf and three piglets.

Sunday 11 November

All listened to wireless for Cenotaph Service. Marian and I went for a walk, do like her so much. Dick with his big dog went off after dinner.

Thursday 15 November

Lilian gave notice. Felt very annoyed as it is unkind to the children to leave. Just at Christmas, also inconvenient for me and hard on Nannie.

Saturday 17 November

Went over to Abington after breakfast taking a picnic lunch with us, which was horrid with cold coffee. Gertrude's impossible. Most depressing day. Dad took one look at the place and loathed it. In fact he had made up his mind before we left. Bill felt it was creepy and found out there was a headless ghost! Too depressing as Mum decided she will now have nothing more to do with it.

Monday 19 November

Bill left early to go back to Hornchurch. A gap in the fog that came down again after breakfast and was impenetrable here by 3.30.

Tuesday 20 November

Off on 2.49 to Cambridge to Claude's shoot. Catastrophe when I discovered once on the train I had forgotten to bring Bill's gun. So hastily telephoned that it should be put on the next train. [How things have changed, no chance of that being allowed now!] Margaret met me at Cambridge. Met Bill at the house, Abberley House quite attractive, but oh so cold!

Wednesday 21 November

Very cold and foggy. Could not get warm last night. Off to the shoot at Brandon. Rang up Mother to say I could not get back till tomorrow. Good shoot, we got over 80 pheasants by 3.00, seven guns one of whom never shot a thing! Except one so close to him that he blew its insides out. Loved being with Bill all day and he shot quite well. Back to the 'ice well' for tea. Such a pain in my back.

Friday 23 November

Wrote to Bill of my row with Mother. Mother impossible and cleared off to London on 9.50 train. Dad very frosty. Mother home after dinner. Atmosphere still very tricky, but she is nicer.

Monday 26 November

Had excellent night and feel much better. Green medicine makes me sleep and good for my nerves. Shopping with Mother in Ipswich then went over to Playford Mount to view the sale on Thursday.

Wednesday 28 November

Went over to Playford Mount for the Sale. The linen is lovely and some of the furniture. Weather bitter and foggy. Bought a pair of scent bottles at the sale.

Thursday 29 November

Royal Wedding. [HRH Duke of Kent and Princess Marina of Greece)] I went over to Cambridge to Bill's Confirmation. Old Hopkinson, Mrs and Philip there. The Bishop preached a nice and very practical sermon. Then we set forth in the little car and motored back here arriving for dinner. Bill returned to Hornchurch, poor dear, he must be very tired.

Friday 30 November

Went over to Playford Mount to see what I had got at the sale. Delighted to find that Mother had obtained the mahogany wardrobe for £8.15 shillings. It's lovely. I got some sheets, tablecloths and napkins and some glass oddments. Quilters came for the weekend arriving in time for dinner. Mrs Marshall served a very nice dinner.

Saturday 1 December

Find this weekend is rather difficult. Most odd situation to be entertaining one's landlord! However they are very nice and gave Bill a lovely day's shooting. She is too much made up and I find extremely stupid. They all went off shooting at 9:30. Eight guns got 200 head with 180 pheasants. Joined them for lunch at the cottage. Poor lunch of sandwiches and nothing hot at all. Ronnie very cheerful in evening, too much to drink again.

Sunday 2 December

Went to Church with Mum and Dad for Communion, Bill's first. The Quilters spent morning pottering in the garden. He gave me two brace of pheasants. He spoke to Bill about staying on here.

Wednesday 5 December

Worried as no period yet. Nanny had day off. Bill came over for the afternoon and worried about the car as it is not going well.

Mother home late and enjoyed herself at Harold and Ursula's. His new school is lovely [Cheam].

Thursday 6 December

Mrs Marshall had day off. No period yet, took Ergot in case, dare not take any chances now. Worried.

Friday 7 December

Went to Cambridge by train and Margaret met me at the station. Can't feel really happy as no period, very worried about this. Ergot gave me pains. Margaret gave us excellent dinner caviar, sole, pheasant and a savoury. Then on to the dance at the Mess, Duxford. I wore green satin and new fur coat. Enjoyed it very much as it was great fun. Bill and I left at 2.00 and went home. Poor little car getting very done. Loved dancing with Bill. No period, oh dear!

Saturday 8 December

Woke at 10.00 and delighted to find I have my period. Spent happy day filled with relief with Bill. Mother's Birthday with cake, candles and children down to tea, great fun.

Sunday 9 December

Had breakfast and the morning in bed, which was very pleasant. So relieved have period. Bill took family to Belstead Church. Mrs Marshall produced a poor lunch, she sometimes cooks very badly. Bill had great difficulty leaving, as car would not start. Feel this must be end of the poor little motor.

Tuesday 11 December

Pepper ill having eaten lead pencil.

Wednesday 12 December

Bill arrived after lunch in ghastly looking old Ford V8 4 seater. Quite hopeless.

Friday 14 December

Went up to London with Mother, then to lunch with Mary Wilson at Ovington Square, Bill met me there and we went to the lost property office and retrieved Bill's attaché case. Then to Shrimptons, (Motor car dealer in Berkeley Square), to see Salinson car which Bill is thinking of. Like it but wonder how we shall afford it! Home and met Mum who is giving Bill £100 towards the car.

Wednesday 19 December

Parcels flowing in for children and general excitement everywhere.

Thursday 20 December

More presents and cards arriving. Dad home from King's Dinner in Tunbridge Wells in the evening.

Friday 21 December

Busy doing final Christmas shopping and preparations for the party. Bill arrived in a green Morris ISCS saloon, looks nice but Bill says is very slow! Lovely to have my darling here. Adore him.

Monday 24 December

Children very happy and excited over the Christmas party. After lunch did final touches to the tree then at 4.00 Mrs Pulman, her two boys and the Barlows, their nanny and two boys all came. It was great fun. Children and nurses had tea in drawing room and us in library. Then Dad appeared by the Christmas tree dressed as Father Christmas to the children's delight. Presents and then games. Then servants came in for their parcels.

Tuesday 25 December

Christmas day. Mary and Merlin began the day by singing carols outside our bedroom! Then Bill and I unwrapped parcels. Merlin thrilled with his motor, Mary with her log trolley. Mum gave Mary dress and Merlin a train. Dad a Noah's Ark and dresses for the twins. Went to church and Communion at Belstead. Lovely happy day. Excellent lunch and dinner in the evening.

Thursday 27 December

Bill had to return to Hornchurch in the evening to return the car to Shrimpton as it is no good. Sad he is gone.

Saturday 29 December

Went to London for a matinee for Mother's birthday. Met Bill, Mum and Dad at Piccadilly Grill where we lunched. Home for dinner.

Monday 30 December

The last day of the old year. A very happy one with my darling twins safely here. Mary and Merlin so well and happy. Having Mum and Dad here makes me so happy. I love my darling Bill more than ever each year if that is possible. He is more perfect to me and good to me than anyone knows. Only unhappiness is that we are not always together. I wish it could be so and then my happiness would be indeed perfect. This house too I love and have been so happy here. Tomorrow I shall go to London to be with Bill again. I hope the car will be nice. We must house hunt and sell Walton Place and I wonder if Bill will go to Andover this time next year. I do hope so, God is very good to us all and I'm afraid I don't pray enough but will do better next year.

Leckhampton Cambridge 1933-1934

All four with Cesca 1934

Twins Christening April 1934 Leckhampton

Mother, Cesca, John & Mary Wilson
Royal Show week 1935

Ralph Millais' 30-98 Vauxhall
Mary & Merlin 1939

Mary and Merlin

Belstead the twins 1936

1935
Belstead and Malta

The first day of 1935 finds Cesca in London, staying at the Hotel Meurice with Bill where they danced and dined. The next day after a busy morning shopping in Bond Street, having her hair washed and set at Harvey Nicholls and lunching at Fortnum & Mason, they went to Shrimptons to try new motor cars. The Lanchester and Standard Waymarker. 'The second hand Lanchester reg. YY is lovely and we have decided on it. Expensive but so nice and comfy and I do hope it goes well'.... On the 12 February their 6th Wedding Anniversary is shattered by terrible news.

Saturday 5 January Bill arrives back at Belstead in the new car. Very thrilled with it. It is a Lanchester 18hp, dark blue body saloon, room for 5 and upholstered in blue leather. It goes like a dream and is so quiet, fluid flywheel so hope I may be able to learn to drive it. Car is really lovely and so nice to have Bill here.

Monday 7 January
Bill returned to Hornchurch in the Lanchester. Woke to find snow falling. Mary and Merlin very thrilled over it and gazing at snowflakes! Dad very cross since last evening's discussion about taking on this house permanently.

Thursday 17 January
Very cold and foggy. Bill and I had a sleep in the afternoon before changing for our party, wore my satin dress. Left Belstead at 4.45 and had horrible drive up to town in pouring rain arriving late at the Ionides house by 10 minutes. Dinner and then to 'The Dominant Sex' a poor play which we did not much care for. Home in the car, which went beautifully by 3.00.

Friday 18 January
To Duxford by car leaving at 9.00, feeling a bit pop eyed, but lovely cold frosty day so soon felt all right. Shot 9 brace of partridge, various hares and rabbits and motored home after lunch.

Thursday 24 January

The cook, Mrs Phillips, has decided to stay. Left for London with Mum and Dad. Shopped hard. Ordered ham and smoked salmon from Selfridges. Then lunched with Aunt Edie and was shocked to see a great change in her. Went to Harrods House Agents about 2 Walton Place. Then home met by Sturgeon. Snow falling on and off all weekend, bitterly cold. Children tobogganing on trays down the slopes. Twins very cross. Bill left and had awful drive back to Hornchurch taking him three and a half hours.

Tuesday 5 February

Went to London by train then by bus to Harvey Nichols where I did some shopping and then to King & King about the house. Taxi to Gabriel's where I arrived for lunch. Bill came up for dinner and we went to see "The Man who Knew too Much", quite a good film.

Wednesday 6 February

Bad night. Kept awake by her child howling. Terrible the way Gabriel brings up her babies. Left at 11.00 with bad headache to go to Hornchurch where Bill met me with the car. Bitterly cold. Back home and babies all well. To bed early with my Billy.

Monday 11 February

Lovely day. Bill and I went into Ipswich in the Austin. In afternoon took the children over to Felixstowe to see about rooms for when we leave here where we can send children and nurses. To bed early, so happy.

Monday 12 February

Our 6th Wedding Day. Such happy six years with my darling Bill. Present of £50 from Dad, tulips and theatre tickets from Mum. Pot plant from Nannie, snowdrops from children. Lovely carnations/my bouquet from my darling. Spent the day quietly and happily. I drove the car again in the afternoon. Children came down for tea. Bill and I went up to have a bath and then as I had finished, I was called to the telephone. It was Lena on Dandy's behalf ringing to say Peter had been killed in air collision off Malta this afternoon. Felt quite faint. Told Bill and we then rang and decided not to go up until tomorrow. Felt so upset over it all.

Wednesday 13 February

Went off to London by car at 7.30. Poured all the way and the windscreen wiper would not work. However eventually arrived at 11.00 at Dandy's flat. Found her quite calm. Pat in a stew, poor girl. We saw them and left to see Bill's mother. Bill spent an hour with her. Terrible for her. Then went to put notice in the *Times*. Then went with Bill to Lloyds Bank to see about Peter's balance, and then to solicitor as apparently he has left no Will. Came home by train and went to bed.

Thursday 14 February

Felt better after a good night. Very upsetting and harrowing, however and had many letters of condolence and misery from friends. Twins 1st Birthday, the darlings. Still feel upset and so worried about Bill. Don't know how I shall put up with his flying nowadays.

Friday 15 February

Fay and Richard are coming tomorrow. Have asked R for details of Peter's death. Had a bad night and felt upset and worried. Wild day. Went to meet Bill in evening, but to my sorrow he rang up to say he could not come till after dinner. He arrived after 10.00 looking very white and tired.

Sunday 17 February

Bill, Mother, Dad and I went to church at St Mary le Tower in Ipswich, good sermon. Fay and Richard left after tea to return to London. Loved having them and she is returning next Wednesday. Bill and I busy writing letters still.

Monday 18 February

Felt extraordinarily depressed when Bill left early this morning and cried a lot. Babies came in to comfort me. Better later but headache and tired and worried all day. Cannot get over this tragedy of Peter's death and feel so sad. And the peculiar way his mother and family behave. My poor darling.

Tuesday 26 February

Lovely day. I took nannie into Ipswich in the car and shopped myself. Also
had my hair washed. (Why is it there is never a good hairdresser in any county town?) Isobel Durham, daughter Jane and her nurse arrived before lunch. Did up parcels for Mary's birthday tomorrow. Good dinner; Tomato soup, loin of lamb (excellent), chocolate soufflé and cheese board.

Wednesday 27 February

My little girl's 5th Birthday. Sweet child is so happy and had lovely presents. Gardening tools, seeds, plants etc from Mum and me, Liberty dress from Dad. Pinafores from Bill, woolly dogs from Dandy. Busy morning preparing for party, bitterly cold and so different from yesterday. Party great success, lots of toys and games. Bill arrived with Fay.

The next day Fay is rushed to bed as threatened with a miscarriage. The doctor is sent for and Cesca rings Richard and the London doctor. The whole household is worried and rather upset. Cesca fears the worst may happen.

Friday 1 March

Isobel decided to go early and left by 10.00 train. Mother also left for London. Dad, Bill and I lunched alone and worried over Fay. Bill and I worried and rang up Richard. During evening Fay in pain. Richard's car broke down so unable to come tonight.

Saturday 2 March

Nannie woke me at 2.00 and said Fay in great pain. I hurried along and found her groaning and making an awful fuss. However stayed with her for a good time and went back to bed afterwards. Went to her again in the morning. Rang Dr G. and he came about 8.30. Soon after he left, baby came away and all was over. A dead baby according to Dad and Dr G. All very upsetting as Richard arrived at 12.00 and had to be told all that had happened. Decided to keep Fay here for a short time. A nurse installed for her.

Sunday 3 March

Fay better but does make such a fuss and the nurse is awful. [Cesca's lack of sympathy for Fay who has just lost a child can possibly be explained by Cesca's worries over the imminent removal of all the Quilter's furniture and her Mother and childrens' health]. Feel worried as Mother too is not at all well, and Merlin still has a bad cough. Richard is rather trying and pedantic. Went over to Framlingham with Bill in the afternoon in the Lanchester as feel must get away from it all for a bit. Heaven knows for how long we shall have Fay ill here and the move and all coming, it is a worry. Lovely to have my Bill here though.

Monday 4 March

Fay better but still inclined to think herself half dead. Nurse is really awful. Mother is in bed and Merlin ill with temperature of 103. Feel very worried and am afraid it's flu. Bill and I took Mary with us to Felixstowe to see the rooms to install the children when we leave. Mary sleeping with us. Bill returns to work tomorrow. It's been a miserable leave for him, poor dear.

Tuesday 5 March

It definitely is Flu. Mum, Mary and Cecily all in bed with temperatures. Nannie too with cough. Told Richard he had really better remove Fay as if she gets it in her present condition it could be very serious. So he ordered ambulance and arranged for Nursing Home, and finally she and R and the miserable nurse left after lunch. Poor Mum feeling very seedy, Mary bad and Merlin better. Bill left early evening.

Wednesday 6 March

Mother, Merlin, Mary are all in bed, and Cecily too. Bill returned in afternoon. Lovely to have the house to ourselves again. Feel tired and have been taking Ergot again. All well in the evening. Have been so very worried about this and worries never come singly. Mum better in evening.

Cesca wishes she could have the day in bed. Mary continues to be ill, Merlin coughing still. She visits Fay, who is better, at the Nursing Home, taking eggs and lilies. Mary is still ill, poor child and coughs a lot.

Saturday 9 March,

Bill, Dad and I all flared up. He says he won't take any responsibility and that is that. Worried about poor Mary who coughs so much. Rang Dr Banks and the London Hospital and tried to get Nurse Griffen to come. She could not so Bill and I met Nurse Foster at the station. Moved Mary to end spare room with big fire, all very cosy. Bill and I went to dine at the Barlows. Have never felt so cold. Everything seemed frozen on the plates before it reached us.

Sunday 10 March

Mother seems very much better, Merlin too. Clare has it now and is seedy and coughing. Mary improving. Am very glad I have this nurse. Dr Banks came, I like him and he seems very efficient. Feel rather seedy myself. Family are trying but I suppose they are worried too.

By Tuesday Mother and Mary are both better, but Cesca has a temperature and is afraid she is in for the flu. Wednesday and Thursday both she and Bill are ill in bed with the flu. Cesca still feeling rotten on Saturday, Mary back in the nursery and nurse Foster left in the morning. Cesca has a temperature of 100 on Monday and Doctor Banks visited.

Tuesday 19 March

Bad night and feeling rotten. Still got temperature. Mum cross with me and Bill. Felt furious with her and Dad and did not speak to them all day. Felt very weak and rotten. Dr Banks came. Wept all day. Bill left in morning. Can't bear it.

On Wednesday, another bad night but a dose of castor oil has improved things. Dr Banks and Bill arrived in the afternoon. Arrangements for the move are getting sorted and she hopes to be up by the end of the week. The last ten days of March are taken up with the Quilters having their furniture all removed and the children being installed in comfy rooms at Felixstowe.

Monday 25 March

Up early and the house was full of men. Men everywhere, from Frazers, Abbotts, Mrs Quilter and the sweep. Terrific. Went off to Felixstowe in the car arriving after going to the laundry. The children and babies all well. My room very comfy but I feel lonely and wish my Bill was with me. Hate having to go down to dinner alone.

Tuesday 26 March

Had a very good night and feel much better. Lovely day and had breakfast in bed and was delighted to get a letter from Bill saying he is coming tonight to be with me. He arrived in time for dinner. So lovely to be with him. Lovely night, close to my darling.

Lovely warm sunny weather both Wednesday and Thursday. Cesca goes over to Belstead by train in the afternoon, met by Sturgeon in the car.
Found the house pandemonium! Frazers men very slow and nowhere near moved out yet. Mother tired and having giddy attacks. Cesca feels worried about her. Southgate gave Cesca a large box of rhubarb, flowers and apples for the children.

Monday 1 April

Returned to Belstead with Bill in the car after saying goodbye to the children.

Mother greeted us in a fury and I felt totally and utterly miserable when Bill left and wept. Mother horrid and so bossy. However she soon said she was sorry. Poor Belstead looks so queer. Frazers men still removing. Went into Ipswich for lunch as the Esse not in its place yet. Had a very busy day getting things from station and getting our room ready, the oak room for our bed and sitting room.

Tuesday April 2

The superintendent of the Esse cooker arrived and saw stove going well. It certainly cooks extremely well so far. Mother and I busy unpacking. Very cold with snow showers. Ceiling in my old bedroom fell down today.

Wednesday 3 April

Bill came over for the afternoon and evening. I went over to Felixstowe to see the children in the morning and found them all flourishing. Dropped Mother at the station to go to London. When she returned from London she was as cross as could be and was perfectly beastly to poor Bill. I had it out with her afterwards and had a row ending by my saying I would leave the house in the morning.

Thursday 4 April

Decided that really I cannot put up with Mother and her behaviour any longer. She said she would prefer Bill and me to leave. Decided to do so. Went into Ipswich (snowing hard) to find out about trains to Shenfield where Bill could meet me and go together to London. However, just before lunch she said how sorry she was so all was well again and she could not bear me to go. Martins Removals bought another load in the evening. Still snowing. To bed very tired.

Friday 5 April

Decided to go to Felixstowe for weekend with Bill this evening. Busy all day. Basil Ionides came and stayed until after tea leaving for Colchester with the car. Mr Hempson and Mr Snell manager of Frazers came to complete the schedule. Men getting on well with the decorating. Bill arrived and we all had dinner together. Mum very nice to us both. Off in evening to The Felix for weekend.

Saturday 6 April

Children came round to see us before breakfast. Lovely to see them. Went over to Ipswich and took Mary and Merlin with us. We spent the afternoon and evening with Mother. Unfortunate contretemps when Esse chief arrived and I interviewed him before she did and she felt slighted. Most awkward. Mum is terribly touchy and I suppose it is due to her overtired condition. Back to the Felix and a good dinner. This hotel is most comfy.

Sunday 7 April

Bill so sweet and good to me, and I do miss him when he is not here. Spent afternoon with children and had tea with them in the rooms. Also watched twins have their bath. Dinner at the Felix, then back to Belstead where I found Mum very tired and done up, but much more pleasant. Bill returned to Hornchurch and I to bed early.

Monday 8 April

Mother and I off in the car to Colchester to see Sheraton settee recommended by Basil Ionides. Bought this for £7. A bargain. Mum and I delighted. Had busy afternoon with carpet and curtain men. Laying carpets, linos and measuring curtains. Dining room carpet down and looks lovely.

Tuesday 9 April

Lots of letters including one from Bill, and a tiresome one from Patricia, who writes an illegible hand. Martins arrived with another load (the 4th) today.

Wednesday 10 April

Went over to Bury St Edmunds with Mother to see Rutter about these dilapidations. Also to Collins Agency about parlour maids and head house maids. Called at the antique shop and Mother bought a very nice set of oak chairs. Bill came and stayed for tea and dinner. More ceiling came down and in the bathroom.

Thursday 11 April

Unfortunately Aunt Edie can't put Bill up for the weekend. Am very upset about this but it can't be helped. Went to Felixstowe where I spent the afternoon with my babies. Aunt Edie rang up in the evening to say Bill is bringing his own camp bed so we shall have the weekend together.

Friday 12 April

Went up to London and met Bill at Romford and had tea with him in the Mess. Then we motored up to London together to Aunt Edie's. She was delighted to see us both. Gave us comfy room and excellent dinner. So happy at being together. Bill rather upset and cross as he did not sleep well, poor dear as his camp bed was damp.

Saturday 13 April

Lovely to be together. Went off to shop in Bond Street and Harrods. Then to His Majesty's to see Henry IV which was poor, but enjoyed because we were both together. Went to see Mary and John Wilson before returning to dine at Aunt Edie's. So happy with my Bill.

Sunday 14 April: Palm Sunday

Bill and I breakfasted together, Aunt Edie in bed. Then we went to church at St Mary Abbots, in Vicarage Gate. It was very high church so we came out early. Took Aunt Edie to St. Martins for evening service. Bill left after dinner for Hornchurch.

Monday 15 April

Up early and went to Hamleys to get Merlin's Birthday presents. Then packed and bade farewell to Aunt Edie. Took taxi to 2 Walton Place and found Miss Ussher still there complete with a vast staff of maids. Back to Ipswich after seeing Martins safely into Walton Place to pack up.

Tuesday 16 April

In the evening Martins brought their first load from Walton Place. Things look very dirty.

Wednesday 17 April

Off to London again to see to Walton Place and Martins. Got to Walton Place but no sign of Martins. Returned at 12.30 to find that both carpet men and Harrods, with the table, had called when the house was empty. Very annoying and had to do much telephoning. Lunched at Gunters with Dad then returned to the house to find Martins getting on. Returned to Ipswich.

Thursday 18 April

Footman's came to see about my carpets. We had a hectic day and never sat down as Martins arrived at 9.00 and from then on no peace. Bill arrived unexpectedly on Easter Leave which was indeed lovely. Slept in our old bedroom in very comfy new beds.

Saturday 20 April

Bill went to fetch children before lunch. Nannie had arranged a van to bring their things over. Lovely to have them back and all looking so well. Bill and Mum hard at work hanging pictures. Dad returned after lunch. His room is now straight.

Tuesday 23 April

Bill returned in YY [the Lanchester YY 3864] to Hornchurch.

Wednesday 24 April

My little Merlin's 4th Birthday. Mum gave him two rabbits and a lovely hutch. Bill and I gave him a fire engine, Jim a Rolls Royce, Fay a scrap book, Dandy a level crossing, and Mrs Lunn porters and camels etc. Bill flew over in the morning and dropped a birthday message that unfortunately caught in the topmost Elm tree. He stayed the night.

Friday 26 April

Bill has tickets for State Ball. Went to meet Bill at Martlesham for the Glemham Hunt Ball. I wore my green satin. We set off for Glemham at 9.30 in the Austin arriving at 10.00. Enjoyed the Ball very much and danced together all the time. Met Pat Ainslie and others there.

Saturday 27 April

Felt unaccountably miserable and depressed at Bill's departure for Nottingham and wept a lot when I left him at Martlesham. It's most foolish of me as it's only for a short while. I suppose I am tired after last night.

Tuesday 30 April

Off to London, went to Harrods then to lunch with Mum at Gunters before going to Miss Gray to choose my Ball dress for State Ball. Chose a lovely pale pink dress with embroidered silver lace and tulle cape. Mum is very kindly giving it to me. Arrived home and found Bill. He has flown down for two days leave.

Wednesday 1 May

Oliver came to lay the carpet in Library. Paid all wages. Bill and I had a lovely ramble with the children, bird nesting over the fields.

Found thrush and chaffinch and showed Bill the moorhens with the 6 eggs. Back in our own room which is lovely.

Friday 3 May

Off at 9.30, having paid wages, to London for day. Worried over my Hawker shares which are rising and rising, can't decide whether to sell or not. Sold my Roll Royce on Monday and of course since then they have risen steadily! Frightful crowds everywhere. Bought three lovely rugs. Shopped at Harrods, Harvey Nichols and to Fauchon where I bought shoes for State Ball. Home.

Saturday 4 May

Joyce back here which is nice. Two new housemaids came this afternoon. Mother busy hanging pictures in Drawing Room. Walked to Copdock in evening with Dad to see a nursery maid. My mattress arrived from Harrods. Everything is full of the Jubilee. [King George V and Queen Mary.]

Sunday 5 May

Mother terribly cross and tired. Furious with me for standing on a chair with heels on with the result she cleared off to bed with no lunch. She gets very trying. Children all most sweet and happy.

Monday 6 May: Jubilee Day

And a most glorious one for the King and Queen. Very hot and lovely here. Bill rang and said he would come up. So he arrived at 3.00 and we all went up to the sports together at Belstead and had tea with the village people in Mrs Wilson's barn. The Gurneys and Milbanks were there, lovely evening. Bill and I spent it in the garden.

Wednesday 8 May

Bill at Rochester being entertained by Mayor and Corporation. In afternoon went for walk with children and found the sweetest willow wren's nest in field.

Thursday 9 May

I went off to London on 9.00 train, frightfully full. Shopped before fitting at Miss Grays at 12.30. My dress looks lovely. Later met Bill at Gieves where he tried on his tunic for the State Ball. Home late so babies all asleep.

Friday 10 May

Oliver here all day laying carpets. We are getting on at last, but house in great muddle after Martin's last load here yesterday. Window cleaners here. Bill arrived early, surprised to see him so soon. Lovely that he is on leave.

Saturday 11 May

Took children for a picnic in afternoon to Holbrook Bay and then to a lovely picnic spot lovely. Children so good and we all had a happy time together. Dinner excellent tonight. Asparagus soup, boiled turbot, hollandaise sauce, roast duckling, peas. vanilla ice and choc sauce.

Monday 13 May

Bill and I left on 12.20 train for London. Excellent journey to London, Ist class most comfy. Went to Miss Grays, my dress for the State Ball tomorrow is really lovely and I am delighted with it. Met Bill at Gunters for tea. Had an ice each. Went then to the Richards where we went to bed early after a good dinner of dressed crab, roast saddle of lamb, and meringues.

Tuesday 14 May

Very cold, but fine. Very thrilled about tonight. Had my hair shampooed and set after lunch at Hugo's. Rested. After dinner changed for the Ball. Bill looked awfully nice in his full dress uniform with sword etc. My dress looked well I think, but I expect we both looked a bit dull compared to all the marvellous dresses and jewels at the Ball. The Queen looked marvellous in lovely blue dress with emeralds and diamonds. Bill and I simply loved it. The palace too was indescribably lovely, a mass of crimson and gold. The string band was good too and so was the buffet supper. We stayed till the end and then returned in a large Daimler to Sloane Street, where we felt as if it had been a rather wonderful dream.

Wednesday 15 May

Returned to Belstead and had lunch on the train. Great disaster! Pepper had eaten one of Merlin's rabbits. Everyone very thrilled to hear about the State Ball.

Thursday 16 May

Bill returned to Hornchurch early. Bill had put up my bedroom curtains yesterday and they do look lovely.

Friday 17 May.

Bill came back for weekend leave this evening which was as unexpected as it was lovely. Had a good dinner. Soup, roast shoulder of lamb, vegetables, asparagus and ginger pudding. Very cold.

Saturday 18 May

Such a severe frost last night as has not been known here for over 40 years. So Southgate [gardener] says and all green stuff and new potatoes blackened. Very cold. Took children into dentist. Mary and Merlin have a good many teeth that will have to be filled. I am worried about this.

Sunday 19 May

Bill and I got up early and went to Holy Communion at Belstead. The new vicar was inducted yesterday. He is an old King's man called Ussherwood.

Monday 20 May

Bill returned to Hornchurch. Ada Tong, new under nurse came to take Lilian's place this evening. Do not much care for her and have had poor references.

Thursday 23 May

Ada Tong came to me and said she wished to leave immediately. I said this was quite impossible and that she must stay her month. Took the children to the dentist.

Friday 24 May

Worried over Hawker shares that after the government's announcement on Wednesday to increase the RAF are falling. Can't understand why they should. Went to London with Mother.

Took presents to Pontifex's for Claude's wedding. We bought a rug from Harrods and went to the Royal Tournament at Olympia which we both thoroughly enjoyed.

Saturday 25 May

Heard from Bill he is coming late tonight. Took M. and M back to the dentist to have their teeth done. Both very good and were given vanilla ice cream which they did not care for! In spite of looking forward to it immensely! Then took Nannie in who departs for her holiday and Lilian returned. Ada hopeless.

Wednesday 29 May

Off to London by train arriving 11.30. Shopped at Harrods, and went to the bank to do some finance which I hate as it makes me headachy. Met Bill 2.30 at Fortnum & Mason and went to the Academy which we both thought rather poor and terribly tiring as so hot and stuffy. Back to Liverpool Street after saying goodbye to Bill. Hate these short times together.

Thursday 30 May

No news from bank about sale of my Hawkers shares. Busy sending off invitations for party. Have advertised in East Anglian for nursery maid and am getting lots of replies, four girls came to see me this afternoon.

Monday 3 June

Off at 5.30 to London with Bill for Trooping the Colour. Arrived in the Mall at 7.30 and found already a lot of people there. Had breakfast at Park Lane Hotel, then hurried down to the Mall with our camp stools. Sat and read papers till 11.00, when the parade and procession started. The King arrived punctually and we saw everything extraordinarily well. To lunch at the Rembrandt. Rested and then in the evening we dined at Pruniers.

Tuesday 4 June

Bill left early to return to Hornchurch, and I shopped returning to Ipswich on 12.20 train, met by Sturgeon. Dad away for the night in Tunbridge Wells. Went over to Thorpeness to see the Ian Smiths for tea.

Wednesday 5 June

Mum and I busy sending out invitations to our party and hope the weather will be nice. Bill arrived for tea and Dad after dinner. Very cold and wet so had a big fire. It has not been warm since Jubilee day. Ada Tong left and I have new under nurse called Olive. Does not seem much better than the last one. Spent quiet day with Bill.

Monday 10 June: Bank Holiday

Lovely to have Bill still here.

Tuesday 11 June

Bill left early as he goes to Sutton Bridge today. Very wet. More answers to our party, not many coming which is unfortunate.

Friday 14 June

Busy with preparations for Aunt Edie's visit. She arrived at teatime complete with bags, cushions and Richardson [her companion]. Both highly excited. Nannie returned from her holiday, very brisk and Lilian left. I was sorry to say goodbye as I always liked her so much. Aunt Edie enjoyed her dinner which was excellent.

Saturday 15 June

Pouring wet day. Aunt Edie unable to go out until just before lunch. Then came a downpour and sure enough the entire Ussherwood party turned up for tennis! It is wretched bad form and a sickening bore to have to talk to people all afternoon. However Aunt Edie enjoyed it and they all ate an enormous tea. Bill rang to say he would be arriving this evening. Great joy. Waited up for him.

Sunday 16 June

Bill left to return to Sutton Bridge and Olive, the miserable under nurse, decamped and did not return.

Monday 17 June

Aunt Edie went off with Dad to inspect the churchyards at Belstead church and St Peters. Cold nasty day and had library fire again. Richardson is a trial and I dislike her.

Tuesday 18 June

Aunt Edie left after lunch! Poor old dear, she really looks very old and white and there is such a nasty smell in her room now she has gone.

Wednesday 19 June

New under nurse came with her mother and appears to be very stupid. However perhaps Nannie will get her into shape.

Thursday 20 June

Busy preparing for our party. It rained all day, if it continues it will be awful for our party on Saturday. Dad however predicts a change.

Friday 21 June

Busy getting the house nice for tomorrow. Mum doing flowers. Mrs Sutton arrived at teatime. Bill and McKenzie here at 4.00 having motored down from Sutton Bridge. Lovely to see Billy again. But stupidly we got cross with each other and I went to bed sad. Marian arrived from Newcastle, hot and tired as it is suddenly hot today. Good dinner salmon trout, roast saddle of lamb, asparagus, and praline ice.

Saturday 22 June

Our party this afternoon was a great success. About 35 people came and 17 played tennis. Mum, Dad and I received visitors in the Drawing room and Bill up on the courts. The tennis went well and so did the tea. The twins in their new smocks looked too sweet for words. All departed at 7.30 and we dined at 8.00, tomato soup, roast spring chicken, globe artichokes and chocolate creams.

Sunday 23 June

The weather is still lovely. Went to church at Belstead. Sat on lawn almost all afternoon and read. Played tennis after tea.

Monday 24 June

Bill and Mac left early to return to Sutton Bridge. It is very hot and I am sunburnt. Went to the Ussherwood Wedding at Belstead. The bride looked dreadful and so did the bridegroom!

Wednesday 26 June

Bill arrived in evening and we had a picnic in the fields below the house and Dad found a partridge's nest.

Belstead High Summer 1935

Belstead and the children 1936

260

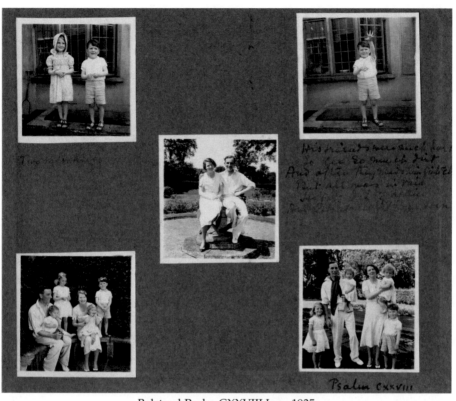

Belstead Psalm CXXVIII June 1935

Family picnic Egypt 1937

Sunday 30 June

Went to tennis at the Schreibers and enjoyed it until Bill had a jug of boiling water upset all over his leg. Worried about it and when we got home Mum, Dad and Nannie looked after it for him. He returned to Sutton Bridge. There is still no news of Staff College.

Tuesday 2 July

Spent an extremely busy day in London. Arrived and took strawberries with me for Mrs Lunn, but when I got to Wigmore Street found the house to let and they had gone! So gave the strawberries to the Durhams.

Wednesday 3 July

The most wonderful news. Bill rang up and said would I look in the Times for the announcement as he is selected for Staff College and Claude Pelly too. Too good to be true. Frightfully pleased over this excellent news. Bill arrived in the afternoon. It is wonderful.

Thursday 4 July

My clever Bill went back to Sutton Bridge again for the last time as the Squadron [No 19 Fighter Squadron] returns to Hornchurch on Friday.

Friday 5 July

Mother went off for her weekend to Cheam by train. Children well apart from getting rather cheeky do not appear to mind the changes of nursery maids, as the last one Ida, departed this morning. Sent box of roses and sweet peas to Mrs Lunn.

Saturday 6 July

Dad and I getting on very well. Bill arrived and we had a lovely time together making plans and feeling very happy. New nursemaid came. Mary rather naughty with all these new girls.

Monday 8 July

Mother returned from Newbury looking seedy and tired, with a painful hand that had been stung. Terrible place on her hand, poor dear. New girl decamped after lunch but is not much loss.

Tuesday 9 July

Went to London to celebrate the result of the Staff College Election. Met Bill at the Club. We went to the Mask of Virtue with Vivien Leigh which was very good indeed. Then on to the Berkeley where we had supper and danced. Had dinner first at Pruniers. Enjoyed our evening.

Wednesday 10 July

Went to lunch with Bill at my new Club, The English Speaking Union. Went to Sir Phillip Sassoon's Garden Party at Trent Park. [He was a politician, art collector and social host and died in 1939 aged 50.] We enjoyed it as we met so many people we knew. Motored home in the evening back for dinner at 8.00.

Sunday 14 July

Bill turned up for lunch and the Ussherwoods came to lunch too and we had a little service in the hall and had the house blessed. [My mother, Mary and uncle Merlin always believed Belstead to be haunted.]

Monday 15 July

Dad's 76 Birthday. He was rather cross. I gave him linen basket, Mary and Merlin a waste paper basket and the twins a biscuit box. Bill away night flying.

Thursday 18 July

Went over to Aldeburgh with all four children arriving at Ann Page's cottage in the High Street at 1.00, where George and Mrs Lunn are staying as the Business has had to close down. A sweet little cottage and we had an excellent lunch. The children had two helpings of everything. George seemed older. Home after tea all four children sleeping all the way home.

Friday 19 July

Mum has not been feeling very well but has gone to London for a family meeting. Went to meet her at 6.15 and found her in tears and terribly upset after stormy meeting and row with Alfred. Went on to meet the Pellys in their Moth at Ipswich Aerodrome. Bill rang to say he would be very late.

Saturday 20 July

Bill arrived at 3.30 am. I was dead asleep but it was lovely to be together again. Bill took Mum, Dad and Claud into Ipswich and Margaret and I spent the morning together. Played tennis in afternoon. Dinner was excellent. Melon, Salmon trout, roast saddle of lamb, peas, new potatoes, vanilla icecream and raspberries.

Sunday 21 July

All went to church. After tennis the Pellys had to leave in the Austin back to their Moth and fly back to Duxford. Enjoyed seeing them very much.

Monday 22 July

Bill left early for Hornchurch. After lunch a terribly upsetting telephone call from Nellie's sister to say her other sister had fallen down dead on Sunday. Poor girl went into hysterics and I eventually got her to bed.

Tuesday 23 July

Nellie ran away this morning, so now I must find another one I suppose!

Thursday 25 July

Nannie had day off in London and Lillian came to help with the children. Interviewed 2 more girls whom I engaged.

Friday 26 July

Interviewed maids all afternoon and evening. John Peel arrived at teatime for the weekend.

Saturday 27 July

A hectic day. Bill and McKenzie had to be fetched from Martlesham by John as the car was busy elsewhere. In afternoon Mum, Dad and I went to Mrs Gurney's funeral at Belstead. Mr Ussherwood took the service and the little church was crammed. Then went to the Shawcrosses for tennis who have a swimming pool. Bill, John and Mac all bathed. Back for dinner, Mum upset after the funeral.

The next few days are taken up with tennis parties, maids arriving (Queenie Lumpkins) and others departing. She interviewed "a useless old woman" as head house maid. Cesca is longing for Bill's month-long leave to start.

Thursday 1 August

Ivy packing all my things while Mum and I went to London to Pat Ainslie's wedding at All Souls Langham Place. Pat's wife is quite pretty and young looking but has rather nouveau riche looking parents. Met lots of old friends and talked a lot to Hugh Lang and his little daughter Oenone, who was a bridesmaid in yellow. Returned home by train and Bill and I, all being packed, set off for Grantham where we arrived at 11.30 at The George.

Friday 2 August

Left Grantham after sending P.C.s to the children. In Harrogate we lunched at The Grand, a nice hotel and a good lunch for 10/-.
Sent the children some Harrogate toffee. Then went on our journey to Bleasdale over the Yorkshire Moors, best part of the drive so far. Arrived at 6.00 after bad map reading on my part. House is in a lovely position and glorious view over the Fylde to the sea. Mr and Mrs Silcock very nice to us and Marian sweet. She has a nice brother Dick, but queer sister Mary who has married an impossible man, Tommy Watson who is a clergyman though no one would ever think it.

Friday 3 August

Felt this is going to be rather an odd visit. The Silcocks though charming are entirely self made and with no background. Evidently very wealthy and all is very well done. The house is small but comfortable, wash basins in all bedrooms and maple furniture. The food too is lavish and good but without the personal touch which one misses when a housekeeper is employed. Mrs S. remains in bed till lunchtime. Went out shooting with the guns. The bag was 32 snipe, 24 rabbits, 19 wild duck. It was lovely hot weather. Tennis in the evening.

Sunday 4 August

All went to Bleasdale Church. Marian and I spent a quiet afternoon in the garden. Dick has got a most super Rolls Bentley which is Bill's idea of perfection in cars and he and Dick took it out today. They also have a new Ford V8, an Essex and a little Morris.

Monday 5 August

Marian and I went out with the guns and came in for lunch. Played tennis after tea. I am improving. We played charades after dinner.

Tuesday 6 August

Out shooting again but so hot only went for a short time. Tommy Watson was affected by the heat. I should have thought it was too much drink!

Wednesday 7 August

Our last day here. Out shooting again. Marian took me on a lovely drive over the moors at the back of Bleasdale Tower.

Thursday 8 August

Packed and left at 10.00. Sad to go as they have been so kind to us but feel Carbeth is more 'us'. Had a rather unpleasant drive as far as Scotland when it started to rain and the windscreen wipers would not work! Rather tiresome, got through Glasgow arriving at Carbeth at 6.00. Mary and John as nice as ever, the Richards arrived soon after and were in great form having motored from Borough Bridge.

Cesca and Bill much enjoy their stay with the Wilsons at Carbeth and the excellent dinners. A most glorious 12th and perfect weather and Mary and Cesca walk up, but very tiring so sit basking in the sun and watch Bill and John shoot 10 brace of grouse. Cesca got terribly burnt and bitten. A tiresome letter arrives from her Mother about the servants.

Thursday 15 August

Left dear Carbeth after many farewells to all. They are so kind and good to us and we left with a brace of grouse and a large basket of grapes. We went via Peebles, Jedburgh, Otterburn, Scotch Corner and arrived at Spennithorne at 6.30 to find Aunt Freda and Aunt

Ruth much the same but the house slightly more aged and tumbledown. Food poor. Gave Aunt Freda the brace of grouse. Uncomfy bed.

Friday 16 August

The last day of our holiday. Lunched at The Bell at Barnby Moor. Then on to Thetford where we stopped for a cup of tea. Arrived at Belstead at 6.30, lovely to be back. Mum in a spin and going away tomorrow. Babies all well and so very sweet.

Saturday 17 August

Took cachet about 4.00am as headache so bad. Mum off at 9.40 upset at leaving Pepper and all of us. Dad went with her to see her off on the *Arandora Star* at Tilbury. Bill and I very busy doing accounts and writing letters. Children very good and sweet, I do love them so. Bill plunged in The Eunuch of Stamboul [written by Dennis Wheatley published that year.]

Monday 19 August

Nannie came to tell me that poor Ivy had lost her young man and that he had been found dead in a ditch near Haughley. Arranged for her to go home.

Tuesday 20 August

Very hot indeed. Worried about Ivy and rang Haughley Police Station. The inquest will be tomorrow evening. Bill and I took Nannie and the children to Felixstowe and bathed. I paddled! Then had a picnic tea near the aerodrome. Lovely day, so happy.

Wednesday 21 August

Engaged a temporary head house maid and sent Ivy her wages to date. In afternoon went over to Leiston, then to Sizewell and had tea with Mrs Lunn and George in their tiny cottage there. George and Bill both bathed at Sizewell beach. Mrs Lunn is buying a house at Saxmundham.

Thursday 22 August

Had my hair washed and Bill took the children to the sea and bathed. Mum seems to be much enjoying her cruise.

Friday 23 August

Bill has given me a lovely 'Swingy" in other words a hammock for the garden which is most awfully comfortable.

Saturday 24 August

The Burleighs arrived in time for lunch and were very thrilled with the house and everything and are most easy to entertain. Hutch and his wife arrived at 6.00 and I think she is frightful and do hope I can bear her over the weekend. Impossible woman. Played bridge after a very good dinner.

Sunday 25 August

Church at Belstead and some good tennis in afternoon. The Burleighs and Schriebers are very good.

Monday 26 August

My 31st Birthday. Such lovely presents! £50 from Mum and £20 from Dad. The children had Happy Birthday written on cards round their necks. Bill gave me a lovely cookery book, 'The Ideal' which I saw at Mary's. Our guests left after breakfast not tipping well. A call for Bill saying he must return tomorrow night.

Tuesday 27 August

A dreadful day of alarms and misery. Another call at 12.45 to say Bill need not return. But there were rumours that the squadron was to leave on the 3rd for Malta or Aden. This was frightful. [Italy invades Abyssinia October 3.] Another call at teatime to say Bill must return forthwith as they were definitely sailing. This was confirmed by the Air Ministry. Felt miserable and both of us wept during dinner. I cried myself to sleep.

Wednesday 28 August

Bill left at 6.30. Felt utterly miserable and cried all morning. He rang at 9.30 to say it is definite. He sails on Tuesday in the *Neuralia* for Malta taking the squadron with him. The AOC says he can return for Staff College provided there is no further trouble and war is averted. Took children to the sea to distract myself.

Thursday 29 August
Dad went to meet Mum at Waterloo on return from her cruise. Bill rang wondering whether he should go overland to Malta if the AOC will permit it. I said yes. Bill returned home at 7.00 and stayed the night. Both Mum and Dad came home. She looks very well.

Friday 30 August
Mother as grumpy as a bear with sore head. Bill returned from Hornchurch in evening. Mum still furious and has gone to bed. Feel so upset. Bill sweet to me. To bed after doing some packing.

Saturday 31 August
Mother and Dad still difficult but had it out with Mum and we were mutually sorry for being upset and cross. I feel ill and miserable, do not know how I shall bear this parting. It's awful. Bill and I took in his luggage and sent it off.

Sunday 1 September
Life is as black as it can be and I feel utterly miserable. Oh dear Oh dear! Bill wonderful and so sweet to me but it's awful he has to go and to all places Malta. Do not know how I shall get through the next two days….then the awful blank without my darling.

Monday 2 September
Our last day together, busy packing then we left on 12.20 train. Bill said goodbye to the children. When we got to London I went to Harrods where I got some books for Bill, then fetched the luggage from Liverpool St, got a taxi and met Bill at Waterloo. He had seen Dandy as it's her birthday, and also said goodbye to his Mother. Nice journey to Southampton where we had a room at S.W. Hotel, depressing and noisy. Walked to see the *Neuralia*, awful old boat. Met Potts who is to share cabin with Bill. Back for dinner and bed, so sad, so sad.

Tuesday 3 September
Blackest of days. Tried hard to be brave and was till last moment. Can't write anymore. **Awful. Too awful**.

The next five days go by in a sea of misery and tears. Bill sends a wire to say they are passing Gibraltar on Saturday. Cesca enjoys her day in London on Monday and secured a cook. Descaling started at Belstead so the house cold and no hot water that night. Tuesday Cesca drives to Burnham Overy Staithe to stay with Margaret Pelly for two nights. 'Frightful journey by train', left at 2.30 and arrived over 4 hours later. A sweet little cottage and Claud is away at Sutton Bridge. 'She is so nice, already feel less miserable'.

Wednesday 11 September
Margaret's cottage is right on The Staithe which is covered by the sea twice a day. A dear little garden and sweet cottage nicely furnished. Wrote to my dear love. Miss him so.

Thursday 12 September
Mother rang to say that Bill had safely arrived at Malta and had received my letters. Such a joy to know he's safely there.

Friday 13 September
Margaret motored me to Thetford and was met by Mother with YY and Sturgeon. Also received the cook's references which appear satisfactory in every way.

Monday 16 September
Mum and Dad's 44th wedding anniversary. Terrific gale all night, quite unable to sleep.

Wednesday 18 September
The weather is frightful and almost impossible to stand up. I am so thankful Bill is out of these gales safely at Malta.

Thursday 19 September
The poor old Acacia tree is almost down, very wobbly and expect it to go over at every gust. Mrs Marshall cooked an excellent dinner.

Friday 20 September
Went off to a sale at Cantwell Road and bought a lot of things. An oil painting inscribed R. Wilson, wonder if it is Richard Wilson if so I could sell it on quite well. I thoroughly enjoyed myself.

Tuesday 24 September

Went to London with parcels on 9.00 train. Went to Miss Gray's dress show which I enjoyed and also to Fortnum & Mason. Ordered new corsets at Marianne Jacks. Left Merlin's mug at Shaplands. Returned wet and cold in the evening.

Wednesday 25 September

I have secured a cook at last. She comes tomorrow from Norwich. She's called Mrs Judy. The children of course call her Mrs Punch and Judy! The car fetched her in the afternoon, a very large and stout party.

Saturday 28 September

Had letters from Bill. The situation does not appear to be much better. Everything very uncertain and the papers pessimistic. What will happen one wonders. Mother very cross. Altogether these old people are very lacking in understanding.

Monday 30 September

Feel frightfully depressed and miserable. Mother very cross and unsympathetic. [Mrs Judy who only arrived on 25 September was clearly a disaster.] Went into Ipswich where I interviewed another cook who I engaged, nice old thing but absolutely deaf. Wonder whether she will do.

Tuesday 1 October

Had lovely letters from my Bill, which I read over and over again. Do love and miss him so. Felt very tearful. Mother too is not a ray of sunshine! Paid servants and decided to go to London for a few days. Went for long walk with children to the farm and saw the cows milked. They were thrilled. Put them to bed as Nannie out.

Wednesday 2 October

Went off to London by train. Went to Shapland's [in High Holborn specialising in antique silver and fine jewels] first with my picture and am having a report on it. Had lunch at Gunters. Home in evening.

Thursday 3 October

Family still very cross and difficult. However all was well at lunch as I had it out with Mum and we both forgave each other and got over it. Went over to Bentley Manor to view sale that takes place tomorrow. Still no letter from Bill. Worried about news of Abyssinia and Italy who have started war.

Friday 4 October

The news is bad as Italy and Abyssinia are now definitely at war. The cook is impossible and shall be thankful when she leaves. Went over to the sale at Bentley. Mum bought a small antique mahogany mirror and some china. Came home to find two letters from Bill.

Saturday 5 October

Went into Ipswich with Mary to buy her a hat for Harvest Festival tomorrow. Succeeded finding a sweet one in brown tweed. Went up to Belstead church to help with the flowers. Letters from my darling with some photos enclosed.

Sunday 6 October: Summer Time Ends

Lovely autumn day. Dad had such fun last night putting all the clocks ON one hour!! I took Mary and Merlin to Harvest Thanksgiving. They loved it.

Monday 7 October

Went up to London, the train late owing to the fog. Went to Yorkes to choose hats, shopped in Bond Street and lunched at Isobel Durhams. Enjoyed it very much as I do like seeing my friend. Posted letter to Bill in London. Ronnie Quilter sent down a pheasant and four partridges from the shoot on Saturday. Full of shot and all old birds.

Tuesday 8 October

Dispatched the awful old cook, Mrs Judy, a blessing as have never had such a terror to deal with before. Wrote to my darling boy and had airmail letter from him. Italy seem to be having no end of a party in Abyssinia. It's awful. [Emperor Haile Selassie had pleaded in vain with the League of Nations to react.] New cook, Mrs Edwardes arrived. She is deaf as a post.

Wednesday 9 September

Mum and I went to London together. I enjoyed my day enormously. Went to Pierre's and Yorke's for fittings. Lunched at Gunters and had tea there also after seeing a show. Came home via Colchester, changed and home at 9.00. Awful wild night, gale and rain in buckets.

Thursday 10 October

Old cook is rather mithered with the Esse. Met Isabel Smith in Ipswich, she and Ian have just moved to Thorpeness.

Saturday 12 October

Ronnie Quilter shooting at Belstead. They got 120 brace and sent us two brace partridges and a pheasant. Fay and Richard arrived and were thrilled with the house. I put them in the oak room. Ralph was fetched from the station by Sturgeon. It is fun having guests and cheers me up. Poor dinner. This old woman is quite hopeless cook and sent everything in very badly presented.

Sunday 13 October

Richard most selfish and tiresome, did not say a word about the situation or Bill. Mum and I talked over the weekend and decided Fay thinks of nothing but herself and her ailments. Ralph was, as always nice.

The week goes by, Cesca writes to her Bill every day, the cook does not improve and Cesca decides as she is only temporary she must go within the week.

Friday 18 October

Went to London as have had offer for 2 Walton Place that I must see about. Ordered new dress at Leila Reads in South Molton Street and then saw Hughes re the offer for the house which he turned down as not good enough. Very disappointed as do so want to sell it.

Saturday 19 October

Nannie's day out in London so in charge of the children. Dad returned after lunch. News seems better from the war. Do so hope my darling may soon be home.

Wednesday 23 October

General change over. Lucy now takes on the twins. May returns tomorrow and Mrs Edwardes, this hopeless and impossible cook goes. I shall be thankful.

Thursday 24 October

Bitterly cold. Went over to lunch at Marks Tey at Mrs Carr's. Nice lunch and enjoyed it. Home in YY and Sturgeon more stupid and dense than usual. He is a trial. Car going well.

Friday 25 October

I went to London for fitting and shopped at Fortnums and ordered groceries and chocolates to be sent to Bill. Also to Floris for soap for Bill. Very fortunately secured a cook, Mrs Beasley who came back with me.

Saturday 26 October

The Esse not going well, in fact almost out. Worried about this as the cook is so nice and adaptable. Rang up Esse and they are sending a man down here on Monday.

Sunday 27 October

The Esse ceased to function altogether. In desperation we lit the little Range in the scullery. Rather doubtful it would work as Abbotts said it would not. However we had an excellent lunch and dinner. Have thought of Bill all day.

Monday 28 October

The cook is doing her best. The Esse man arrived this afternoon and found all the chimneys blocked. Rang up the sweep. Really lovely to have three letters from Bill today. A scene with Clare who was very naughty after tea.

Tuesday 29 October.

Sweep came to do Esse, also Abbotts men.

Wednesday 30 October

I went up to London to have fittings. Hughes has no further information on 2 Walton Place. Tea at Debenhams and like an ass left my engagement ring in washbasin place. Realised on train, so upset about this. Sturgeon met me and home in time to say goodnight to my babies.

Thursday 31 October

My new cook, Mrs Beasley has decided to stay permanently at £70. Very pleased about this. Also delighted to hear when I rang up Debenhams that they have my ring. Heard Mrs Milbank has had a heart attack.

Saturday 2 November

Colonel and Mrs Ian Smith to lunch. Mrs Beasley gave us an excellent lunch. Cauliflower au gratin, roast pheasants, cold coffee soufflé, and apple tart, cheese and celery. Sent Bill a letter by airmail. I am much cheered to know he is more hopeful to get home for Christmas.

Sunday 3 November

Woken early by the noise of the pheasants, such a lot about. Went downstairs to get my book and found at 6.45 no sign of any maids about. Annoyed about this. Went to short children's service at Belstead this afternoon. Merlin and Mary loved it because we sang 'All Things Bright and Beautiful'. Bill is my everything but the children are sweet and dear to me.

Monday 4 November

Busy morning, seeing Mrs Beasley and packing. After light lunch went up to London. Took my luggage to the Club and went to have my hair shampooed and set. This they did very badly. Set off for Berkeley Square arriving for tea with Basil Ionides. Mrs Ionides in bed with gastroenteritis. Went to the theatre which was very well acted. Came back and found Basil had forgotten his keys. Great difficulty to get let in.

Egypt Avro 504

Bill flying

Bill with Top Brass ?

Bill

Bill's Bristol Bulldog 1932
commanding C Flight No 19(F) sqn. RAF Duxford

RAF College Cranwell

Bill posted to Malta
Sept-Dec. 1935

Tuesday 5 November

Shopped in the morning and lunched with Marian and then went to see Mrs Currie [Dandy, Bill's grandmother]. The tiresome old thing kept on about my going to Malta till I could have murdered her. Saw that two faced cat Elizabeth there. Can't bear her. Odd as Bill likes her better than the others. Back and changed for dinner at 7.15. Mrs Ionides better. Then went to 'Call it a Day' at the Globe which I loved. Delightful.

Wednesday 6 November

Went shopping and lunched with Mary Wilson and Marian. Basil Ionides and I went to Curzon Street cinema and saw Hungarian film, dined together.

Thursday 7 November

Miss my Bill so. Wrote to him and received another from him forwarded from Belstead. Gave Gabriel coffee at Fortnum & Mason. Lunched with Basil at Berkeley Square. Home for tea to see my babies who are all so sweet.

Friday 8 November

All is going well with Mrs Beasley. Had three letters from Bill which was lovely, the darling, darling boy.

Sunday 10 November

All went to church, Mum is quite recovered and Dad very jolly. Pat Ainslie and his wife arrived for lunch in Pat's Ford. Much enjoyed having them. Bill always in my thoughts, wrote him long letter as soon as they had gone. I wish he was here. I can't bear it.

Monday 11 November: Armistice Day

Miss Morse arrived after breakfast complete with poppies. All the maids bought them and she must have done very well indeed. I have been terribly happy all day as I had three letters from my Bill this morning and another on my return this afternoon from visiting the Brocklebanks at Giffords Hall, a lovely Tudor part Georgian house that Basil has been decorating. [Basil Ionides, architect, who published two best-selling books, *Colour and Interior Decoration* and *Colour in Everyday Rooms*. Best known for his 1929

278

interior design of the rebuilt Savoy Theatre. He died in 1950 at the age of 66.]

Tuesday 12 November

Felt so happy with letter telegram from Bill saying he hoped to be home for Christmas! Too good to be true. Two more letters on my return from Cambridge in the evening. Off to Cambridge, Sturgeon driving, to lunch with Margaret which was nice. Then went to Dr Budd who said my headaches were due to nervous exhaustion and I must rest and drink more glucose.

Wednesday 13 November

Went into Ipswich with Mrs Beasley to choose meat for weekend dinner party. Gale again and terrific rain. Reading Dorothy Sayers new book called 'Gaudy Night'.

Thursday 14 November: Election Day

All passed off quietly here. Mum, Dad, Nannie, May and Mrs Sturgeon went to record their votes at 10.00 at Copdock School. I went later with Sturgeon and Mrs and Mrs Ely. Voted for Walter Ross-Taylor. No letter from Bill. I write to him as usual every day.

Friday 15 November

Mary and Marian both arrived at 6.00, nice to have them here. Rested all afternoon as Dr Budd said I should. Mrs B. sent in good dinner. Whitebait, roast pheasant, crème caramel and cheese straws. To bed after hearing more election results.

Saturday 16 November

Very wet day, Marian, Mary and I went out for a walk in the morning and got soaked. The Hawkers, the Wises and the Barlows came and all went off very well. Mrs Beasley sent in an excellent dinner. Clear soup, salmon mousse, roast saddle of lamb, pineapple ice and prawn fritters. Mary looked so nice in black and Marian in red.

Tuesday, 19th
1.15. p.m

love Bryan
and the Baltic
your own
Billy

[left margin, written sideways] Got in my cigarette Case. Bye Bye for the moment Sweetest I must talk Pott now and keep him cheerful. Much Much

My Precious Darling

The budget of letters from you yesterday really were marvellous and I am so glad you are cheered up and thrilled with the news. It really is agony waiting! I do hope to be able to signal a date shortly. An official letter came in this morning from H.Q. saying they were applying for a passage for me as soon after Dec 1st as possible! It's all too too exciting! Darling Darling Darling.

I wrote a very incoherent letter last night after receiving the mail and it went first thing this morning. I am going for a walk at 2. p.m with Pott and will post this before I go to catch the afternoon post, then write again to night which will go first thing to-morrow!

How tiresome and foolish of Sturgeon about the lights on the Car. ~~You~~ He should not take it out at night unless the spot light is working, its absurd trying to drive on the side lights. Perhaps he has not discovered the special switch! Underneath the "arm" on which are the two horn buttons is a switch which turns off headlights and puts on spot light.

2 Horn buttons
and switch!

if nothing happens on working this either
the bulb on the spotlight has broken or
there is a fault in the wiring or switch
or both and he should be able to locate
it. The main switch on the dashboard
merely puts the side and Head lights on
or off. Twist him!!

I do not know where I shall arrive
I expect it will be Tilbury! then perhaps
we could stay the night at the Hyde Park?!
or ought we to go straight home?! I
feel it will all be too too Overwhelming!
Darling Darling. I am so glad Mum
has got a Piano Hurrah! it is good
of her.

The Court Martial went off alright yesterday
but I couldn't do much for my poor
client who is i'm afraid a confirmed
sinner. No other news I flew all this
morning and the days do seem to be
going. Oh Moppet won't it be Heaven.
Keep Faith and I shall be in your arms
before Christmas. I enclose a letter
from a female at Andover sounds
rather ghastly! I do hope I don't get
thrown off the course for incompetence after
all this battle to get there!

I love you so much and feel
so desperate about you its quite quite
impossible to tell you "of Same" in a letter!!
My own Precious elic-like Moppet. I do want
you so! and long and long for you and adore
the sweet little pictures of you which I have now

281

Sunday, Monday and Tuesday passed by uneventfully. Wednesday 20 November Cesca discloses that the exciting letter with good news came on Saturday. The only surviving letter from Bill was tucked in this diary. He had had an official letter from HQ saying they were applying for his passage as soon after Dec 1 as possible.

Saturday 23 November

Headache very bad made worse by Frances being rude and giving notice. Tiresome rat. It means she will leave two days before Christmas which is nice. Two letters from Bill and also a small bottle of scent! Lovely! To bed early with shatteringly bad headache.

Monday 25 November

Three letters from Bill which was too lovely. Such a joy especially as he hopes soon to wire his departure date. Went into Ipswich with Mum to interview kitchen maid. Thick fog all day.

Wednesday 27 November

Bill wired to say he sails on Wednesday 4 Dec and due to arrive at Tilbury on 13 or 14 December. I shall be quite batty with delight. Simply cannot get over Bill's return, simply can't believe it at all, it's marvellous.

Thursday 28 November

Nannie went out so I had charge of babies which I enjoyed except Clare was cross in evening. Am getting desperately thrilled and excited over his return. I shall go completely utterly mad with joy.

Friday 29 November

Doris did my packing. Went off to London, busy day shopping in Peter Jones. Also did some telephoning to Bill's bank to sell some of his shares. Sold his Associated Equipment for exchange into Associated Electrical. Almost finished Xmas shopping. Posted letter to Bill to Marseilles. Then left on 4.50 train to Maidstone where Betty met me with the car and we went to Boxley. Nice to be back again.

Saturday 30 November

Wet morning. All went out shooting thickly clad and big shoes on.

The bag was 31 pheasants, 88 rabbits, 3 partridge, 3 woodcock, 2 pigeon and 1 plover. I enjoyed it but felt so cold. Good lunch.

Sunday 1 December

Do not sleep well in this house. Do not know why as I'm beautifully warm, comfy and have big fire and every comfort. Went to early church with all Style family. How I long for Bill. In a fortnight we may be together.

Monday 2 December

Left the Styles at 9.30, they were all so nice to me and I do like them.Train arrived at 11.00. Very cold and unpleasant. Went to Harrods to enquire about the *Moldavia* and was worried to be told she did not sail till 11 Dec. Awful shock so I went to P.O. offices and found it incorrect and that she leaves on 4 Dec arriving at Tilbury 13 Dec. How lovely! Lunched at Fortnum & Mason. Ordered new dress at Miss Gray's. Home to find six letters from Bill. Such heaven.

Tuesday 3 December

All babies well, but Nannie turning rather tiresome. Mary and Merlin sweet. Have written last letter to Bill. Went over to interview kitchen maid at Rushmere taking the twins with me. Both very tiresome. Nannie very trying and has the day off tomorrow in London with Mrs Beasley.

Wednesday 4 December

Somewhat hectic with Nannie, Mrs Beasley and May all away but all babies miraculously good. Bill sails today and do hope and pray to God nothing stops him and that by now he is at last coming nearer to me at every moment. Wrote party invitations for children's party on 28 December.

Thursday 5 December

Can't think of anything else but Bill's return. It's all so lovely. Busy doing up parcels for Christmas.

Friday 6 December

Very cold and foggy. Heard my Hawker Siddeley shares sold for 26/-. Bill's Associated Electrical going up by leaps and bounds. In

a week I shall be in Bill's arms. Oh I do love him so. Mum bought
two budgerigars from Mrs Broomfield for children's Christmas
present. Most exciting. Drove home in thick fog. I hung my head
out of the window most of the way.

Saturday 7 December
Cold and bitterly hard frost and thick fog. Doing up parcels in
afternoon and cards. Letter from Bill, the last I shall have from
Malta.

Sunday 8 December
Mum's Birthday. Gave Mum a linen bin, the children vases.

Monday 9 December
Have secured kitchen maid. Two letters from my darling this
evening from Marseilles. Lovely to know he is on his way. So
excited, feel all queer.

Tuesday 10 December
Went to London for fitting at Miss Gray's and ordered a dress in
eggshell blue chiffon. Went to P&O office. My love arrives at
Tilbury at 3.30 am and is allowed off at 8.30 am so I must be up
early and motor down to be with him. Awful gale tonight. He
must be having an awful tossing poor darling. I feel so worried
about him. Cross Channel boats are not allowed to sail. Home to
find Mum seedy and cross but Dad all right.

The next two days Cesca got all 'mithered' and muddled the days up. Lots of
crossings out.

Thursday 12 December
Went up to London and stayed at the Mayfair. Terribly excited.
Had face treatment at Elizabeth Arden. Dined with Mrs Ionides.

Friday 13 December
To bed but could not sleep and soon it was 6.00 am. I dressed and
tried to eat a bit of breakfast. Set off for Tilbury and arrived after
perilous drive and saw my darling leaning over the side of the ship
waving. Too lovely. He soon disembarked and we sped away in
the car for London. Simply too lovely to be with him again. Can't

get over it. Went to 'Espionage' in evening after dinner at the
Berkeley Grill. Everything perfect being together again.

Saturday 14 December

Up early, very sleepy but so happy and went off to Belstead.
Arrived in bitter cold and snow at 12.00. Children delighted at
seeing Bill again, also Mum and Dad. Feel whirly with utter joy
and excitement and so happy. Everything is perfect.

Sunday 15 December

Stayed in bed for breakfast. Then to church with Bill and Dad.
Spent the day quietly with family and children. So much to say
and do together and we are all utterly happy.

Monday 16 December

Very cold, frosty and foggy. So happy just to be together, and all
anxiety over for time being. Although news about Italy is not very
reassuring.

Tuesday 17 December

Went over to Rendham see Mrs Lunn and George at their little
house which is quite sweet though in the depths of the country.
Had nice tea and came home. Roads frosty and very cold indeed.

Wednesday 18 December

Sent off all Xmas cards and parcels. Bill and I went to London, he
to Air Ministry and I to Miss Gray's for fitting. Then to Dandy's for
lunch. Found her very well and cheerful and she gave us an
excellent lunch of soup, roast beef and apples in jelly and a soufflé.
Then we went to Harrods, bought some things for Christmas.
Home after having tea on the train.

Thursday 19 December

Mother seedy with bad cold and trouble inside again. She was
unable to go to the de Haviland's Lunch Party which disappointed
her very much.

Saturday 21 December

Frances Greenacre left after being with me nearly two years. New
girl Edith Forsdyke arrived and though young seems already to

make atmosphere less electric with Mrs Beasley. Parcels and cards arriving by every post.

Sunday 22 December

Very cold, all roads frozen and ice everywhere. We shall have a real white Christmas. Twins at last getting good with Bill!

Monday 23 December

Have a tiresome cold. Bill skating. Went over to collect budgerigars after lunch at Mrs Bromfields. Her son Patrick and daughter Betty are joining our party for the Hunt Ball. Cold so bad on my return that I retired to bed with aspirins after a mustard bath.

Tuesday 24 December

Had breakfast in bed, feeling better. Busy doing things for Christmas. In afternoon went over to Mrs Vivian's children's party at Foxborough Hall which Bill, Mary, Merlin and I thoroughly enjoyed. It was great fun and very well organised. Mary got a nice book and Merlin an aeroplane. Both looked very nice. Mary in pink silk and Merlin in green (Rowes) trousers and silk shirt. All home by 6.30. Busy getting presents ready for tomorrow.

Wednesday 25 December: Christmas Day

So glad to be with my darling. It has just made all the difference and made it perfect. Bill and I went off early to Holy Communion taking Nannie and May. The Ussherwoods all came to lunch and tea and we enjoyed having them so much. All the children had wonderful presents. I had a cigarette case and pen from Mum and Dad £25. The children went off happy to bed, the sweet darlings.

Thursday 26 December

Busy letter writing. Mother and Bill decorating Xmas tree in preparation for party on Saturday.

Friday 27 December

May's day off and four maids went to theatre tonight. Another four go on Monday. Preparing for party. We expect 26 children and a good many adults.

Saturday 28 December

The children and mothers, nurses and friends started to arrive for the party. Tea in dining room. Grown-ups had theirs in study. Dad dressed up as Father Christmas and gave away presents. Twins were terrified and were carried screaming from the room with several other children. Barlow played the piano and we played musical chairs, nuts in May, Musical bumps, and blind mans buff, general post etc! Exhausted afterwards when they all left at 6.00.

Sunday 29 December

Bill and I went to Carol Service and brought the Ussherwoods home to tea. Mum much better. She has not been well lately and her inside trouble has been worrying her. So happy with my darling boy at home.

Monday 30 December

Wet day, flooding at bottom of the hill. Children went to Fancy dress party at the Parkers. They went as a Dutch boy and girl, Mary in red and white check gingham, white cap and clogs and Merlin in large baggy red trousers, black waistcoat and black hat and pipe.

Tuesday 31 December

Mother and I went to London and saw 'The Rivals' which we both much enjoyed. Bill met us at station. It is so lovely to have my Billy home with me. This year is ending so happily after the miserable autumn.

1936
Belstead
Cesca used 'The Boudoir Diary' purchased from Harrods for 5s 6d

Cesca, Bill, the children and her parents are living together, not always harmoniously, at Belstead. The death of George V, held in high esteem and affection by the people, affected everyone. The abdication of Edward VIII followed. The cook, Mrs Beasley, gave notice in January, a frightful bombshell. In July Merlin falls from the swing, resulting in a four-inch cut to his head The hoped-for sale of 2 Walton Place does not materialise. This prevents Bill and Cesca finding a home together. Bill is now based at Andover at Staff College. More separations. A burglary at Belstead frightens Cesca. Bill takes a little shoot for the season at Hemley. In October Cesca has a call from Bill. He has been appointed to Staff Headquarters Cairo after he leaves Staff College. Although this means leaving their babies, they make plans to live in Egypt together from January 1937. And a pony makes her appearance, to Mary's joy.

Wednesday 1 January
Have been in charge of the children all day as Nannie had the day off. Bill, John Peel and I went for a long walk, along the bottom of the hill up Sandy Lane and home. A lovely day, and perfect views of this beautiful bit of country. Nannie returned while I was busy bathing the children.

Thursday 2 January
Ordered food for weekend party. John left after lunch. Bill fetched David Atcherley from the station at teatime. He is nice. He and Bill talk and talk! Excellent dinner.

Friday 3 January
Very cold and rather foggy, felt worried about getting to Bury for the dance this evening. Claude and Margaret arrived from Duxford by car. Wore my new bluey green chiffon dress from Miss Gray. We had an excellent dinner and I thought it was a lovely dance.

Saturday 4 January

Bill, the Pellys and David went off by train for Twickenham to see the All Blacks beaten by England. Dad returned from seeing the same match at 7.30 and the others at 8.15. All very tired. Mrs Beasley sent in a poor dinner owing, I'm afraid to this wretched little kitchen maid.

Sunday 5 January

The Pellys, Mum, Dad, Bill the children, Nannie and I went to Belstead Church. Very cold. David and Heather went for a walk and left later by 5.40 train to London. I find her difficult but David nice but wild. Claude and Margaret very jolly and we spent a happy evening together.

Monday 6 January

Claude and Margaret left for Andover via Duxford. Mum and Dad rather cross and difficult. Set off after lunch to go to London by car. Having shopped arrived at the Durhams at 5.00. Isobel very cheerful and well but Uncle Bill definitely aged since his illness and looks tired.

Tuesday 7 January

Bill slept in Uncle Bill's dressing room and I in the tiny spare room. Set off early for Andover arriving at lunchtime at the Pellys' very nice small house called Penton Manor. We had a nice spare room and the house very comfy. Spent afternoon looking at houses, flats and rooms in heavy rain.

Wednesday 8 January

Wired Mum to tell her returning home tomorrow and spend the day seeing the agents in Andover re The Old Farm Cottage and made an offer of 35/- for this. Went to see Ursula after lunch. Her new house is very fine. Frightful afternoon with gale and pouring rain.

Thursday 9 January

Motored home via Uxbridge, Hertford, Bishops Stortford and Colchester arriving about 2.30. Enjoyed our drive in spite of the rain and wet roads. Found family rather bolshy. Servants all right except for Mrs Beasley and the kitchen maid who is impossible.

Friday 10 January

Had fuss with Mrs B and she nearly gave notice. Can't find any other kitchen maid. Mum and Dad go to Bath tomorrow which will be a blessing and do them good as they are very difficult.

Saturday 11 January

Mum and Dad departed with much fuss at 9.30. Really lovely to be alone together, and with the children. Went for a walk together. Edith, the kitchen maid left in the morning. I was pleased as since then things are far smoother. Lovely to be together and to have another week's leave.

Tuesday 14 January

Rather worried about Merlin who does not sleep well so rang up Dr Banks and asked him to come tomorrow. Went to Yaxley to interview under nursemaid who I engaged. Merlin sleeping with us, very restless and dreaming, poor little boy.

Wednesday 15 January

Doctor B came, ordered him medicine, to stay in bed and sleep with me. Letter from Mum and a box of Bath Olivers and Bath Buns. They both appear to be enjoying themselves.

Thursday 16 January

Had sweep in library, chimney bad again. Heard that our offer has been accepted for the cottage near Andover. Heavy fall of snow and bitterly cold.

Friday 17 January

So happy with my Bill and all the time he is so good to me. Wire from Mum to say they are returning tomorrow owing to the cold.

Saturday 18 January

We went to meet Mum and Dad from their train. Bitterly cold and much snow and frost. The King is very ill and great concern for him is shown by everyone and the press. Busy preparing for our move to Andover on Monday. Excellent dinner slip soles, roast chicken and cherry cream.

Sunday 19 January

Mary and Merlin are much better, so I shall not worry about leaving them while I'm at Andover. Terribly cold. Went to Flatford to see skating and Bill skated. New kitchen maid satisfactory. Children busy painting with us in Library. Mum and Dad flew into a rage about the cottage and the fact I shall be away. It really is unkind of them and beastly our last night here.

Monday 20 January

Bill and I had disturbed and agitated night over the horrid and peculiar way in which the family are behaving. We would far sooner be on our own, but cash is the trouble until 2 Walton Place sells. Set off after icy coolness from family. Arrived at the Pellys at 3.00 and Bill and Claude went off to tea in the Mess. The King is very ill and the bulletin at 9.30 stated he is not going to live.

Tuesday 21 January

Bill and Claude went off early. Heard The King died last night at 11.55. All papers black edged and everyone feeling miserable. Shall have to buy black. Dined with the Pellys and Margaret sent me some daffodils to put in our cosy little room.

Wednesday 22 January

Mrs T cooked nice breakfast and Bill went off to The Mess. I finished tidying and gave Mrs T instructions and left at 11.45 to walk to the station. Met Bill and felt so sad at leaving him, just like last parting on a platform when he went to Malta. Excellent journey from Basingtoke, went to Fortnum & Mason and got some black things there. Sturgeon met me at the station and the family were quite amicable but cool.

Thursday 23 January

Everyone everywhere in black or grey for The King. Things will be very gloomy and sad for next few months. Mother and Dad much nicer and all seems well here.

Friday 24 January

Frightful bombshell this morning. Mrs Beasley late again with nursery and staff breakfasts. I blew her up and she gave notice and at breakfast kitchen maid ran away! I rushed around to get a new kitchen maid and cook, not much success so far.

Saturday 25 January

Went into Ipswich, interviewed and engaged temp cook. Mrs B impossible. No news except depressing details of King's funeral.

Monday 27 January

After having my hair washed in Ipswich I saw a kitchen maid who I engaged. This was very lucky.

Tuesday 28 January

King George V funeral. Listened on wireless to it all morning. Everything very sad and depressing. Told Mrs B she could go tomorrow.

Wednesday 29 January

Pouring wet depressing day. Papers full of George V funeral. Went for walk to see floods with Dad. Paid Mrs B who departed peacefully and left kitchen all beautifully clean. Collected Mrs Worly and new kitchen maid. Such a relief to have a pleasant woman and all going smoothly in the kitchen.

Friday 31 January

Mrs Worly, blasted woman gave notice and all because she has not got a fire in servant's hall. After lunch I went up to London by train. Took my luggage by underground to Waterloo where I interviewed Mrs King, a cook who seems good and keen to come. Bill met me at Andover and am so happy to be at our dear little cottage. Very warm and cosy though Bill says it is damp.

Saturday 1 February

Nice morning but very damp in cottage and it smells musty. Bill and I shopped in Andover then had lunch. Had dinner with Margaret and Claude then onto the cinema to see The King's Funeral. Both had some Ovaltine and went to bed. It's lovely to be together and all alone with no servants or children, sometimes.

Sunday 2 February

We got up very late after breakfast in bed and went to Penton church. Went to see the Gilmores at their little house in

Winchester Road. Looked at cottage at Abbotts which we both liked. May have to leave Charlton as it's so damp.

Monday 3 February

Sad leaving Bill again, also concerned about the damp of the cottage. It seems so musty, smells nasty and is full of beetles. Then back to Belstead, all well.

Tuesday 4 February

Woke in the night several times, worried about the babies and the under nurse. Mum went into Ipswich to see royal funeral at the cinema.

Wednesday 5 February

Nanny rang early to say her mother had died therefore she could not return until the end of the week. Lucy can't stay either. Too tiresome. Bill rang up to say his daily help had decamped and he was in a mess. Poor darling. Mrs Worly left and Mrs King arrived. Poor dinner but perhaps she will improve.

Thursday 6 February

I am in the dark as to when nanny will return. Mum and Dad most helpful in every way and so good to me. Mum gave me lovely new nighty and white crepe housecoat for my 7th wedding anniversary.

Friday 7 February

Letter from Nanny saying funeral not until Monday so she cannot return until Tuesday. Children are all very good, but of course it's a great tie. Mrs King sent in better lunch today. Met Bill at station, lovely to have him home.

Monday 10 February

Cecily has diarrhoea but better in afternoon. In evening Merlin was terribly sick and then Mary. I had them both with me. They were sick on and off all night.

Tuesday 11 February

Bill sent me lovely scent spray from Floris for our wedding anniversary tomorrow. Seem to be very broke still and no news of 2 Walton Place. M and M recovered. Nanny wired, she is returning later! She really is the limit and I am fed up with her. Nanny returned just before I left for Andover. Snowing hard and bitterly cold.

Wednesday 12 February

Bill sent me the most lovely bouquet for our seventh wedding anniversary. The carnations and lilies smelt lovely. Dad sent us a very generous and kind cheque for £50. Looked at some more cottages with Margaret then Bill and I came home after dinner at Star and Garter.

Thursday 13 February

The cottage still terribly damp and cold. Had taxi to station after saying goodbye to Bill and lunched on train to London. To Ipswich on 4.54.

Friday 14 February Twins Birthday

Slept like a log until I was called. Lovely day for my darlings' second birthday. Do love them so. In afternoon had tea party in dining room and Mrs K made two lovely iced cakes for the twins, white and pink with Clare and Cecily written on them. I went to meet Bill. Exceedingly cold.

Saturday 15 February

Bill and I spent lovely day together. Ipswich in the morning and rested in the afternoon and he went to sleep in the library.

Friday 21 February

Decided suddenly that something must be done about 2 Walton Place. Decided we must do it up and refurnish it. Went up to London and shopped hard. Went to Miss Gray's for a fitting then Harrods, Fortnum & Mason. Met Bill after having looked at 2 Walton Place. I told him my plans. Arrived back home to find a rather frosty atmosphere and the kitchen maid who was desperately seedy this morning much worse. I rang up the doctor who came to see her.

Saturday 22 February

Worried about Daisy who seems really ill. Rang Dr McEwan who said she must at once go to hospital and be operated on for appendix. Mother absolutely sickening and most tiresome. Felt furious and went into Ipswich shopping. Bill and I went to see Gay Divorce in the evening.

Sunday 23 February

Same exceedingly frigid atmosphere. Am getting a bit tired of it. Bill and I went out for a walk in afternoon. After tea he had to go and caught the 5.13 back. Felt miserable.

Monday 24 February

Mother and I had it out and all was well afterwards. Had sweet letter from my darling which cheered me up. Went to the sale at The Grove, Bealings. Had a long walk there from the main road. Caught bus back.

Tuesday 25 February

Very busy preparing for Mary's party on Thursday, cakes etc. Mrs K. exceedingly cross and sent in cold coffee. I complained with the result that she gave notice. More work to find another.

Wednesday 26 February

Went over to the sale at Bealings which I much enjoyed. Mum helping me with cash for the moment and I spent £16.0.0 on sofas and chairs. I did love it and feel very pleased to have had an excellent day. Walked home as no buses.

Thursday 27 February

Mary's 6th Birthday. My sweet pet. It can't be as long ago as 6 years. Lovely presents. I gave her coral necklace, a new dress and hanky. Mum a pram, Dad a dress and hairbrush, Merlin books, Dandy, Mrs Lunn books etc. Went over to 2nd day of sale at Bealings and then home at 3.00. Birthday party of 26 and all went off very well and Mrs K sent in lovely cakes.

Friday 28 February

All the goods came over from Bealings and I was pleased with them. Then went to London and had lunch with Aunt Edie. Went in the car with her to Walton Place and met Tilbury and discussed the house with him. Met Bill and came home on the train together having dinner on the train. Family very pleasant.

Sunday 1 March

Lovely day. Bill and I went to Belstead church. He left in the evening to return to Andover.

Monday 2 March

Letter from Bill written last night from the In and Out Club. Interviewed kitchen maid called Doris Sheldrake whom I engaged to come on Wednesday. Then went with Mum to Playford Hall to see furniture there.

Tuesday 3 March

Woke to find two letters from my darling. Lovely of him when busy to write twice to me. Went for long walk with children and Nannie. Lovely warm sunny afternoon.

Wednesday 4 March

Went to see Tilbury and agreed his estimate after more discussions. Had fitting for my black dress with Miss Gray. Home early as London was so cold.

Friday 6 March

Went to the Sale at the Arcade all morning, Mother collected me. I bought a set of 5 chairs, a mirror, china and glass. Bill arrived home for the weekend. Lovely.

Sunday 8 March

Went up to London by train where we were met by car from Shrimptons. Inspected Brown's Hotel and The Flemings in Clarges Street and decided to stay at the latter. A nice room and bath for 24/- per day. Lunched with Mrs Ionides which was excellent. Bill worked with David Atcherly, then we had tea in the club. We dined at the Berkeley and then to cinema, 'Captain Blood'.

Monday 9 March

Bill off with the Staff College to Dagenham to see Ford Works. I had busy day shopping, seeing the house and lunching with Gabriel. Bill returned and we dined with the Ionides, afterwards going to dance at Quaglinos. To bed 1.00.

Tuesday 10 March

Bill off to Croydon to see London Airport. I met Mum at Miss Gray's and returned home with her in the evening. Very warm and lovely day.

Wednesday 11 March

The car took me over to Playford Hall for the Sale there. I enjoyed it but found things were fetching rather high prices. Walked to Woodbridge Road for bus, home by teatime.

Thursday 12 March

Second day of Sale at Playford. Better prices and got a good deal of stuff. Letters from Bill. Children all so well and sweet.

Friday 13 March

Arranged for things to be delivered from Playford. They arrived at lunchtime.

Saturday 14 March

Bill celebrated his 30 Birthday at tea this afternoon with cake etc.

Tuesday 17 March

Wrote letters. Mrs King terribly cross and bolshy. Shall have to get rid of her. Wrote to Bill for his Birthday tomorrow. Marriage Allowance starts which will be helpful.

Wednesday 18 March

Went up to London with Mother to Walton Place. Saw the foreman and carpet man. Work progressing well. Had tea with Gabriel where I met Margaret with whom I motored down to Andover in her Alvis. My Billy's Birthday, the darling boy. Found him and Claude both so tired with very heavy week of work.

Thursday 19 March

Margaret had lunch party and her in-laws came over from Wincanton for the day. Claude and Bill are both working hard. Decided to motor home together tomorrow. Enjoying myself.

Friday 20 March

Bill and Claude at work in the morning. We left for Belstead after lunch and much enjoyed the drive. Took us four and a half hours. All well at home.

Saturday 21 March

Lovely weekend. No carpets in Library and Drawing Room as spring- cleaning starting this lovely weather. Went over to Bury to view the Sale at the Corn Exchange. Drove over hump on way home and knocked my head on car roof. Had headache.

Sunday 22 March

Bill returned to Andover after lunch, lovely weekend together and these warm days are so nice after the winter. He is so good to me.

Monday 23 March

Lovely day, up early and over to Bury by train. Lots of people at the Sale and most things fetched big prices. I got a sofa, a wardrobe, two beds and some oddments and lots of nice curtains.

Tuesday 24 March

Man down from London to lay Library and Drawing room carpets. And had excellent old man from Belstead here all day to beat carpets in Dining room, Study, stairs and landing. Bevan here loading up from 4.00 until 5.30.

Wednesday 25 March

Left for London early with May. Took taxi to Walton Place and was furious to find the painters had not finished so Mrs Webb had not been able to do all she should. However soon set to work. Bevan arrived and unloaded first load. Staying at Isobel's which is a comfort. May staying at Mrs Ottaway's.

Thursday 26 March

Went to Walton Place at 9.30. Man has installed telephone, also boy has now cleaned and installed gas cookers and stoves. Electric to be connected on Monday. Went to Maples for bedsteads and Peter Jones for lamps and shades. Tea at Mary Wilson's.

Friday 27 March

Slept well and up early. Said goodbye to all at Hans Crescent. Then to the house which is really getting on splendidly. Another load from Bevan. Painters have finished and May is excellent. Had two Americans to view the house. May and I returned to Belstead on

3.40 meeting Bill and had tea in our carriage. Very tired indeed. Aunt Freda arrived at 6.30.

Saturday 28 March

Babies all seem very well and none the worse for my absence. Aunt Freda is a dear and Mum likes her too. Mrs K cooking so much better and is more pleasant. Excellent dinner both evenings. Lovely warm day so took children in garden after tea. Am so pleased with Library carpet. To bed after playing Lexicon and L'Attaque.

Sunday 29 March

Bill and I got up early and went to Communion. Philip and Henry Van Straubenzie, Aunt Freda, Mum and Dad all went at 11.00. After tea my darling boy left and I saw him off. Philip and Henry left after dinner.

Monday 30 March

Went over to Stowmarket with Mum and Aunt Freda to interview a kitchen maid and secured her to come on April 8. On our return, stopped at Coles in Stowmarket and bought a nice antique screen and a small mirror for Walton Place.

Tuesday 31 March

Up early and did up several parcels of things to take up to Walton Place. Aunt Freda and I went up by train and shared a taxi to Walton Place. She went on to Weatherby Gardens. Found the house all in a hopeless muddle. Carpet men not finished and everything messy. But was terribly thrilled to get an offer from the American couple called McCabe who saw it last week.

Tuesday 2 April

To London with May to the house again which is getting on very well indeed. The Americans have signed the agreement and are paying £236 until October. Most satisfactory. Shopped for the house all day.

Friday 3 April

Up to London, I hope for last time. May, the daily and Mrs Webb all there finishing off everything. Went to Elizabeth Arden for face treatment after which I felt much better. Home 6.15 and Bill arrived soon after. Worried as the American rang saying he could not move in unless there was adequate furniture.

Saturday 4 April

This worried me all night until we rang this morning and found he was moving in and all well. Much relieved. Claude and Margaret arrived at tea time. Very cold and fires lit everywhere.

Sunday 5 April

David was expected last night but arrived by air just before lunch and we met him at Ipswich Aerodrome.

Monday 6 April

Heard from agent that Mr McCabe still seems to require an enormous amount of things. Bought a lovely Chippendale bureau bookcase, a chair and a table from Coles in Stowmarket for 2 Walton Place. David returned to London by air in evening. Mum and Dad very cheerful and the weekend was a success.

Tuesday 7 April

Bevan took up another load last evening and Mr McCabe has received it all. Bill, and the Pellys all left for Andover in the Alvis. Rather depressed with so much to do, tidying up all day long. The kitchen maid left and Mrs K much better tempered.

Wednesday 8 April

Spent most of the morning in Ipswich, went in the Lanchester with Mother and collected new kitchen maid. No cheque yet from the agent which is a bit steep. Finished tidying my bedroom drawers and cupboards.

Thursday 9 April

Horrors and very worried as the kitchen maid walked off this morning. Awful job now to get another. Bought very nice bow fronted chest of drawers from Stammers Sale. Mum came with me to find a kitchen maid. No luck in spite of motoring over half of Suffolk. Collected Bill at station.

Friday 10 April Good Friday

Lovely to have Bill home. All went to church. Busy preparing for guests and doing accounts.

Saturday 11 April

Lovely day though very cold and big fires everywhere. Betty Cripps arrived, and John Peel in his new baby Ford. I have secured 2 girls from the village who are a great help. Mrs King cooking well.

Sunday 12 April Easter Sunday

Bill and I and John went to Holy Communion taking Mrs K, Nannie and May with us. Food is very good this weekend. I have a lovely ham from Selfridges. Children overwhelmed with Easter eggs.

Monday 13 April

All went over to Woodbridge Horse Show. Bitterly cold but we loved it. The Suffolk horses were lovely also the Hunters. In afternoon display of trick riding and jumping. Home at 5.30.

Wednesday 15 April

John left. Bill and I went over to lunch with Ian Smiths at Aldeburgh, then on to Mrs Lunn at Rendham. Found her and George in and had tea with them. Bill invited them to come with us to Badingham Pt to Pt on Thursday.

Thursday 16 April

Had the sweep in Nursery and Mum's room. Took Mary, Merlin, Nannie and the twins to tea at Mrs Mason's at Northcliffe, Felixstowe, while Bill went to see shoot at Hemley Hall. Bill most taken with the shoot. The asking price is £60 and they need a decision quickly.

Friday 17 April

Bill and I feel we cannot decide in such a hurry. Busy packing for our weekend at Buxted Park. By train to London, then the Ionides car met us at Buxted station. A lovely house and we have a lovely bedroom but it is so cold. Large fires but no heating.

Saturday 18 April

Just one other guest, Lady Hood, quite nice, but rather a society woman.

Sunday 19 April

Bill, Basil, Lady Hood and I went to Buxted Church. The house is so very cold.

Monday 20 April

Bill and I left and caught 11.00 train, terribly slow, arriving in London at 1.00. Inquired about rooms at the Hans Crescent Hotel for the Royal Tournament on May 12. Home by 3.10 after lunching at Searcy's. Children all well and Mum and Dad very pleasant.

Tuesday 21 April

Busy day getting straight. The Turners, and Dr and Mrs Banks came to dinner. Salmon mayonnaise, mixed grill, strawberry ice and cheese wafers. All stayed up late and listened to the Budget.

Wednesday 22 April

Bill made offer for shoot and heard it was accepted, for the next season.

Thursday 23 April

Bill and I set off for Badingham Pt to Pt with a picnic lunch and picked up Bill's Mother and George. Lovely warm day. We had an excellent lunch of salmon pates, sandwiches, cold chicken, cake and jam puffs, coffee, beer etc. George and Bill had luck. Actually Bill's horse won and as we left the ground he managed to give half to George who was delighted.

Friday 24 April

My little Merlin's 5th birthday. Bill and I gave him a bow and arrow, a cannon gun and a platinum tie pin. Dandy sent him a water pistol and a football. Mum a cricket set and Dad 10/- and Mrs Lunn 10/-. Mrs King impossible and so rude. She leaves on Monday.

Saturday 25 April

Have secured Mrs Worly for Monday and the kitchen maid, fortunately, is staying on. Walk in afternoon and had a bad headache.

Sunday 26 April

Bill, Mum and Dad all went to church but as I still have a headache, I rested in the loggia. Mrs King asked to stay on, worried about this but feel I shall be better off without her.

Monday 27 April

Mrs K left and Mrs Worly returned here. Peace in the kitchen at last. Busy looking for a permanent cook and kitchen maid. The Acacia tree is being taken down which is very sad.

Tuesday 28 April

Merlin's 5 birthday party. Great fun. Bill in splendid form playing with children. We had a treasure hunt and parcels hidden all over the garden then lovely tea and cakes. And then games in the garden, hide and seek, blind man's buff and grandmother's footsteps. Merlin loved it. Mum cross.

Wednesday 29 April

Mother in London all day and home late, still very cross indeed.

Thursday 30 April

Decided to go down to Andover tomorrow. Paid wages and packed in evening. Took Mary and Merlin over to the shoot and had picnic which was great fun.

Friday 1 May

Mum still very cross and I felt rather upset about it. Bill is so sweet to me which makes things all right. Set off at 9.30 and car went well. Lunched at Dandy's, nice to see the old lady again and we had an excellent lunch. Arrived at Andover at 6.00 and found our rooms very nice and cosy. So happy to be together. Food not very good.

Saturday 2 May

Busy morning getting our rooms straight and unpacking. Poor Mrs Taylor is obviously very badly off and a bad manager too. It is rather down at heel, poor things. We have made our rooms very nice and if only the food would improve all would be well. Saw Claude and Margaret and the Gilmores.

Sunday 3 May

We were woken early by the howling child. I went to sleep again. Very cold so had fire in our sitting room. Had excellent lunch with the Pellys after church at Penton. Then Bill finished his holiday task and we all went for a walk together.

Monday 4 May

Went off to the station with Bill after breakfast. Excellent train to London. Busy shopping all day. Saw a man run over which was horrid. Lunched at Cordon Bleu, very good food there. Home on 4.54. Mum very cross when I returned as I had not left our address with her.

Wednesday 6 May

Mlle Roger Machart [governess] arrived this evening by train. She is very slim, quiet little thing but I was slightly staggered at her asking for £1 a week pocket money. Said this was quite impossible.

Thursday 7 May

Dad went down to Tunbridge Wells. Mlle settling in and children like her which is the great thing. Spent evening with Mother in library over big fire.

Friday 8 May

Went into Ipswich and took Mlle in to register her at the Police Station. Aunt Alice and Uncle Henry arrived followed by Bill at about 5.00. Mrs Worly gave us an excellent dinner, soup, roast lamb, asparagus, strawberry gateau, coffee and dessert.

Saturday 9 May

Very cold for tennis. However had a nice party, 22 in all. I am enjoying this weekend. The Bromfields came to dinner and we had Lobster a la Newburg, chicken Maryland, chocolate ice and cheese soufflé.

Monday 11 May

Nannie came along to my room to say Mary was ill with acidosis. Too sickening as were to have gone to London today for the Royal Tournament tomorrow. Bill decided we must keep to our plans and go up early tomorrow morning. Mary still sick.

Tuesday 12 May

Left Mary in Dad, Mlle and Nannie's charge. Merlin, Mum and I went off on the 10 train. Merlin terribly thrilled over it all. Had car to meet us and take us to the Hotel. Took asparagus and flowers to McCabes and Durhams. Had lunch and then to Royal Tournament where we met Bill and David. Excellent show and we had a box and enjoyed it enormously. Poor Mum not feeling well.

Wednesday 13 May

Woke up early, breakfast in bed. Then Mer and I went to the toy department at Harrods and we bought a spear. Then to Hyde Park by bus where we fed the birds and ducks. Then we all lunched at Isobel's. Home by 3.10 and found Mary better but twins sick all last night. Dad very cross.

Friday 15 May

Poor Merlin has got this horrible sickness. He has been sick since 5.00 am. Spent busy day dealing with the invalids. Bill home this evening. Mary in my room as Merlin so seedy.

Saturday 16 May

May and Nellie down with it this morning. Worried about Merlin, his temperature is 101. He said to me 'Mummy, if my temperature goes up to 105, I shall die, shan't I?' Played tennis with Mlle and Bill in evening.

Sunday 17 May

Sent for Dr Banks as Merlin still seedy and temp. of 100. He thinks it is a horrid germ but wants a specimen in case of paratyphoid. Mother still seedy, poor dear. Mlle also sick last night. Dad in bed for breakfast. Left with Bill in evening for Andover as Merlin better. Had a good run down arrived at 12.15

Monday 18 May

Woke at 7.00. Everything very nice and cosy. Bill went off to work. I wrote letters and enjoyed a quiet morning. Lunched with Pellys.

Tuesday 19 May

Very hot and lovely. Bill back for lunch which was very good today. Before I left I wrote out a list of foodstuffs Bill likes for Mrs

Taylor. Bill and I went to watch the flying of visiting squadrons at the Aerodrome. Left at 4.48 by excellent train to London and caught the 6.39 home arriving 8.30. Found Suzanne Ploquim [Cesca's old governess] had arrived. Delightful to see her again. Dad well but Mum pale and has to have all teeth out.

Wednesday 20 May
I did enjoy my stay with Bill at Penton but it's now lovely to be back with the children. The cook seems to be no good. Went for walk with Suzanne. Mlle not much use I feel with children.

Thursday 21 May
Mother and Nannie to London by train (the latter loaded with eggs, chickens and lilac). After lunch Suzanne, Mlle, Mary, Merlin and I went for a walk. Mary complained of feeling cold and having a headache. I was horrified to find she had a temperature of over 102. Put her straight to bed and sent for Dr Banks. He thinks she has a relapse. Felt very worried about her.

Friday 22 May
Had to put off having the children photographed again by Miss Compton Collier. Mary still temp of 102 and Dr Banks did not come till 5.30. Poor Mary very seedy. Merlin too has a bad cough. Lovely to have Bill home. Played bridge in the evening.

Monday 25 May
Esse cooker giving trouble again and can't make it out. Cook too, is hopeless. Suzanne left after lunch. Much enjoyed having her with us as she is a dear. Mum seedy and cross over Mary being ill.

Tuesday 26 May
Children all with snuffling colds. Mary the worst. No temperature however. Arranged for them to go over to Mrs Gorts at Felixstowe on June 2 for a week. Mum in better temper. Shall really be thankful to get children and nurse out of the house. Esse cooker man came and fortunately fixed the cooker again. Felt like a cold so took aspirins, hot whisky and a hot bath and went to bed.

Wednesday 27 May

Lovely to go off to Andover to be with my darling. But had a very tiresome journey as just missed my train at Waterloo and I had to wait over an hour on the platform. Bill met me and we went for a walk. To bed feeling rotten.

Thursday 28 May

Woke up feeling very sick and dizzy and head all buzzy. Stayed in bed till lunchtime. Bill busy writing and doing prep. To bed early, still feeling queer and have an awful cold.

Friday 29 May

Up and had early lunch before leaving for Belstead in the car. Had tea on the way at Hertford. Still feeling pretty rotten so on getting home went to bed. Children are fortunately all better. Mum also less cross and difficult.

Saturday 30 May

Mrs Bowyer (cook) came to stay for Whitsun. Poor Mary went with Bill to the dentist to have a tooth out and gas. She was however quite all right. Mrs B sent in quite a good dinner of soup, fried sole, chicken cream, asparagus and lemon soufflé.

Monday 1 June

Mrs B is a dear old thing. She is staying on till Wednesday. Mum not very nice to her. Busy preparing for children to go over to Felixstowe tomorrow.

Tuesday 2 June

Very busy packing up for children. Arranged for carrier to take their cots. Mrs Worly returned fortunately. Peace in the kitchen at last and the Esse going perfectly. I set off with children, Nannie, Winnie, and Sturgeon in the Austin to Felixstowe. Settled them in and saw twins starting their bath. On my return to my fury I found that May had forgotten to send the mattresses and blankets. Was really very vexed. Had to go back in the car with these.

Wednesday 3 June

Was very tired last night and could not sleep. Kept worrying about the children as Mary was upset at my leaving her and kept dreaming of the forgotten mattresses. Mrs Bowyer and I set off to London by 9.30 train. I went with her in a taxi to Waterloo where I left my luggage. Then shopped and went to agencies about a cook. Finally had my hair washed and lunch and took the 3.30 down to Andover. Dined with Commander and Mrs Broad, she was not a good hostess. Margaret and Claude there, the latter very bucked as he had just been promoted. We got back from dinner about 11.30. It was such a cold evening, no fire and I felt quite sick with cold.

Thursday 4 June

Letter from Nannie saying children were well. Was really terribly upset when Bill told me at lunchtime that he has had another flare up with the Commandant, Barratt, who said his work was not good enough and that unless there was an improvement he would not last the course. So upset. Bill had to go back in evening and work.

Friday 5 June

Both feel miserable about Bill's trouble. After breakfast with him, off back to London. Shopped at Harrods and then to bank about my John Brown shares which have risen to 26/- Then bought myself a new mac. Joined Bill at Liverpool St. Both feel better getting away from Andover. Then we had tea in comfy 1st class carriage. Sturgeon met us.

Saturday 6 June

Mother seems cross again. There seems to be a great frost on! Bill and I both feel much better after a good night and a lovely morning too. In afternoon we went over to tea with children and found them all the picture of health. Merlin and Mary looking quite brown. Have arranged for Mrs Lunn to see them tomorrow and Elizabeth.

Tuesday 9 June

Lovely day and quite hot. Went to fetch children from Felixstowe after lunch. Paid Mrs Gort £6 and 16/- for food also the man who brought their cots to and from 12/-. And so it has cost me £7.10.0.

The great thing is the children are all so well after their time there.
Motored home in time for tea. Bill rang in evening.

Wednesday 10 June

Lovely to have babies all home and so well again. Mum in London.
Mlle has bad earache so put her to bed with oil in her ear.

Thursday 11 June

Went into Ipswich looking for under parlour maid to take
Dorothy's place. Ivy, kitchen maid left and new girl, Jean Clark
came, who is a nice type of girl.

Friday 12 June

Mother took children to Pin Mill and I went to London in the
afternoon to join Bill and help him pack up at Penton. Arrived at
7.30 in pouring rain. Settled into the rooms for the last time.

Saturday 13 June

Pouring wet and exceedingly cold too. Took Bill's things into the
Mess. Then to Andover paying bills and shopping. Then lunch,
roast chicken but the food is terribly poor and I'm sure Bill will be
much better off in the Mess. Went over to Ursula's [Cheam School]
for Old Boys Reunion Party. Met a lot of nice people there.

Sunday 14 June

Went over to church at Penton and lunched with the Pellys
afterwards. Bill and I returned and did more packing up and he
did some prep. Still so cold.

Monday 15 June

Up very early and paid our account with poor Mrs Taylor before
leaving. Pleased to be going as it is so dirty and squalid. Bill
returned to the Mess. Caught 8.35 and had a busy day shopping in
London. Lunched at Gunters and went to the Academy which I
enjoyed before returning home. Children all well and so sweet.

The rest of the week is spent searching unsuccessfully for maids and preparing
for the weekend.

Saturday 20 June

Very hot day. Tennis party in afternoon and it went off very well. Mrs Worly sent in marvellous cakes. Pat and Ursula Ainslie arrived at teatime. She does not play tennis and is very big. Mrs W. gave us an excellent dinner of grapefruit, Lobster à la Newburg, chickens and vanilla and blackcurrant ice.

Sunday 21 June

Lovely weekend. Am much enjoying it and it's lovely to have Bill home here. Very hot all day and then cooled down after violent thunderstorm in evening. Poor darling Bill, John and the Ainslies all caught in it on their way home. Nannie left for her holiday.

Monday 22 June

Very busy all day looking after children and trying to find maids as Nellie gave notice. Poor Mrs Worly was knocked off her bicycle Saturday and her leg is so bad I have had to take her home so am cookless and nurseless and am terribly busy. Out in car with twins in evening searching for maids.

Tuesday 23 June

Went over to Naval Review at Shotley in honour of the King's Birthday today. Mum and I went and we much enjoyed it. Very hot and met a good many people there that we knew.

Wednesday 24 June

I went into Ipswich with Dad, shopped and then went to a Sale at Old Museum Rooms. Awful place but most satisfactory sale from my point of view as I got some lovely sheets and linen. Also some china and glass. Home for lunch, having been there most of morning and spending £7.0.0. So pleased with my purchases. Put babies to bed.

Friday 26 June

Very busy packing for London. Must get a cook as heard Mrs W. is not yet well enough to return which is a plague. Nannie arrived back. Arrived in London at 2.00 and went to Park Lane. Then to E. Arden for face treatment. Bill met me and we had tea together at Fortnum & Mason. Then to Park Lane, changed and had light dinner at Pruniers where the Allinsons joined us. Then to 'The Frog' and then on to Café de Paris which was lovely. Bed 3.30.

Saturday 27 June

I wired a cook from Watsons to come on Monday. Then Bill and I set off for Pageant at Hendon leaving our car in the Staff College car park. Met quite a lot of friends there and had excellent packed lunch from Fortnum & Mason. Tea in Staff College Enclosure. The flying too was marvellous especially Broadhurst's display. We got away easily reaching Shrimptons [car dealership in Berkeley Square] at 6.30 and then home by 9.30.

Monday 29 June

Wet all day with thunderstorms. Busy getting house straight. New cook, Mrs Taylor, arrived at 1.30. Ursula arrived at 9.30 and seemed charmed with the house.

Tuesday 30 June

Mrs Taylor cooked a very good lunch. Then to see some friends of Ursula's at Chelsworth. A queer establishment but house contains some lovely things. Babies all well and Ursula thinks them wonderful.

Wednesday 1 July

Heard Barbara has had a son by caesarean operation, poor child. Hope she will go on all right. Went to British Legion Fete after lunch and saw the flowers which were really quite lovely. It's a joy to have such a marvellous cook again. All maids went to the Fete to see the Fireworks.

Thursday 2 July

Ursula left and Mum and I went into Ipswich shopping. Wrote to Bill. Worried about maids. It seems impossible to get any young ones. Miss C Collier came to photograph the children after lunch and took a lot of groups. Then after tea, an AWFUL thing happened. Merlin fell off the swing and on to the path cutting his head open four and a half inches long. Blood all over everywhere. Fortunately I got Dr Banks to come out at once and we got Dr

Golders to give him an anaesthetic and all was stitched up by 7.00. Mary with me. Merlin was very sick but slept well.

Friday 3 July

Merlin better, Thank God. Spent the night walking from my room to his every few hours to listen and check on him. Rang Bill to say I would come to Worplesdon this evening but not to lunch. Dr Banks came and said he was much better, no sickness or temperature. Bill and Mrs Harvey met me and we have a nice room. Unpacked and had a good dinner. Lovely to be with Bill.

Saturday 4 July

Spent a quiet morning and then in afternoon went to Aldershot Horse Show which we both enjoyed. The Count and Countess de Bortsch-Grave came to dinner and afterwards we played games. The Harveys are charming and house most comfy and a good cook.

Sunday 5 July

Woke feeling very weary. Bill and I left after lunch and returned to London. He saw me off and arrived home at 6.19 met by Sturgeon. Am pleased to find Merlin really himself again.

Monday 6 July

Mum at dentist in morning. She had four teeth out but all well and in evening had new ones fitted. Mlle leaving on 23 July. Bill rang to say he was at Greenwich.

Thursday 9 July

Went to London and had a busy time at Harrods doing sale ordering. Lunch at Searcy's and then to the Seligman Wedding where I only stayed for a short time.

Monday 13 July

Dad much better and up again. Still pain in my back. Merlin's bandage off now and his head much better.

Tuesday 14 July

Still awful weather but managed to pick lots of currants and raspberries for jam making. The agents wired with an offer for Walton Place for 7 guineas for 3 months. Rang to tell them I would accept £7.17.6. A large and enormous cheque arrived for Bill from South Africa. This is a great joy. Miss Worsfold arrived to paint Clare and Cecily. She is charming in every way.

Wednesday 15 July

Dad's 77th Birthday. He is very well and more cheerful. I gave him silk socks and Mum a wireless. A letter from the agents confirming Commander and Mrs Edwards offer of £7.17.6 for 3 months. Very pleased about this. Pouring with rain all day. Only went out with Pepper for half an hour in afternoon.

Thursday 16 July

Went to see Barbara Carr who is in the nursing home and getting on well after her caesarean. Baby perfectly sweet too. In afternoon busy unpacking things from Harrods.

Friday 17 July

Merlin and I off to London together with our suitcases which we left at Paddington. Then we shopped at Debenhams and had an excellent lunch of fried Dover soles and fruit salad. Then by train to Newbury where Ursula met us and drove us to Cheam School. Put Merlin to bed in the blue room. Then Bill and I went to the dance at Andover after dinner with Ursula. Lovely dance which we both enjoyed enormously. Danced mostly with Bill.

Saturday 18 July

Woke at 7.00 to hear bells being rung all over the school and boys leaping out of bed over one's head. Merlin ensconced in Harold's bed as he had upset his milk. Went into Newbury with Ursula and then played bridge in the evening with their senior master Mr Pearson.

Sunday 19 July

All went to church in the school chapel in the grounds. Harold took us in the Ford V8. Merlin rested after lunch and then went for a walk.

Monday 20 July

It is lovely to have Merlin with me and he is such a dear good little boy. No trouble. He had a PC from Mary which pleased him a lot.

Bill and I had lunch at the Barratts, it was really nice and everything well done. After lunch I motored with Bill to Basingstoke but found the train not running but replaced by an earlier one. Unfortunately Harold brought Merlin over too late to catch it so we had to wait for an age to catch slow train to London. Arrived Ipswich at 8.30 and a tired little boy got into bed at 9.00.

Wednesday 22 July

The weather is hopeless this summer. Miss Worsfold hopes to finish the twins' portraits tomorrow. In Ipswich with Mlle at Police Station in morning.

Thursday 23 July

Mlle left on 9.50 train. Interviewed a cook, Mrs Constable. Miss Worsfold showed us twins' portraits, really lovely and quite perfect.

Friday 24 July

Miss Worsfold left this afternoon and it is decided that she is to do Mary and Merlin in August. Do like her so much. Bill arrived at 6.30 and we had to do a quick change to dine at the Turners at 7.30. A very nice simple dinner then the Turners drove us to the dance at Flatford Mill. Enjoyed it but Bill and I were so tired.

July 25 Saturday

Went into Ipswich to shop and met Patricia [Bill's sister] who arrived for the weekend. Bill slept in the afternoon. We feel Pat is very bored with us.

Sunday 26 July

Pat and Bill did not go to Church. I went with Mum and Dad. Nannie being extremely trying. The cook, Mrs Taylor, leaves tomorrow which is sad. She is an excellent cook. Bill left at 5.00.

Monday 27 July

Pat left at 11.30. Quite pleased as she is not an easy individual to deal with. Bill at Southampton all week. The poor darling, does look so worn and tired. It will be a mercy when he comes on leave. Nannie being exceedingly boring in every way. Simply longing for

Bill's leave to start. Then shopped and went to agents for a French governess.

Saturday 1 August

Went into Ipswich and got myself a Driving Licence. Tennis in the afternoon at the Hempsons. Courts very wet and slippy but we had some quite good tennis and enjoyed it. I drove there!

Tuesday 4 August

Dandy and the Caldecotts came down to lunch and then to Rendham for tea. The old lady seemed to enjoy herself and was charmed with the house, children and the parents. The old lady went all round with Dad who embraced her on her departure. Bill and I then went over to the shoot at Hemley. Rather fun as we succeeded in getting a rabbit and a hare, 1 wild duck and 1 pigeon. Home for late dinner.

Wednesday 5 August

My period at last. Was getting worried about this. Went over to Cambridge to collect Bill's dog, Simon, a lovely Springer, black and white and has been trained by Curtis of Whittlesford. We had to go slowly as the car had been decarbonised, and so we cannot exceed 30 mph. Miss Worsfold arrived in evening to do Mary and Merlin's portraits.

Thursday 6 August

A tea party this afternoon. I am having to buy all the cakes as the old cook seems unable to get through the work. I have had to give her notice.

Friday 7 August

Wrote letters and shopped in morning. Rested before going to dance at Crowe Hall in evening. It was great fun and we both enjoyed it. I danced with Captain Alexander and also Mr Turner, otherwise with Bill. Home about 3.00.

Saturday 8 August

Bill and I went over to the shoot and were delighted to get a duck, some rabbits and hares. Miss Worsfold getting on with children's portraits.

Monday 10 August

Frightful shock this morning to find we had had burglars last night and that they had taken £2 of mine and some things of Mother's. Cosway miniature of George III, a corkscrew, old watch and a Dresden box. The police were soon here, we found the robber had entered through the cloakroom window and out through the drawing room.

Tuesday 11 August

The police here again, and no sign of the thief.

Shooting with Bill and children's parties fill the rest of the week.

Saturday 15 August

Mrs Constable the wretched cook left. And new cook from the agency Mrs d'Albuquerque (black!) arrived. Miss Worsfold left. Mary and Merlin's portraits are absolutely charming.

Monday 17 August

All went over to the sea at Bawdsey in two cars after lunch. Lovely afternoon and picnic tea. Bridge in evening.

Thursday 20 August

Bill, Mum and I went up to London for the day. I interviewed four awful governesses in afternoon and did not much care for any of them. Lunched at Fortnum & Masons. Bill chose me a very nice evening dress.

Friday 21 August

Nannie out for afternoon. Bill and I took picnic tea and Mary and Merlin to the sea at the shoot where Bill shot a mallard and a shelduck. Unfortunately Bill did not quite finish off the duck and we were afraid it upset Mary.

Sunday 23 August

Bill left to go to Tidworth attached to 3rd King's Own Hussars for a week. Miss him dreadfully and do love him so. Poor Mary not very well and was very sick again. She is in my room in her little bed. Still very sick in evening. Gave her dose of Castor Oil.

Wednesday 26 August

Mary up for lunch for my Birthday, 32 today. Bill sent me a wire and a very nice new brown lace evening dress, also a bottle of E.Arden scent. Mum gave me a lovely old cut glass compote, sets of mats, lavender pillows and a new entrée dish. Children all came in with presents and Clare and Cecily had lunch on the dining room and were so good. A lovely happy day only I miss my Bill so.

Thursday 27 August

Went to Sale at Stammer's Rooms and bought a butlers tray for 2/- and a toilet set for 8/6 which is very nice. Lovely hot day.

Friday 28 August

Very hot day. Bill arrived quite unexpectedly for dinner. So lovely to have him home again and looking so well. Mary seems quite well again.

Saturday 29 August

Had my hair shampooed and set by Miss Scutt. Bill working. Went over to the shoot after tea to see Hill who has a dog and also to learn how to run the shoot. Fetched Mum off the Aldeburgh bus. She had had a very jolly day. Very hot evening.

Monday 31 August

Had a pretty hectic morning preparing for the shoot tomorrow. David Atcherley arrived at Martlesham later than planned. He is very nice but as usual his own arrangements come first. A good dinner.

Tuesday 1 September

Bill and I most excited. A lovely golden morning and all set for our 1ˢᵗ day's partridge shooting. Arrived at Hemley Hall at 10.30 to find Hill and his Labrador and Col. Bromfield and his loader Ken there. David in frightful checks and Douglas did not arrive till 1.00 owing to missing his train. Lovely day and very hot. Arrived home at 5.30 with 8 brace partridges, 5 hares, 3 rabbits, 1 pigeon and a young pheasant. We had an excellent lunch in an old barn. Cold chicken, potato salad, hard boiled eggs, lettuce, tomatoes, apple puffs, cheese and biscuits, coffee. Saw David off at Martlesham.

The birds were rather wild and David a hopeless shot. Bill and I both adored it all.

Wednesday 2 September

Felt so very tired, must have walked too far. Went off to London, to Victoria where I had arranged to meet 2 governesses. Only one turned up so I interviewed Miss Haverson and engaged her. I hope I have done the right thing. Then down to Maidstone to Boxley Church for Ursula and Dick White's wedding. She looked sweet and behaved so charmingly. Lots of people I knew there. Home by 8.30 met by Bill.

Friday 4 September

Bill out shooting with the Bromfields and only got two brace partridge all day. I met Jean MacGregor at the station. I hated it as I do so loathe having to cope with strangers, especially Americans. She is pretty frightful too.

Saturday 5 September

Very rough and wild morning after pouring wet night. John, Anthony, Jean, Bill and I went over to the shoot arriving to find Wallis there already. Poor day. Very few birds. Poured with rain. The American girl is awful. Anthony shot well, Wallis never touched a feather and Hill's dog was useless. Mrs d'A. sent out a very good luncheon and an excellent dinner. Mum very cross indeed on her return from London.

Sunday 6 September

Wet morning and Mary not well with very swollen glands and sore throat. Dr Banks says she must stay in bed, poor little girl. Tennis party after lunch, twenty one of us. Too awful because this wretched American girl came down in the shortest shorts (quite disgusting) and Bill and Mum so horrified they asked me to tell her to change. So I did, then to my horror both the Alexander girls came in shorts too so I had to tell her to put them on again. Never have I felt so embarrassed.

Monday 7 September

Thank heavens Jean McGregor left at 9.30. Never have I felt so thankful to say goodbye. Bill completed his holiday task. Mary still ill.

Wednesday 9 September

Lovely morning, after the gales of last two days. Mary's neck still terribly big poor little girl. Feel so worried about her. Dr Banks came again.

Friday 11 September

Jim and Gabriel arrived soon after 7.00, all the way from Northumberland to see us. Lovely to see them both.

Saturday 12 September

Mary definitely better, such a mercy. We all went off to the shoot and had a delightful day shooting 5 brace partridge, 4 rabbits, 1 hare, 1 dove and 2 snipe. Birds quite plentiful. Home to tea after a very good picnic lunch. Good dinner of clear consommé, roast saddle, baba of fruit and cheese soufflé.

Sunday 13 September

Lovely day. Walked up to church at Belstead. Dr Banks came and said Mary may go outdoors. All sat in garden till tea time. Jim and Gabriel took brace of partridge and a rabbit with them. They all left and seemed sad at leaving. Glad to be alone with my Bill again.

Monday 14 September

Another lovely day. Family very cross and bolshy especially Mother who was quite impossible before she left for Aldeburgh to stay with Lottie. Let's hope she comes back better. Bill out shooting with Douglas Packard and got 10 brace of partridge.

Tuesday 15 September

Men came to start descaling, awful job. New parlour maid quite hopelessly inefficient. Told her she could go after Monday. Mum and Dad both bolshy. To Frinton with Bill, great fun. We found excellent rooms for children and me.

Wednesday 16 September

Mum and Dad's 45 Wedding Day. Both improved in temper but latterly have been really most trying. Played bridge with them in evening.

Thursday 17 September

The most lovely day. Mum and Dad in London. Bill, Merlin and I went over to Hemley after picking up Douglas Packard. Had most successful day getting 6 brace partridge, 1 hare, 4 rabbits and 1 snipe. Merlin very much enjoyed himself. Bill shooting awfully well.

Friday 18 September

Another perfect autumn day. After shopping early with Bill in Ipswich, sat in garden reading before lunch. Dr Banks came and said Mary could go over to Frinton next week. Family more cheerful.

Saturday 19 September

Bill and I went over to the shoot meeting Gordon Wordsworth at the Fox Inn and had a very jolly day. Partridges were very wild and scarce but still succeeded in getting 1 brace. Bill and I had tea and so loved our day together, one of the last of Bill's leave.

Sunday 20 September

Another lovely September day. We are both very sad that leave is so nearly over. Walked up to church and then after lunch Bill left for Andover in the car. Very sad but busy preparing for going to Frinton on Tuesday. Do hope it keeps fine.

Tuesday 22 September

Lovely morning. Such a joy and what a lot of good it will do the children if it lasts. Set off at 10.30 well packed into the car, Merlin on my knee in front. {How scary, no seat belts]. Nannie, Mary, the twins and luggage in the back. Arrived at Frinton at 11.30 and found mist there which cleared later and gave us a perfect afternoon. Everything awfully nice and most comfy, excellent rooms and good food.

Wednesday 23 September

Spent all day on the beach with the children enjoying ourselves. Such a nice peaceful spot. Everything most comfortable and well managed at Oak Cottage. Mrs Alton is a widow and does all the cooking herself.

Thursday 24 September

Another nice day. Saw my babies on to the sands and then caught the 11.29 to Ipswich via Colchester a long and tiring journey. Dad met me. The family very cheerful and happy. A letter from Bill saying unable to come up this weekend.

Saturday 26 September

Dad said Mum and I should have the car so we went over after breakfast and spent the day there and I took my things for the weekend. Very cold and wet however and not much fun. Children all very well.

Monday 28 September

Very cold still and so wet. Went out with the children and got soaked again. Went off home by 3.00 train, Dad met me at 4.30.

Thursday 29 September

Headache all day and such pains in my legs. Rang up Bill who is very depressed over his work, poor boy. Wrote to him. Took aspirin in evening and felt better after a hot bath and dinner.

Wednesday 30 September

Still a slight headache which got worse all day. Had a long and frustrating day in London searching for a carpet for Bill's room without success. Wrote to Bill on the train home and found a letter from him on my return.

Thursday 1 October

Went to London again today. This time with Mum and had a very pleasant time. Was delighted to find 2 Walton Place had been left most beautifully clean and tidy and nothing broken or damaged. Mum having lunch with Lottie with whom she is going to America.

Friday 2 October

Busy preparing for the weekend. Mother went to Frinton and fetched home the children and very sweetly paid for their last week there. They returned looking very fit and well. But Mary had been sick in the car of course! Claude, Margaret and my darling Bill arrived at tea time and ate a large tea. Pat and Ursula Ainslie arrived later and we had an excellent dinner of tomato soup, chicken Maryland and cheese soufflé.

Saturday 3 October

Went off to Hemley. Douglas came too and we went in Claude's Alvis as well as D.'s car arriving at 10.00. Col. Bromfield and Betty and their boy Ken there. So altogether with the two dogs we were a party of 15. Mrs d'A. packed excellent luncheon and we all enjoyed ourselves and got a good bag of 17 pheasants, 12 partridges, 3 rabbits, 4 hares and 2 pigeons. A perfect day, quite hot. Excellent dinner cooked in great style by Mrs d'A of clear consommé, lobster newburg, saddle of lamb, and praline ice.

Sunday 4 October

A perfect autumn day. Poor darling Bill does not seem to be enjoying the weekend very much and looks seedy. Went to church with Pat and Ursula. Bill, Claude and Margaret all left after lunch in the Alvis to return to Andover. Pat and Ursula left after dinner. Enjoyed the weekend very much but feel tired.

Monday 5 October

Busy preparing schoolroom and Miss Haverson's room, also giving out extra blankets for staff and selves.

Tuesday 6 October

Walked up to view the sale at the Gurneys. Not much there except a nice picture which we fancy. Also a little 20 bore shotgun by Purdy I hope to buy.

Wednesday 7 October

Spent day at the sale at Stone Lodge. I bought the picture for Mother for £5.7.6. And also the gun, a print, a coal scuttle, and a hot water can. The schoolroom is now nearly ready.

Thursday 8 October

Miss Harverson arrived at 3.15 and I met her at the station. Mary and Merlin have taken to her already, a great joy. Fetched things from Gurney sale. So relieved Miss H. seems to have some common sense.

Friday 9 October

Mum had to go to London about her passport as she is off on the *Queen Mary* on Tuesday. Spent a long morning doing accounts and writing letters. Miss H. seems to be successful in the nursery, at least in winning the children's confidence. Bill arrived on leave this evening. He seems tired and depressed about his work.

Sunday 11 October

Bill and I both awoke feeling terribly sad at the prospect of his going abroad at the end of this course. He had to leave early at 11.00 to get prep finished at Andover. Took the children and Miss H. to the childrens' service at Belstead church in afternoon.

Tuesday 13 October

After early lunch, Dad, Mum, Merlin and I went up to London by car. There Dad left us to do some shopping and we went on to Waterloo. Arrived Southampton at 5.00 and had nice rooms at the S. Western Hotel which conjures up such miseries of last year when Bill went to Malta.

Wednesday 14 October

Woke to find it pouring with rain. Had taxi after breakfast to the *Queen Mary*. The most enormous and marvellous ship. I was very thrilled and enjoyed seeing over her but found Merlin got very tired. Mum had a nice cabin and met up with Lottie. Then we said goodbye and watched the *Queen Mary* slowly leave and the tugs pull her out. A very fine sight. Lunched on the train back to London but the train to Ipswich brakes failed so not home till late.

Saturday 17 October

Very cold last night, had a big fire on our room. Went off to Hemley taking Douglas with us and had the most delightful day, getting 9 pheasants, 9 partridges, 1 snipe, 1 pigeon. Enjoyed it very much but felt tired in evening and fell asleep in library after dinner so to bed late. Lovely to have Bill here.

Sunday 18 October

The 'Haversack' did not speak at lunch today and Bill and I worried about her. Bill left for London then to Camberly.

Monday 19 October

Miss Haverson gave notice so that's that and we know where we are now. I am not sorry although it is such a bore to find another and sort out all these frightful females. Decided to have female lunch party on 29 October. So busy writing invitations. Bill rang and I told him about the Haversack. Mum sent a wire saying she had arrived safely after very rough passage.

Wednesday 21 October

Heard from five females all refusing my invitation. Shall have no one here when day comes.

Thursday 22 October

Engaged a new third housemaid, she seems a nice child. Lovely walk in afternoon and then Pepper had fight with another dog. Most awkward. Dad upset. Have a streaming cold.

Saturday 24 October

Went over in Austin to Hemley and got 2 pheasants, 8 rabbits and 1 hare. I took the little 20 bore gun with me but was not successful in shooting anything. Good lunch but both got bored ferreting after lunch.

Sunday 25 October

Pouring wet night and garden a wreck. Bill and I rather depressed and worried about what will happen when Staff College is over. I saw Bill off at the station at 4.30. Wild and windy night.

Wednesday 28 October

Went to London on 10.00 train. Went to Shaplands, The Times Book Club, Debenhams for clothes, then to Harrods and then interviewing governesses at the agency. Liked two. Home with many parcels! Bill rang to tell me that he has been appointed to

Staff Headquarters in Cairo after he leaves Staff College. Very pleased, but a bit of a shock.

Thursday 29 October

Woke up wondering what was bothering me, then remembered that we are going to Cairo and I shall have to leave my babies behind. This is rather hateful and felt sad. Busy with my lunch party, Mrs Alexander, Mrs Turner, Mrs Banks and Mrs Wallis all came. Mrs d'Alberquerque cooked an excellent lunch. Lobster salad, pheasant, then pineapple en surprise and cheese beignets.

Friday 30 October

Felt so sad and upset. Met Bill who arrived at 4.50. Both feel very miserable and depressed. We both love our home and our children and it seems awful to have to leave them. Dad rather tiresome too.

Saturday 31 October

Woke up early and cried my heart out. Can't bear it. Went to sleep in afternoon as had had such a bad night. Bill has a lot of work to do.

Sunday 1 November

Felt dreadful again in the morning and so unhappy at thought of leaving the babies. I cried a lot. Bill had to leave at 5.00.

Monday 2 November

Felt better after taking two doses of green medicine. Also looking forward to seeing Mum home tomorrow. Rang up Bill and he gave me lots of news and details about Egypt and altogether things are very much brighter.

Tuesday 3 November

Dad went off to London to meet Mother. Busy preparing for her return. Mum home at 8.30. So pleased to see her but do not think she looks well at all.

Wednesday 4 November

Had a long talk to Mum about Egypt. I think she will be helpful. In afternoon took Mary and Merlin to tea party for Guy Fawkes which they loved.

Thursday 5 November
Pouring wet day. Have decided to engage Mlle Lutz so wrote to
Lady Child for references.

Saturday 7 November
Pouring day and terrific gale so not very promising for our shoot.
However very pleased to find a lot of birds and we had an
excellent day shooting 26 pheasants, 3 partridges , 4 rabbits, 2
hares, 1 moorhen and 4 pigeon. Douglas shot well and we had 4
beaters and Hill out. I loved it. Had a good dinner soup lobster and
prawns, roast chicken and raspberry ice.

Sunday 8 November
All went to church. They all left after lunch. To bed early, very
tired but had bad night owing to the terrific gale.

Monday 9 November
Had Mlle Lutz reference which was not very satisfactory. Worried
about this. Nannie returned from her holiday looking well and Mrs
Haverson left. Took children to dancing class which they loved.
Bill rang to say he thinks we shall leave in the *Somersetshire* on 6
January. Central heating switched on.

Wednesday 11 November
Armistice Day again. I remember so many. Bill and I on the steps
in Brompton Road with Merlin on the way. Mary with Nurse Lice
and I in the Park and Mary cried. Myself at Leckhampton
expecting the twins. Myself in London, trying on underclothes as a
girl. I wonder where I shall be next year? Met Mlle Lutz, she is
very smartly dressed and quite pleasant.

Saturday 14 November
Pouring wet day. Really the weather is awful. Bill and I spent all
day talking over Egypt with the family. Went for a walk with Bill,
Mary and Merlin. Bill had two doses of green medicine and feels
better.

Wednesday 18 November

Nannie gave notice and refuses to stay here any longer. Says she can't stand the country and dullness of it. Might have thought of this sooner. Nannie out

so I had charge of the twins who were so sweet and good.

Thursday 19 November

Second lunch party was a great success. Excellent lunch. Lobster salad, Chicken a la Maryland and praline cream. Took Nannie and the twins over to tea at the Bealings.

Friday 20 November

Went off early to the sale at Arcade House and bought some china and silver. Bill had been inoculated so not feeling well.

Sunday 22 November

Bill quite well again. Bill and I had a good talk in the car about Egypt and the future. Felt much clearer as a result. Bridge in evening.

Tuesday 24 November

Mlle gave notice, the beast, just when I've got enough to do. Went over to tea with Mrs Anderson at Capel and there we saw the sweetest pony which Mum has bought for Mary and Merlin for £12.12.0

Thursday 26 November

Went into Ipswich with Mother who went up to London to see the Doctor as her eczema is very bad again. Mlle lost the children. Really these incompetent women are the limit.

Friday 27 November

Peggy and Ralph Heathcote and Jim arrived after tea. A good dinner and to bed early, as we have a long day's shooting tomorrow.

Saturday 28 November

Lovely day, so lucky after the awful weather we have had. Set off for Hemley after breakfast, Jim and I in his car, Peggy and Ralph in theirs. Fetched Bill and Gabriel at the station. Guns were Gordon, Ralph, Jim, and Bill and we had three men, Hill and two dogs. Got

27 pheasants, 1 Partridge, 2 rabbits and 3 hares and 4 snipe. We all enjoyed our day. Good dinner.

Sunday 29 November

Everyone left after lunch. Bill and I had a quiet afternoon getting straight before he left at 7.30 for Andover.

Monday 30 November

Took children to dancing class which they much enjoy and are getting quite good. Sent off pheasants to Dandy, Mrs Lunn, Aunt Edie and Isobel. Also sold four brace. Dr Banks came to vaccinate me in the evening.

Tuesday 1 December

Went into Ipswich and had fitting at Miss Jekell's. Went over to Martlesham to see Medical Officer who had to sign a paper saying I was medically fit to go to Egypt. No trouble on this.

Thursday 3 December

Went tea at Mrs Mason's at Felixstowe taking Mary and Merlin with me. They had Mickey Mouse film and we enjoyed very much. But my arm was painful.

Friday 4 December

Went to London and interviewed three governesses none of whom I liked as much as Miss Wyatt. Met Bill on the train and had tea together. Lovely to see him but worried about his bad foot after playing hockey. The nail has turned septic and is coming off.

Saturday 5 December

Pouring day. Bill resting his foot, poor dear and not feeling very grand as it is very painful. Very worried too over this business of the King and what will happen. [King Edward VIII, 41 and unmarried, and Wallis Simpson, an American with one divorced husband still living and another whom she hoped to divorce].

Sunday 6 December

Bill's foot better but went to church in the car. Mum had her birthday party and we had cake and candles and presents. Dad has given her a lovely sapphire ring.

Monday 7 December

Dr Banks came and inoculated me. Nannie is very trying. Went to bed early as arm rather stiff and painful.

Tuesday 8 December

Dear Mum's 73 birthday and she seems wonderfully well. She and Dad off to London for a Matinee. Dad then down to Tunbridge Wells for the night. General gloom everywhere over the situation. Will the King abdicate, if so will the Duke of York carry on or will he chuck Mrs Simpson?

Wednesday 9 December

Wrote a good many letters and cards for Christmas. Rumours that the King is going to abdicate.

Thursday 10 December [Following his abdication the Duke of Windsor played often at Worplesdon, he was captain in 1933, and was sufficiently fond of the course to attempt to buy Mingary. He often took tea with Hugh Lang's Mother and asked one day if the house might be for sale. Mrs Lang asked 'Will you be bringing that woman here?' and when the reply was in the affirmative, she flatly refused to contemplate any offer from the former king.]

Spent all afternoon writing letters and cards. Heard that King Edward VIII had abdicated in favour of his brother the Duke of York. I must say I think the Duke of York will make a much more suitable King and we shall have a Queen and princesses which seems the right thing. Listened to the Proclamation.

Friday 11 December

Mlle Lutz left and we both went to London on 10.00 train. Pouring wet day and very cold. Everyone talking of the King's Abdication. Went to Golanski and Harrods for fittings. Had lunch at the Green Lizard, poor sort of place. Bought final Christmas presents. Met Bill on 4.54 train.

Saturday 12 December

Had another fitting in Ipswich. Bill out shooting with Ronnie Quilter here. They shot 78 pheasants, 30 partridges and he enjoyed his day very much. Miss Wyatt arrived in afternoon. Am not very impressed so far. Bill's nail has now come right off and is better.

Wednesday 16 December

Man came to do packing of all glass and china and spent all day here. Dr Banks came again and inoculated me a second time for Typhoid.

Thursday 16 December

Spent all day in bed. Feel very upset about Nannie going tomorrow. It's a wrench after 5 years. Bill rang to say he had been interviewed by Barratt, he would get his PSA but not for 6 months which is sad. My arm is very painful. Miss Wyatt seems quite useless and I saw her pummelling Merlin and she keeps on nagging him. Poor child.

Friday 18 December

Nannie left at noon without a word of goodbye to anyone. She seemed very upset but I must say behaved in an extraordinary way. Felt very upset and exhausted and have diarrohea after this miserable inoculation. Anyhow I must cheer up as Bill is coming home tonight. Winnie arrived after lunch, nice to see her pleasant smile again. I think Miss Wyatt is useless.

Sunday 20 December

Bill and I had the whole morning clearing out desks and drawers and seeing what we have to do. Mum and Dad out to lunch. Took children for long walk in afternoon.

Monday 21 December

Went up to London with Mother and had frightfully busy day. Shopped hard and had fittings and eventually just caught the train and arrived home at 6.19 with Mother. Merlin had slight cold so put him to bed with a fire.

Tuesday 22 December

Merlin has a temperature, looks like flu and in bed all day. Miss Wyatt says she has sore throat. Everything very hectic added to which I am trying hard to pack for Egypt.

Wednesday 23 December

Mary has flu now so put her in with Merlin. Miss Wyatt says she feels rotten. Went over to Rendham to see Mrs Lunn and George and took some jams, jellies and mincemeat. Twins out with Winnie.

Thursday 24 December

Mary worse but Merlin better. Dr Banks came to see them both. Miss Wyatt in bed. Have put off the party until 31 December. In evening servants had their Christmas tree, parcels and party in servant's hall and we all sent in our presents.

Friday 25 December Christmas Day

A sad Christmas with both Mary and Merlin in bed. Went to Holy Communion with Bill. Clare and Cecily had lunch with us, turkey and a nice Christmas pudding and crackers which the babies loved. Poor Mum very depressed as there is to be no tree and party after all and we must cancel it altogether. Mum gave me a new white suit, Dad £25 and the children have all had lovely presents.

Saturday 26 December

Bill and I went over to the shoot as everyone seemed much better. But when we returned with 6 pheasants, 6 rabbits and 1 hare all shot by Bill, we found the family fairly spinning. Miss Wyatt in bed, children's temperatures up and Pepper being sick having eaten holly berries. Clare and Cecily also ill.

Sunday 27 December

Miss Wyatt still in bed so what's the use of her? Asked if she would prefer to go home and she agreed best thing to do. So her people came to fetch her after lunch…She then got up pretty brisk so I asked her if she would prefer to leave and she agreed, so I paid her up to date and she left. Looking after children all day. Bill slept with them.

Tuesday 29 December

Bill took me to the station laden with parcels. Interviewed governesses and decided on one and hope she will be all right. Went to 2 Walton Place and saw the tenant Mrs Edwardes. Home very tired.

Wednesday 30 December

Bill is so sweet and helps me such a lot and really through him the children are much better as he has slept with them for three nights and keeps them quiet in early mornings. Shall miss them so when we are away as do love them so. All heavy luggage left.

Thursday 31 December

The last day of the old year. Mary and Merlin both better and back in their own rooms. Went over to say goodbye to Mrs Lunn and George and found them both in bed. It is so sad to be leaving all those I love so but I shall be with my darling Bill and home again in 4 months time.

At the end of 1936 there is an account of game sold at Hemley. A total of £6/5/6. Two brace partridge fetched 6/6 sold in September and 5 pheasants sold for £1/3/9 and hares 2/- each.

FEBRUARY 15 1929

MARRIAGE OF MISS BISSHOPP

Ceremony in London.

LIST OF PRESENTS.

BRIDE AND BRIDEGROOM LEAVING THE CHURCH.

A GROUP OF BRIDESMAIDS.

HAPPY WEDDING DAY
16 ANNIVERSARY